HE
KILLED
THEM
ALL

ROBERT DURST AND MY QUEST FOR JUSTICE

HE KILLED THEM ALL

JEANINE PIRRO

GALLERY
BOOKS

New York   London   Toronto   Sydney   New Delhi

G
GALLERY
BOOKS
Gallery Books
An Imprint of Simon & Schuster, Inc.
1230 Avenue of the Americas
New York, NY 10020

First Gallery Books hardcover edition November 2015

GALLERY BOOKS and colophon are registered trademarks of Simon & Schuster, Inc.

For information about special discounts for bulk purchases, please contact Simon & Schuster Special Sales at 1-866-506-1949 or business@simonandschuster.com.

The Simon & Schuster Speakers Bureau can bring authors to your live event. For more information or to book an event, contact the Simon & Schuster Speakers Bureau at 1-866-248-3049 or visit our website at www.simonspeakers.com.

Interior design by Renato Stanisic

Manufactured in the United States of America

10 9 8 7 6 5 4 3 2 1

Library of Congress Cataloging-in-Publication Data has been applied for.

ISBN 978-1-5011-2500-3
ISBN 978-1-5011-2503-4 (ebook)

To Kathleen Durst and all the women silenced
by the men who said they loved them.

~~~

To Cody Cazalas, who stands tall among the men and women
in law enforcement,
who fight every day to protect victims,
and whose moral compass never wavered.

~~~

To Gilberte Najamy, who, for thirty-three years, to her
dying day, led the charge to find Kathie.
I hope she has her answers now. RIP Gilberte.

~~~

To my mom, Esther Ferris,
who taught me never to remain silent
in the face of injustice.

"If Ms. Pirro had kept her mouth shut, none of this would have happened."

—Michael Ramsey, criminal defense attorney for Robert Durst

CONTENTS

| OPENING STATEMENT

As I write this, Robert Alan Durst is rotting in a federal facility. But I don't want him to die.

And, no, I am not relying on his lawyer Dick DeGuerin's statements about his client's poor health.

If Dick DeGuerin told me what time it was, I'd check my watch; if he told me the sky was blue, I still wouldn't believe him.

All you have to do is look at Robert Durst to see that he's not long for this world. The man is seventy-two years old, but he looks like a thousand. His physical disintegration from when I first laid eyes on him in 2001 in Pennsylvania to 2013 when he filmed the HBO documentary series *The Jinx* to now is startling. He's stick thin, weak looking, and shuffling. A strong wind would topple him.

On one side of his shaved head, he's got a shunt to drain out excess brain fluid. The condition is called hydrocephalus. It might kill him. It might not. If the brain fluid doesn't do him in, his esophageal cancer will. For now, Durst is being held in a federal facility, having been transferred to St. Charles Parish's Nelson Coleman Correctional Center to be treated for his illnesses, in Hahnville, Louisiana.

I'm praying his brain and cancer treatments work. I want Robert

Durst to live long enough to stand trial in Los Angeles and be convicted for the December 2000 murder of his friend Susan Berman in that city. I want him to live long enough to be indicted for and convicted of the murder of his wife, Kathleen, who vanished in 1982. And then I want to dance in my Manolo Blahniks on his grave.

As district attorney of Westchester County, New York, I took a fresh look at Kathleen's case in 1999 when new questions about it came to light.

The decision to reopen that seventeen-year-old cold case was like kicking a hornet's nest. Sixteen years after that, the hornets are still buzzing, louder than ever, and a lot of people have been stung in the interim.

I kicked that nest because I knew it was hiding a man who killed his wife, a woman who disappeared without a trace. I knew it then, and I know it now. How? Guts and instinct. When you've done enough of these cases, as I have, you just know. There's a second sight, a déjà vu, an overwhelming sense that you've been here before and you know how it ends. The dots are all over the place, but the lines aren't yet connected.

But pure guts and instinct aren't enough to bring a criminal down. You need evidence, pure and simple. And Robert Durst, for some reason, is expert at getting rid of evidence. Actually, he doesn't deserve that much credit. He was aided by money, power, society, and a culture (including the police) willing to believe that a woman who vanished from the face of the earth probably just fell off. Case closed.

I've been on a mission since 1999 to prove that Kathleen didn't just fall off or run off, but had been murdered and disposed of by her not-so-loving husband. Not just that. I've been fighting to expose the ineptitude, ignorance, abuse of power, and, yes, cover-up, that have allowed Durst to live free for more than three decades.

He's skated for two other murders since then. He was suspected of shooting his best friend Susan Berman in Los Angeles in 2000. They'd been each other's close, close confidants. But when he feared, heard, and knew she'd talk to the police about him, he was not about to let that happen. He had to shut her up.

He admitted to killing a neighbor, Morris Black, in Galveston, Texas, in 2001. But the half-wit jury—aided and abetted by an out-of-her-depth judge and an odiously brilliant but unscrupulous defense "dream team"—acquitted him of it. I actually believed that kangaroo courts ended . . . But, then again, people were starting to question the criminal justice system. O. J. Simpson: acquittal. Michael Jackson: acquittal. Durst testified on the witness stand that he shot and dismembered his neighbor Morris Black. After he was caught, he jumped bail and stayed on the lam for six weeks. To my mind, and the minds of most normal people—not to mention an accepted legal inference, which, as a judge, I charged juries for years—his flight alone showed consciousness of guilt. He killed Black intentionally, and then the entitled dirtbag thought he could just drive away and never look back. Actually, he did!

One of the jurors who let him get away with murder (and wore it as a badge of honor) visited Durst in jail *five times* while Durst served a year on separate charges of bond jumping and evidence tampering. Why did this man visit Durst so many times? His actions were questionable at best. So much for Texas justice. Isn't Texas where murderers go straight to hanging immediately after arrest?

In a perfect world of equal justice, Robert Durst would be shot in the head and then dismembered with an axe and a bow saw, like Morris Black. ("I didn't kill my best friend," Durst told the jury. "I *did* dismember him.") Or he'd be shot in the back of his head like Susan Berman, one of his other best friends. With friends like him . . . Or he would meet whatever heinous fate was inflicted on Kathie.

I have long been haunted by the question of exactly what he did to her. But I have a pretty good idea. Based on an accumulation of evidence compiled by my team, law enforcement in other states, and *The Jinx* filmmakers, I'd bet my pet pig Kathie was beaten to death in their home in South Salem, New York, hacked up for easy transportation to some remote parkland in New Jersey, and secretly buried.

I've always been a believer that sooner or later the truth comes out. Sooner or later, the jig is up. But Durst is not your run-of-the-mill dirtbag. He's pulled himself out of the fire again and again, thanks to family money and the power to corrupt the justice system. He has gotten away with murder. Not once. Not twice. But three times (that we know about).

In the annals of serial killers, Robert Durst has raised the "Holy Shit!" bar sky-high. To say that he has been cunning, methodical, and devious every step of the way is an understatement. It's no surprise that a man worth upward of $100 million could or would beat the system. What *is* a surprise is the shrewd and outlandish methods he used to get away with his crimes, such as passing himself off as a mute woman named Dorothy Ciner—the girl whose high school yearbook picture was next to his. He assumed multiple aliases, living for months below the radar in a flophouse in Bumfuck, Texas, concocting bizarre ideas for his own legal defense—including the vilification in court of yours truly.

Incredibly, all of these "holy shit!" antics seem to have *worked* for him. For decades, Durst used his wealth to make a mockery of the system of law and order that the rest of us rely on to protect the victim and punish the criminal.

But this circus will come to an end soon. If Durst lives long enough, he'll be extradited from New Orleans to Los Angeles to face charges for the murder of Susan Berman. His "dream team" of lawyers, for yet a few more pieces of silver, will once again attempt to sully a courtroom with falsehoods and manipulation of the facts. But it won't work this time. Prosecutors in L.A. have been building their case against Robert Durst for the last two years. They're doing their job. Witnesses are being interviewed and lined up to testify against him in a Los Angeles courtroom. And along with dozens, if not hundreds, of other reporters, I will be covering the trial, gavel to gavel, relishing every minute of it.

My only regret is that I will not be the prosecutor seeking justice.

So pray that Durst lives! If he dies before the trial, the world will be deprived of the satisfaction of watching that silver spoon of entitlement get ripped from his mouth. If he dies before the trial, the family and friends of his victims won't get to see him pay for what he's done. They deserve that. Like the ripples made by a stone tossed in a pond, the disquieting effects of his violence have lingered for way too long, affecting many, far beyond the immediate victims. Thirty-three years after Kathie's death, those ripples continue to create enormous pain.

I want nothing more than that the victims and survivors of the crimes of Robert Durst get *some* understanding, *some* sense of justice, *some* peace in their lives. I hope their questions will be answered. I hope they can finally put their loved ones to rest, if only in their hearts.

For me, there will be no rest until that emaciated monster is dressed in an orange jumpsuit and then rots to death behind bars.

I, too, have been living with the Durst ripple effect. I haven't suffered the grief and anguish of Kathie's, Susan's, and Morris's friends and family, but I have been obsessed with connecting the dots to prove his guilt. I've been both frustrated and furious over his slippery evasion of punishment. I have also been criticized and vilified—in courts of law, no less—time and again for my "dogged pursuit of Bobby," as if we should just let bygones be bygones. Durst's defense team and other wannabe bit players in the theater of the surreal and absurd that is the Durst story have taken shots at me, accusing me of overzealousness and ambition. They accuse me of being "on a mission" to nail Durst.

Guilty as charged.

I'm *still* on that mission.

This book is the history of my mission as part of the insanity, from the first time I heard the name Durst in 1999 to today, right now. It's the insider perspective of exactly what went down during my fifteen-year investigation of this serial murderer, this pathological liar, this narcissistic, disgusting, fascinating, brilliant, evil little bastard.

There may never be another case as twisted, perverse, and mind-boggling as Robert Durst's.

Thank God, for all our sakes.

| THE FINAL EPISODE

March 14, 2015. I traveled home to suburban Westchester County from work in New York City on a Saturday night, with no clue how crazy things were about to get.

Crazy is generally the norm in my life. My nemesis, Robert Durst, was in custody in New Orleans. I'd just hosted a full hour of live television that included two segments on Durst on my show *Justice with Judge Jeanine* on the Fox News channel. I would be back in that same Studio J the following night, covering Durst for a whole hour.

It was late, but, as usual, when I got home, I gave my handsome standard poodles, Sir Lancelot, aka Lance, and Mikimoto, aka Mickey, a midnight snack. I flipped through the mail. I ate a half pint of Ben & Jerry's Cherry Garcia and, feeling guilty as hell, went upstairs to wash the TV makeup off my face. I began the torturous process of removing the false eyelashes—you've got to hand it to Fox News, they do not skimp on the makeup. I had to be up at 4:00 a.m. to do another live hit back in Manhattan at 7:00 a.m. for NBC's *Today* to discuss the highly anticipated final episode of *The Jinx: The Life and Deaths of Robert Durst*, the riveting documentary series that had been airing on HBO. I finished taking the false eyelashes off, scrubbed my face clean, and felt free of the mask that is piled on my face for those high-def cameras.

I sat down on my bed, bone tired. In addition to speeches and my job at Fox, the past six weeks had been all Durst, all the time. Many of the most rabid *Jinx* viewers hadn't even been born when Kathleen Durst disappeared. Many had never even heard of Robert Durst before. Some people remembered the case, but only sort of. The series got everyone up to speed, and put Robert Durst front and center in the national consciousness again.

It had been twelve years since his acquittal of a murder in Galveston shocked the nation. But for the viewers of *The Jinx*, it was happening as if for the first time.

For me, the case had never been far from my thoughts. It had consumed me the way it had haunted the friends and families of Susan Berman and Morris Black for fifteen years, but not as much as it had tortured the friends and family of Kathleen Durst for thirty-three years. After all this time, two filmmakers, director Andrew Jarecki and his producer partner, Marc Smerling, had somehow managed to do what law enforcement in three states, over three decades, my own office included, had been unable to do:

Nail the bastard.

Was I jealous? You bet I was. But more than that, I was thrilled. Over-the-moon thrilled! The Robert Durst case had been so bizarre, so off-the-charts inexplicable, on so many levels and for so many years—of course it would take two filmmakers to crack it.

Ah, to have the luxury now and then of not being hampered by a little thing called the Constitution.

Now the American public—whether they watched *The Jinx* or not, they sure heard about it—knew what I and many others had known for so long: Robert Durst, the indulged scion to a billion-dollar real-estate empire in Manhattan, was a cold-blooded killer.

It also made karmic sense that it would be the media that brought Durst down. For the entirety of my career, I'd been criticized for being too "media savvy." The media attention wasn't for my own sake. It was part of my job. It was a way of sending a message to both victims and criminals. But where I had been accused of grandstanding, Jarecki and Smerling were seen as simply doing their job.

I first figured out how to use the press as a young prosecutor. The media were responsive to blood and guts, and I was receptive to their attention. I realized that the coverage of my cases would send a message to dirtbags that I wasn't shy, that I wasn't scared, and that I was coming after them. I also realized that the coverage would make victims feel less alone. It would absolve them of misplaced self-blame and give them the comfort that someone would stand up for them.

Damn right, I became media savvy. Reporters used me for headlines—and I used them to crack cases, deter criminals, find victims, and save lives.

During my twelve years as the elected district attorney of a large office in a metropolitan area, as well as the previous fifteen years as an assistant DA, trial attorney, and bureau chief of one of the first domestic violence units in the nation, I learned to use any arrow in my quiver to get results. I brought Crime Stoppers to Westchester— a pay-for-tips system—because the public was a huge, untapped resource for crime prevention, for tips that would solve cases. If people *could* provide information and evidence to law enforcement, they *would*, especially if there was a financial benefit to them.

Were some people uncomfortable with my being "media savvy"? Uh, yeah. Usually, those who squirmed when they saw me in sharp suits and high heels on TV back in the nineties were men who couldn't wrap their tiny minds around the concept of a smart, articulate, attractive woman in a position of power. There was a lot of resentment and jealousy. Did I care? No. It was their problem, not mine. I loved my job and I did it well. I always said I would do handstands in Times Square if it would help a case I was trying to crack.

Fortunately, I didn't have to do that—this time around—to nail Durst. I just had to let Jarecki and Smerling deal with the media glare.

That Durst cooperated with Jarecki and Smerling was stunning to me and everyone else. He stepped right into it. He *volunteered.* He called Jarecki after seeing the fictionalized version of his life in *All Good Things,* a feature film they made about him. He handed himself to the filmmakers on a silver platter. And then Jarecki deftly served him up.

In the fifth and penultimate episode, which aired on March 8, 2015, Jarecki dropped a bombshell. For fifteen years, law enforcement had been stymied by a potentially explosive piece of evidence in the Susan Berman case: a letter that had been mailed to the "BEVERLEY [*sic*] HILLS POLICE." No further address; no return address. Inside the envelope, in more block letters, was a note that said Susan's address, "1527 BENEDICT CANYON," followed by the word "CADAVER." It was mailed on December 23, 2000, the same day it is believed Berman was killed. As Durst himself put it in *The Jinx,* "[It was] a note to the police that only the killer could have written."

Not that L.A. law enforcement didn't pull out all the stops to get a handwriting match on the cadaver note, but the exemplars (other samples) of Durst's handwriting weren't nearly as good as what the filmmakers ultimately unearthed more than a decade later. On camera, Susan's stepson, Sareb, found another letter addressed to her, on Robert's letterhead, which had been sitting in a box all that time, and appeared to be an exact match to the cadaver note, right down to the misspelling of the word "Beverley" on the envelope.

Now, I had also studied a copy of the cadaver note in 2001, as well as other samples of Durst's awkward, boxy hand printing. The expert used by the Los Angeles authorities could not find sufficient similarities between the handwriting on the cadaver note and the exemplars provided. My disappointment was overwhelming. If ever there were a hurdle to overcome in proving Robert Durst's guilt in the Susan Berman homicide, this one expert's opinion would make it almost impossible to scale it.

Most would be surprised to know the cadaver note was written in green ink. To me, that was another telltale sign. Everything I saw that Durst wrote was in green ink. Green—the color of money, the thing he loved so much.

It's been suggested that the killer sent the "cadaver" note because he may have had feelings for the victim. That could be true. It appeared that Susan was kneeling down with a tissue to wipe up dog feces when she was shot in the back of the head. The note may have been written so that she would be found before she decomposed or her dogs ate her.

In the days leading up to the episode-six finale of *The Jinx*, everyone involved was on tenterhooks. Would Jarecki confront Durst with the side-by-side comparison of the two Beverleys? Would it be so huge, people would need to run for cover? What could it be? The finale *had* to be even more explosive than the finding of the note itself.

So when I was invited to join Jarecki and some of the other key players who'd been part of *The Jinx* that Sunday, March 15, at his Manhattan apartment to view the finale, I was champing at the bit. Fox News channel, like everyone else, was anticipating something big, so I had another one-hour live show to do immediately after *The Jinx* aired. Time would be tight, but I'd figure it out. What better than to have all the players in one room, and to drag along the guests to tell the world what I already knew in my heart—that Robert Durst was a serial murderer?

• • •

ON SUNDAY, MARCH 15, a town car picked me up shortly after 5:00 a.m. to take me to NBC for my hit on the *Today* show, and apply another layer of paint to my face. *The Jinx* was such hot news that even the networks were airing segments on what viewers might see on the finale that night. What no one—not even NBC or me—knew at that point was that big news had already happened.

Anchor Erica Hill said, "You said in a recent interview, and I'm going to quote you here, 'I think Durst knows the jig is up.' That's a pretty strong statement."

I discussed with Erica the inconsistencies in Durst's statement to the filmmakers versus what he'd told police investigators when the crime originally happened. Clearly, the series had been building up to reach a resolution. "I think that tonight will take this thing to another level and I'm looking forward to seeing it," I said.

She asked, "In terms of Durst deciding to speak out against the advice of his attorney? Why would he do this now? Is it based on ego?"

I reviewed some of his ego-driven actions over the years, including his stealing of a sandwich from Wegmans when there was an outstanding murder warrant for him. "He keeps pushing the envelope," I said, "and interestingly enough, it's an envelope that may push him."

What I *didn't* say was that Andrew had previously revealed to me that there would be real closure in the finale. But he and his producer, Marc, would only go so far when they appeared on my show, which aired on March 7, just over a week before the finale. "Our job here is to place it in front of the audience for them to see. That's what we're going to do and what people are going to respond to," he said.

Jarecki's goal had always been to find the truth. I asked him if he found it. He said, "I think we did," but he refused to elaborate. Finally, tonight, eight days later, we would all find out what truth they uncovered.

After the *Today* show segment, when I got into the town car heading back to Westchester, my phone rang. It was Cody Cazalas. Cody was the detective from Galveston, Texas, who scrupulously and painstakingly, piece-by-piece as a good cop does, built the case against Durst for the murder of Morris Black. It was as solid an investigation as I had ever seen. Most in law enforcement would have called it a slam dunk.

Except that it wasn't. Durst walked.

But wait: Let me tell you something about cops—good cops, anyway. When they've lived and breathed a case for years, when they've dotted all the i's and crossed all the t's and damn near killed themselves in the process, when they do all that and the defendant is acquitted, it's personal. It's devastating. The one piece of critical evidence that Cody searched high and low for but could not find was Morris Black's head. If he had found that head—which Durst had admitted to severing at the sixth vertebra—with the bullet lodged inside, he would have found the telltale piece of evidence. Without it, forensic experts could not offer their theory of the homicide or evaluate the trajectory of the bullet to establish whether the shooting was an execution (a bullet entry to the back of the head) or otherwise. Without this crucial piece of evidence, the defense was able to promote a self-defense or accident theory. Without the head, it would be difficult to get a conviction, but certainly not impossible.

I picked up the phone, assuming Cody was calling about *The Jinx*. "Hi, Cody."

"Durst was arrested last night in New Orleans."

"What?!"

He had been nabbed in the lobby of the JW Marriott Hotel late that Saturday, March 14, where he had been staying under the alias Everett Ward. He was in possession of guns and pot—the two things this man can't seem to live without—as well as ammunition, a latex mask, a note with a UPS tracking number on it (that package would later be found to contain $117,000 in cash), and a map of Cuba.

Durst was taken into custody and booked while I was on the air, live, talking about whether he'd be arrested soon.

News of the arrest hadn't been leaked yet, but Cody had the inside track.

"Turn around!" I directed the NBC-hired driver to drop me off at Fox News. My 10:00 p.m. live show had just gotten a lot more interesting, and I had work to do. My first call was to David Clark, the head of weekend news at Fox, to tell him Durst had been arrested. Fox was the first to break the story. My next call was to Andrew. He seemed as exhausted as I was, but at breakneck speed, I told him what I knew. When he said he hadn't known about the arrest, I was surprised and said, "Really?"

He said, "I didn't."

Later, there'd be much discussion and hand-wringing over whether Durst would have been arrested in New Orleans had it not been for *The Jinx*.

The short answer: of course not!

Yes, most of us who were in the loop knew the FBI had been monitoring him for a while, in tandem with the LAPD. But more significant was that, after episode five and the two-Beverley stunner, Durst stopped using his phone. They knew he was in Houston, where he owned a condo, and then New Orleans. Someone (possibly his wife, Debrah Lee Charatan) had just wired him a lot of money. Sanctions for U.S. travel to Cuba were being lifted. The first flight out of New Orleans was scheduled for the night they nabbed Durst. Nothing is accidental with him.

Thanks to *The Jinx* and the persistence of the FBI, "Bobby" would *not* be sunning in Havana, smoking his Marlboro Lights or a joint and drinking Jack Daniel's. He'd check out of the JW Marriott and move directly without passing go into the Orleans Parish Prison, a jail unlike anything he'd experienced, on Sunday. Trust me, there are jails and then there are jails. Orleans Parish Prison is the *worst*. Well suited to guests like Robert Durst.

But it wasn't over yet. Not by a long shot. I had a one-hour show scheduled, and I still didn't know what the upshot was going to be. My head was blowing up with the possibilities. Was it a Susan clue? Kathie's bones? Another body? There was no end to what it could be.

At 7:30 p.m., after I spent every moment since the morning phone call from Cody frenetically preparing for my show—except when I changed into Seven jeans and Manolos, my version of casual—Cody and I arrived together at Andrew Jarecki's apartment in a gorgeous prewar building on Manhattan's Upper East Side.

Jarecki is an interesting guy. He comes across as unassuming and down-to-earth. I actually had a hard time believing this hipster in a hoodie is an Emmy-winning and Academy Award–nominated documentary filmmaker (for *Capturing the Friedmans*). Don't let the hoodie fool you. He's worth hundreds of millions. He founded Moviefone and sold it to AOL for $388 million in 1999. Apparently his shabby chic is the official look of New York screenwriters and directors, a group I wasn't familiar with.

He first appeared on my radar in 2003. He contacted the DA's office about Durst and requested a meeting. The call was directed, as any call like his would be, to the press office. David Hebert, my executive assistant DA and most trusted adviser, handled press requests, and agreed to meet him. David, not generally impressed by many, was impressed with Jarecki's encyclopedic knowledge of Durst, his curiosity, and the chutzpah it took to ask for unfettered access to our law-enforcement files.

Jarecki referenced making a fictionalized account of our case.

"I don't see the law-enforcement value," David said to me at the time.

I fully concurred. I had established a hard and fast rule about cooperating with the media—any media—despite what some people might have thought: If the exposure didn't further our law-enforcement investigation, forget it. Jarecki received a hard "no."

But that wasn't the last of Jarecki. He resurfaced in 2005, just before I left the DA's office. He was certainly persistent, and he was smart and, since he seemed to have a vast knowledge of Durst, I'd hoped that maybe he'd found a kernel of information that we didn't have. My concern was that, upon my moving to another career, the next DA wouldn't continue to investigate a case that I had so much invested in. I agreed to meet with him and his team with several high-level members of my staff. The ground rules were established ahead of time. We would give them nothing, but would listen to them. If and when they touched on something that we didn't know about, my staff and I would inconspicuously make eye contact. Their hope was that, if we needed their help, we might assist them in their endeavor. But it doesn't work that way in law enforcement. At one point, when Jarecki's information was too close for comfort, I politely but respectfully asked them to leave. After they did, we couldn't get over how much they knew.

All Good Things came out in 2010. But that wasn't the end of it. In 2011, Jarecki resurfaced with a new project, a documentary about the case, this time with Durst's willing involvement. He promised it would be the first of its kind, with all police, prosecutors, family members and friends of Robert's victims, and even the accused himself. When I first heard that, I thought, *Why would someone accused of so much wrongdoing sit down and discuss his actions and movements when there was such great risk?* Someone was cutting a deal somewhere. But who? Why? It made no sense. Most people don't do things out of good intentions. Murderers never do.

Also, I was less than pleased about how Jarecki portrayed the DA in *All Good Things*, and repeatedly told him "no." It would take a couple more years for Jarecki to wear me down. I finally agreed to participate when Jarecki showed me a link on his iPad with Durst's Texas lawyers having a good old time, talking about how they took license with me and created a mythical character. I couldn't believe they had admitted to their shenanigans. Deal done. Lead me to the cameras!

As Cody and I pulled up to Jarecki's building, we both noticed the three men standing outside. You can always spot a plainclothes security guard. Or at least, Cody and I can. Jarecki told Cody later that even though Durst was in police custody, he wasn't taking any chances. He had a family to protect. Hipster-in-a-hoodie types aren't accustomed to having dirtbags running around the way those of us in law enforcement are.

We took the elevator—old-fashioned with an accordion gate—up to a big open area, where we hung our coats up and then went into Jarecki's apartment. It struck me as elegant, old world, kind of dark with lots of wood. There were seating areas in a huge central room. The high-backed chairs reminded me of something you'd see in an English castle; a huge portrait of one of his kids hung proudly in the center.

I surveyed the crowd of around thirty people. It was like a mini reunion of so many who'd suffered through years of the odyssey that was the Robert Durst case. It was all supposed to come together and I couldn't believe it might end that night. The anticipation and waiting for the conclusion was awful. Cody was anxious as well.

The first person I made eye contact with was Jim McCormack, Kathie's big brother, whose life had been a living hell for thirty-three years.

Grief destroys people. It makes them angry. They lash out at the very people who are trying to help, especially when investigations that *should* be wrapped up quickly continue to drag on; especially investigations starting eighteen years after the crime. I, too, was frustrated about not having sufficient evidence to get an indictment. I tried to move heaven and earth to indict him from 1999 to December 2005, when I left the DA's office after thirty years. Along the way, a narrative formed in this case that I was more interested in self-promotion than in justice. A small cabal perpetuated this notion, including some who were close to the good-hearted McCormacks.

The fact is that I was the chief law-enforcement officer, elected both to investigate and to prosecute crime in a county of upward of one million people. It was my job, and it didn't matter whether a case was cold or otherwise, and that's exactly what I was doing, like other prosecutors across the country. You would be crazy not to take advantage of DNA and advanced forensics to go after cold cases. I had hoped advances in DNA testing would help solve Kathie's case, but I needed something to test.

I smiled at Jim. He smiled back. You could see the anxiety on his face. We embraced. It was a hug of hope and healing.

I wandered a bit. In an adjoining room, a semicircle of folding chairs, benches, and couches were assembled around a huge flat-screen TV. The couches were opposite each other; the benches and chairs were behind them. In another room were a buffet and an open bar with impeccably clad servers at the ready. The food looked delicious, but I was too amped to eat, and I rarely drink, certainly not while trying to put together a live TV show.

Around ten minutes to eight, Nancy Jarecki, Andrew's wife, asked us to take our seats in front of the wide-screen TV in that adjoining room. There were cameras set up, surrounded by studio lights with those big umbrellas. Jarecki is never off duty, apparently. It occurred to me that the odyssey was not going to be over, that they were now going to film our reaction to watching the show.

Cody was directed to his assigned seat on one couch, closest to the screen. He took me with him, and I sat next to him. To my left and perpendicular to us were the McCormacks—Jim, his wife, Sharon, and his gorgeous daughter, Elizabeth. Elizabeth had also been interviewed in *The Jinx* and looked uncannily like her aunt Kathie—a woman she never knew. It was chilling to sit within a few feet of her, but also oddly comforting, because it seemed as if Kathie was in our midst.

The anticipation grew. It was like an adrenaline rush that came pumping faster and faster. Time went slowly. I didn't want to chitchat. I wanted to see what they had.

In the row behind the McCormacks sat Charles Bagli and his wife, Ellie. Bagli was the *New York Times* reporter who'd done a stellar job on this case for years. He appeared in *The Jinx* and provided one of the most memorable lines, recalling the moment when he got a tip in 2001 that a Robert Durst had been arrested in Galveston for chopping up his neighbor. "*OUR* Robert Durst?" he asked. It reflected perfectly what all of us had asked.

The rest of the crowd included suits from HBO, people I couldn't place, and . . . Diane Sawyer? She was dressed simply, but well put together. There was a palpable sadness in her eyes and her demeanor, as she had recently lost her husband, legendary director Mike Nichols. Jarecki dedicated the last episode of *The Jinx* to Nichols, and, as I'd later learn, he had been friends with Mike and Diane for years. Apparently, when he first got Durst on tape, he showed the footage to them for guidance on how to proceed. Diane advised him not to go to a network with it, but to think outside the box. Good advice.

And then there was Cody. In Midtown Manhattan, Cody's Texas definitely stood out. It wasn't just the cowboy boots, his height, thick horseshoe mustache, or western drawl. He was just straightforward and honest. I asked him if he saw Diane Sawyer. His reply? "I couldn't ID her in a lineup."

Sawyer sat next to Jarecki's wife, Nancy, a cool, quick-witted blonde with short spiky hair and an easy laugh. She was far more extroverted than her husband, which should come as no surprise given that she owns a company that sells hair dye for your private parts. Nancy Jarecki is that kind of gal who you immediately know you would want on your side in a bar fight.

The person sitting on the other side of Nancy was Rosie O'Donnell. I said to myself, *Why is she here? What could her connection possibly be?* But, then again, there were plenty of odd characters in the Durst universe, from socialites to drag queens, but Rosie O'Donnell? In about an hour, she'd make her presence known in a very big way. But first, the countdown to the show.

Wait a minute! Where was Jarecki? Where was Smerling?

The host was missing from his own party. My antenna shot up. We were promised closure. It was about five minutes before the finale. And for Jarecki and Smerling not to be there meant something huge was happening somewhere else. Nancy, in our midst, took a phone call. Everyone seated in the semicircle of chairs quieted to hear her end of the conversation. She hung up and relayed the news: "Andrew is upstate working on something sixty miles away," she said. "Something to do with the case." My antenna reached a whole new altitude.

Upstate, sixty miles away? South Salem was about sixty miles away. The place where I believed Kathie had been murdered by her husband, in the cottage they once shared that sat on Lake Truesdale.

Back in 2000, divers searched that lake for evidence. They found nothing, but there were plenty of woods and grounds around the house that might yield a breakthrough.

Cody and I locked eyes. He was thinking the same thing.

"Do you think they're digging up Kathie's body?" I whispered to him. Cody was a true detective. He'd never reveal what he was thinking. I understood. We just looked at each other.

Then I couldn't resist and blurted out, "What are they doing an hour away from here?"

I eyeballed Bagli. We did that little source/reporter dance with our gaze. *What does he know? What does she know?* Oh, my God. The last thirty seconds of this were simply a microcosm of the whole investigation—confusion, incredulity, surprise upon surprise. Was it possible Durst had, in a fit of uncharacteristic remorse, spilled his guts and told police where to start digging?

Bagli wasn't giving up a thing, if he knew anything. I made a mental note never to play poker with him.

Suddenly, the letters HBO and the staticky sound that we'd all become familiar with flashed across the screen. Moments later, the theme song from *The Jinx*—"Fresh Blood"—was playing. This was it. The beat of my heart was keeping time to the music. For weeks now, Jarecki had promised Cody and me that we'd find "some closure" tonight. Durst was already in handcuffs in New Orleans. Would there be more? I had to catch my breath.

As the episode played, the tension in the room was unbearable. They showed the handwriting expert. They showed Jarecki and Durst going back and forth on the phone to schedule a follow-up interview. Bob's arrest for trespassing on his brother's property. Andrew speaking with Durst's lawyer. Andrew and Marc rehearsing for the big meeting with Robert. There were no major revelations in the first twenty-eight minutes of the show.

I thought, *They're really milking it.*

Finally, on-screen, Jarecki calmly said to Robert, "I want to show you some photographs and stuff." The ease with which he said it, knowing the bombshell that he held in his hand, was worthy of an Academy Award, or, at the very least, a gold shield accompanied by a Glock nine-millimeter.

If you were a cop, you knew that Andrew had spent a great deal of time prepping for the takedown. In fact, a great deal of time in episode six was his preparation for that takedown.

Andrew showed Robert the letter he'd written to Susan, and the telltale envelope it came in.

At that moment, all of Durst's carefully crafted control failed him.

He'd always been an evil genius at hiding his emotions. Anyone watching his reaction to the side-by-side envelopes could plainly see terror sink in behind his beady black eyes. He started burping nervously, and put his hands over his face. Adrenaline must have been racing through his arteries at that moment.

He told Jarecki on camera that he didn't write the cadaver note, even though he admitted to writing the letterhead envelope. Jarecki showed him the blowup side-by-side comparison of the handwriting and asked Durst, "Can you tell me which one you didn't write?"

"No," Durst admitted.

There you have it. The accused readily admitting that even he couldn't distinguish his handwriting from the killer's. Not that we needed him to do so. Any layperson with the ability to see could figure that one out.

The episode could have ended there.

Onscreen, Jarecki, clearly shaken himself, said that they were done. Robert asked to use the bathroom. The image onscreen stayed static on the empty conference room table.

I had an odd feeling. This wasn't going to be some weird *Sopranos* ending, was it?

Then Durst's raspy voice came on. He was muttering to himself— as he often had, since childhood—in the bathroom.

"There it is. You're caught," he said. "You're right, of course. But you can't imagine. Arrest him. I don't know what's in the house. Oh, I want this. What a disaster. He was right. I was wrong. And the burping. I'm having difficulty with the question. What the hell did I do? *Killed them all, of course.*"

Fade to black.

As the lights dimmed on the screen, there was no sound. It was dead silent on TV and that silence was mimicked in the room. The shock was settling in for me and everyone else. Cody and I were holding hands, and we squeezed them simultaneously. He dropped his head. I knew how emotionally devastated Cody had been about the case. He had carried the weight of Durst's acquittal for far too long. I let go of his hand, rubbed his back, and asked, "You okay?"

I turned to the quiet sobbing to my left. It wasn't a wail. It was a sob of resignation. The McCormacks on the bench directly across from the screen were shaking, their heads down, and hugging. It was gut-wrenching. People reached out to comfort them.

That thirty-three years of frustration, agony, and unanswered questions were reduced to thirty-eight HBO Special minutes. The proof we had been looking for had actually been admitted by the murderer himself! That may surprise many. But I've always believed that we would find the truth, one way or another. And this time, in a case that had stumped so many of us for decades, that truth came out of the killer's mouth.

Silence in the room. Probably the same silence that Durst experienced after he killed his victims. No one there knew what to do next. It was over. We were right. The only thing left to seek was the final justice.

I wanted to hear the stream of utterances again, to parse each one. Some of it didn't make sense. But most of it was clear as glass:

"There it is. You're caught."

"Oh, I want this. What a disaster."

"And the burping."

"What the hell did I do? *Killed them all, of course.*"

I immediately did the judge thing in my head about whether those statements were admissible in court, whether Durst knew he was being taped, whether Jarecki and Smerling were agents of law enforcement, whether he was entrapped, was there an expectation of privacy—none of those legal niceties mattered to the people who needed closure. They just needed to know.

Then the silence and soft sobbing were pierced by a screech. As a guest in the home of the filmmaker who, along with his partner, spent eight years of his life on the documentary, with Kathie's weeping relatives in the room, Rosie O'Donnell was freaking out. She screamed, "How could they possibly *withhold* this information for so long? It's obstruction of justice! It's illegal! They shouldn't have been able to do that."

I couldn't believe my ears. Based on the incredible admission by a killer on national TV, something I had never heard in my three decades in law enforcement, I started to question my hearing.

Rosie was pontificating that somehow Jarecki had done something ethically improper, if not outright illegal, by not telling the families.

I thought to myself, *There's no legal obligation for them to do anything! There's no obstruction of justice!* I couldn't contain myself and yelled across the room, "What are you talking about?!"

I noticed that Nancy Jarecki was amazingly gracious throughout Rosie's outburst, smiling, trying to quiet her.

Her tirade escalating, Rosie proceeded to get in the faces of the suits from HBO.

I thought, *You know what, Jeanine? You don't have to get in the middle of this.* My fight had been waged for years against Robert Durst. I didn't need to wage another with Rosie O'Donnell.

Rant on, Rosie.

The truth? We don't have Good Samaritan laws in the United States. There is generally no obligation to report information about a crime to anyone unless you're a mandated reporter who suspects that a child is abused or neglected.

I strolled into the dining room. Diane Sawyer had already escaped there and was standing near the buffet table. She asked me, "What do you make of all this?"

"What do I make of all this? What I've always made of all this. He's a murderer!"

She smiled politely. It occurred to me that she might have been talking about Rosie, so I added for good measure, "And by the way, there was no obligation on Andrew to do *anything*." Legally, he could have sat on the bathroom confession for eternity and not broken any laws. But I did have an inkling, as I watched the meticulous way

Andrew and Marc introduced the envelope evidence, the way Andrew handled the envelope when it was unearthed by Susan's stepson, Sareb, and the video of it being placed in a safe deposit box, that they were creating a chain of custody for future introduction at trial of that envelope. Well done, boys.

Did he have a moral obligation to share the spontaneous admission with the McCormacks, other victims' families, or law enforcement? Not for me to say. I'm a lawyer, not a philosopher. Durst was behind bars. That was good enough for me.

I later found out from Andrew that he did advise law enforcement of the admissions.

I was steamed at Rosie O'Donnell for tainting that moment for everyone in the room. Most of us, friend or foe, were all part of a journey to find out what happened to the victims of Robert Durst. Rosie made it about her. *Really? And who invited you?* I wanted to tell her off, but I didn't have time for such luxuries. I had a TV show to put together in less than an hour.

Jim McCormack told me recently that while I was in the other room with Diane, he approached Rosie and quietly introduced himself as Kathie's brother. He told her that Andrew and the FBI had their reasons for what was done, and that he was okay with it. "She reminded me of the classroom bully," he said. "I told her, 'This is not the time or place.'" He wasn't about to back down. "'It's not your role.'" Nonetheless, Rosie continued to rant as if it didn't matter what Kathie's own brother thought about the situation.

Jim McCormack and Cody were already booked to be on my show for the hour, even though we all were unaware of what bombshell we might be discussing. I rounded them up to leave the apartment and get into a waiting car. On the way out, I grabbed Bagli by the arm. "C'mon, you're doing my show," I said with a smile.

Stunned, he said, "No, I'm not. I'm sick." He was. He'd been coughing all night.

I couldn't let him use that as an excuse. He was too important a part of this story.

"You're not too sick to be here!"

"Oh, Jeanine . . ."

With a smile, I interrupted him. "Come on, Charlie. What, is it a Fox thing? Because you're the *New York Times*?" The Gray Lady had a decidedly liberal bias. And Fox News, of course, was fair and balanced. But those at the Gray Lady believed we leaned decidedly to the right. "Come on, Charlie! The news is just too explosive not to comment on, even for you."

I implored his wife, Ellie, standing next to him. He caved with a smile. I was thrilled, and he rode to Fox with Jim. Ellie, however, stayed at Andrew's apartment. Cody and I took my car. As the four of us walked into the building at 1211 Avenue of the Americas, I couldn't wait to get on the air and talk about what had happened. We got to the twelfth floor, where my *Justice* show is filmed, and were surrounded by people who, like us, had just watched *The Jinx*. Their faces and eyes betrayed their innermost feelings. Camera crew, producers, makeup artists, everyone was saying, "Can you believe it? Oh, my God!"

The "Oh, my God" going on in my head was how to break down thirty years in my one-hour special, how to convey not only the disruption, the havoc, and the pain heaped on innocent victims, but also the shock of a guy who had repeatedly professed his innocence for decades admitting he killed them all.

On air, Jim McCormack, amazingly, kept his composure and talked about the time Durst got angry with Kathie at a Christmas gathering at his mom's house. Robert didn't like spending time with the McCormacks, and having had enough family time, he told Kathie he wanted to leave. Kathie wanted to stay. Robert then grabbed Kathie's hair and pulled her out of the party. The guilt Jim felt for not doing something then was palpable, even all these years later. So many people carried guilt in the wake of Durst's homicidal deeds, wondering if they could've changed the course of events. The only one who should have felt guilt was Durst.

When the show wrapped, we were all still so keyed up, we rode back to Jarecki's. Andrew had returned home while we were live on Fox. I went over to him, hugged him, and said, "Damn. You did it. You're a hero."

He smiled a knowing smile of "I told you you'd have closure." He immediately asked where Cody was. Marc and Cody man-hugged, and then Andrew grabbed him and made him sit next to him on the couch. Everybody loved Cody, but these guys in particular had an affection for him. They knew he was in it for the right reasons. He was the moral core, the big Texan who teared up years later because of the overwhelming guilt that the case was lost, the man who understood he worked for God.

Okay, enough boy time. "Where were you guys?" I asked.

Andrew was now sitting with his laptop open. It reflected a faint light on his face. Clearly, every news outlet in the world was trying to get in touch with him.

Marc and Andrew *had* been upstate, sixty miles away, with a separate camera crew—the dude doesn't miss a trick. I later got wind of a search warrant being issued to remove boxes and boxes of Durst's possessions from the basement of a house owned by a woman he'd befriended who'd agreed to store some of his "stuff." The only thing that registered for me was that they weren't digging up a body.

I was exhausted yet elated. It'd been two tumultuous days of covering the story, as a host and as a source. But the law-enforcement blood that still runs through my veins was dancing.

Cody and I smiled at each other and found a corner in Andrew's big room. Now I had a beer. Or three.

Durst's arrest and the admission hit me on a personal level. The

relief and joy truly sank in for me. For fifteen years, he'd been outma-
neuvering some very smart people all over the country, only to admit
that he was a multiple murderer on national TV. Tonight life was
good. Durst was in jail. He was facing charges in New Orleans and
was wanted for murder in Los Angeles. I lifted my beer bottle to Cody
before taking a sip as he took his.

I said, "Congratulations, Detective Cazalas."

To which he replied, tipping his bottle against mine, "Congratulations, Madam DA."

| THE GUY'S ALWAYS IN THE BOX

Autumn 1999. I had already been district attorney of Westchester, New York, a county of almost one million people with forty-three separate and autonomous police departments, for over five years. Westchester is one of the wealthiest counties in the nation, but money doesn't insulate you from crime. We had our share of murder, robbery, rape, domestic violence, hate crimes, drug dealing, gangs, burglary, clergy abuse, arson, racketeering, Internet crimes, environmental crimes, economic fraud, child abuse, along with every other kind of human deviancy.

I was the first woman to hold the position, elected and reelected by then. I was a woman in a man's job. Every one of those forty-three police departments had a male police chief who needed my approval for their cases to be prosecuted, and none of them liked reporting to a woman. My giving them directives, on the other hand, didn't bother *me* one bit.

My office was huge, befitting the title. Wood paneling, mauve carpeting, formal, dead serious, and intimidating. I sat at the big mahogany desk with a badge on the wall behind it that read "District Attorney" in gold letters, just in case anyone forgot. On either side behind me were an American flag and the New York State flag.

The desk was always covered in paperwork and active case files. My phone had ten lines on it, and, at any given time, most of them were blinking.

Roseanne Paniccia, aka Ro, my assistant, was the gatekeeper. She always called me "Judge" because I had been elected county judge before I was elected DA. She had long, curly dark hair—which never changed in all the years she worked for me—an easy smile, a youthful face, and damn good street smarts. A classic Ro outfit was a short black skirt and high black boots. For accessories? A cigarette and a cup of coffee. Ro knew when to open the gate or fill the waters of the moat beneath it. In this case, the gate was a double mahogany door with four words in simple bronze block letters that read, "District Attorney Jeanine Pirro."

One day in late fall 1999, she came into my office and said, "Clem wants to see you and he's got Bender with him." Part of Ro's job was to announce anyone who wanted entry. There was no popping into my office. That doesn't mean I didn't walk across the hall to the trial bureau to eat lunch with my staff or to find out how their felony trial cases were going or if any of my ex-colleagues on the bench were giving them a hard time. But there was just too much going on to have a casual conversation about anything other than crime in my work zone, aka the Bermuda Triangle. Chain of command was something reinforced by my then chief assistant district attorney Francis T. Donohue—a retired two-star general. Frank and I were about as opposite, physically, as possible. He was a serious, tall, fair-skinned Irishman, well over six-foot-three, whose bible was chain of command, and I, on the other hand, was a gregarious, petite, dark-haired Lebanese, five-foot-four, who, because I was a woman in a sea of men, had made it a habit to jump chain of command whenever I could. But Frank and I did a great two-step. I often said that he was the iron fist in my lace glove. Together, we packed a hell of a punch.

Clement Patti, slim, slicked-back black hair (women swooned for him), was the second deputy DA and chief of the investigations division. Steve Bender, six-foot-two and lanky with curly brown hair and a mustache, an Errol Flynn type, was chief of homicide. Both were career prosecutors who did their job without reference to time, the weather, or the state of their marriages. Like me, they were relentless in their pursuit of justice.

"Boss, we're looking to search Lake Truesdale in South Salem," said Clem.

"Why?" I asked.

Steve filled me in on the background. They said a state trooper had received information from a low-level sex offender, something about a body being dumped in the lake years ago. The woman had gone missing in 1982.

"Who's the informant?" I asked.

"Timothy Martin."

"Who's he? Is he one of our CIs [confidential informants]?"

They proceeded to tell me that we prosecuted and convicted Martin of public lewdness. Apparently, he got off on driving up to female pedestrians, calling them over to his car window, and exposing himself. I asked if he was trustworthy. Most informants are dirtbags to begin with. And it was always a question of whether this one was a believable dirtbag.

And what did he want? I assumed he was looking, like every other defendant, to get a reduced sentence in exchange for information.

In most counties, prosecution begins with an arrest and ends with a conviction. My policy in Westchester was to be proactive and more aggressive. We tried to debrief every defendant we arrested, giving him or her the opportunity to shed light on other crimes he or she might know about. If the tip led to an arrest, so much the better for the defendant. You'd be amazed what criminals would divulge when faced with jail time. And you'd be surprised how frequently defendants ratted each other out. Unless, of course, they were looking for three hots and a cot, which for many of them was better housing and food than what they already had.

I'd amassed a large discretionary prosecution fund by aggressively seizing property from drug dealers, car thieves, and the like. My hitting criminals in their pockets or taking their assets and selling them had afforded us both the opportunity and the ability to use additional resources to investigate crime. Money was not a problem. There was always money to use on cold cases.

"By the way, who's the trooper?" I asked.

"Joey Becerra," said Steve.

I knew him. I had hired Joe's brother Pete Becerra as one of my criminal investigators. Pete was a class act—diligent and tireless, a good man with a gentle soul. His brother Joe was a bit flashier and had earned the nickname "Hollywood Joe" for always managing to get his mug in front of a TV camera. (Pete Becerra passed away at fifty-two from cancer in 2012. It was law enforcement's loss.)

In 1999, I had no idea that Joe Becerra would end up being both an asset to the case and a huge thorn in our side. But back then, I knew him as the brother of one of my investigators for whom I had the utmost respect.

"What do we know?" I asked.

Apparently, Timothy Martin's brother Alan used to be married to a woman named Janet Fiske, a housekeeper at the South Salem home. Janet told Alan, who subsequently told Tim, that the man who lived in the cottage murdered his wife and got rid of the body in the lake or buried it in the woods surrounding the property. Of course, it was hearsay. But some cases start like that. You don't expect criminals to confess to their crimes on national TV, do you?

Bender said, "The wife, Kathleen Durst, has been missing since '82."

"Tell me more."

"The husband, Robert Durst, didn't report his wife missing for

five days. And, by the way, the Dursts own half of New York City."
Totally casual.

"Durst? I don't know that name." I would learn soon enough that
the Durst Organization built Times Square and was a third-generation
Manhattan real-estate dynasty.

Wealthy family? Missing wife? Husband didn't report her missing for five days? The bells started clanging in my head. There were
always urgent messages on my desk, at least two phone lines on hold,
meetings scheduled all day, and Ro, standing at the door to tell me
about a previously scheduled appointment. My job was nonstop, 24/7,
a million miles a minute. We prosecuted thirty-five thousand to forty
thousand cases a year. My attention was always divided, at times
schizophrenic. But there was something about this case that made me
ignore all the other pressing demands and zero in.

I said, "How old was Kathleen?"

Steve said, "Twenty-nine, a fourth-year medical school student.
She was supposed to graduate a few months after she disappeared."

"She was in medical school? In 1982?"

Back in '82, I was a few years out of law school, one of the few
women in my class. Although it doesn't seem that long ago, in the
mid-seventies, it was highly unusual for women to go to medical or
law school. Like me, Kathleen must have been a strong, determined
woman. She wouldn't stick it out in medical school for four years,
fighting the way I know she must have, only to run off within sight of
her graduation. Something sinister had happened to her.

I loved being district attorney, leading the charge every day on the
battlefield, where the fight between good and evil unfolds. We were
the cavalry with the white hats, the angels at our sides, avenging the
wrongs that one human inflicts upon another. Yes, I loved what I did.
I loved being DA, settling scores, leveling the playing field for crime
victims who never chose to be victims in the first place.

And I liked cold cases. They were even more challenging and

mysterious because they were dated. I *loved* using DNA testing, the brand-new technology, to solve them. It was like the finger of God pointing down and saying, "You did it," or for that matter, "You *didn't* do it." We had just cracked the first cold case in New York using DNA evidence and even received an award for it, with one of my top prosecutors, Barbara Egenhauser. The case was a 1979 Mount Vernon murder. While an infant girl slept in her crib, her mother was stabbed to death. The murder went unsolved for decades. And then, when DNA technology hit, we had evidence from that brutal slaying pulled from the property clerk's office to have it tested for any match—hair, fiber, blood. A dried blood sample, miraculously viable despite the passage of time, was run through a DNA bank of samples of convicted criminals. Incredibly, there was a match. The murderer was already in prison. It was a classic "Fucking A!" moment, one of the most amazing I had experienced in law enforcement.

I was always a believer that the answer to solving most cases, and definitely cold cases, was already in the box. I would often say, "The guy's in the box," meaning the killer's name was already in the investigation file somewhere. Sure enough, detectives had interviewed the murderer of the young mother in 1979. They couldn't pin him to the crime then. Now? Thanks to DNA, he was busted. There was a great deal of interest in how such an old case could be solved now but not decades ago. So I held a press conference to announce the indictment, twenty years later. The baby who'd been deprived of her mother's love for all those years was now a beautiful young woman who stood by my side at the podium. She, no doubt, never expected justice. But she got it.

I loved bringing justice to victims. I was convinced that we could tap into the DNA data bank and crack dozens, if not hundreds, of cold cases using this new forensic technology. It might even work on the cold case of the missing medical student that Clem and Steve brought to me that day.

I made the decision then and there, saying, "Do it. Search the lake. Keep me informed on this one."

Despite what you might see on TV, reopening a cold case isn't something that just happens. There has to be an assignment of personnel and resources beyond the continuing prioritization of incoming cases. Only the DA can impanel a grand jury and pull the trigger. There were *plenty* of pressing new cases that needed attention. To divert resources to a decades-old missing-persons case might not have interested everyone, but I didn't hesitate on this one. I had that gut feeling. The case needed a second look.

I certainly had no inkling that my spontaneous "Do it" would put me at the forefront of a far bigger story, one that continues to this day.

I brought in some of my best people to chart out the next steps. Senior investigator John O'Donnell (no relation to Rosie O'Donnell), Clem Patti, Steve Bender, and I gathered in a conference room to go through copies of the file collected from the NYPD. Although the husband said he last saw Kathleen, nicknamed Kathie, at the train station in Katonah in Westchester, the investigation began and ended in Manhattan, where other witnesses say they saw her later that night.

During the meeting, a Pandora's box was opened up for me. I saw photos of Kathie Durst for the first time. She was young, pretty, with long, wavy dark blond hair. Her clothes—peasant blouses and bell-bottom jeans—reminded me of my own swinging style back in law school. She was close to my age, and must have jumped countless hurdles, as I had, to pursue a degree in what was then thought of as a man's profession. You could tell she was vivacious and had an easy smile. She came from a modest background, from a close working-class family, also like me. I read that she and her husband used to hang out at the same clubs in Manhattan I frequented, such as Xenon and Studio 54. For all I know, I might have boogied next to her on the dance floor. We even drove the same car, a red four-door 240D Mercedes diesel.

I couldn't *not* feel a connection to this woman.

Somewhere in the files, I'd find the name of the person responsible for whatever had happened to this bright, pretty young woman. I was as sure of that as I'd been of any cold case. Unlike most of the ones I'd investigated so far, though, I was stunned by how little we had to work with from the initial investigation. A murder investigation in my county would produce a full box, a stack of files as heavy and thick as a few phone books. The NYPD box on Kathie Durst was light, the file itself amazingly narrow.

In good time, my investigators would comb through every piece of evidence and pore over every police report and eyewitness statement. We'd become intimately familiar with every friend, relative, and contact of Kathie's. We'd come across many names—elevator operators, doormen, housekeepers, a dean, a drug dealer, neighbors in Manhattan and South Salem—but only one name resonated with me. It jumped out at me and cropped up on nearly every page of the reports.

Robert Durst.

The husband. He supplied all the leads followed by the NYPD detective, one Michael Struk.

The Durst Organization was the employer of all the eyewitnesses who "saw" her in Manhattan the night she disappeared.

He said many unsavory things about his pretty young wife. I recognized it immediately and said to myself, *Here we go again*. The classic blame-the-victim. Blame the person who is not responsible for her demise.

He had also told the detective that their marriage had been on the rocks. Certainly none of the distraught-husband thing going on here.

Struk opened the investigation on February 5, 1982, pursued the case until April, and then dropped it in December. During those ten months, there had been no sign of Kathie. Not a peep or a call to her family and friends. Not a blip on phone records or credit cards.

Struk, along with his superiors, concluded that, apparently, she'd just run away, and that was that. Forget that all the earmarks were there. Marriage on the rocks, and the husband waits five days to report her missing? What were you doing during those five days? Show me how you tried to find her. And that front-page $100,000 reward? We later found out that that was a printing error and Durst pulled the reward back to $10,000 or $15,000, depending on where you saw it.

Ran away? I did *not* get a runaway vibe from what was in the box. It made no sense. Why would Kathie run away from everything she'd ever known and every person she'd ever loved? Not to mention that she was weeks away from becoming a medical doctor.

This woman didn't disappear. She was *disappeared*.

I fished out a photo of the bride and groom and took a close look at Robert Durst, the wealthy, older husband, a man with power and influence, without a modicum of respect for the woman he married.

The seventies were a bad time to be female in New York. Abusive husbands, boyfriends, and fathers could pretty much do anything to their wives, girlfriends, and children. Domestic violence was a family matter. Child abuse was a social issue. They weren't even considered crimes. A rich man with a smart lawyer could get away with a whole lot back then.

Wealthy, powerful husband.

Pretty younger wife with everything to live for.

He doesn't report her missing for five days.

It was obvious to each of us in the conference room that day that something terrible had happened to Kathleen Durst in '82.

The NYPD detective had kicked the case around the block, and then dumped it with a shrug and a whatever.

This missing medical student with the big smile and sad eyes deserved better.

I was going to give Kathleen Durst the investigation she deserved.

| WHERE IS KATHIE DURST?

Until 1977, New York law *prevented* prosecutors from getting involved in cases of abuse between husbands and wives. A woman could be shot, stabbed, beaten, and brutalized, but if she didn't die, even assuming she wanted to pursue it, the case was automatically sent to family court. The legislative intent of Article Eight of the Family Court Act was to keep the family unit together *at all costs*, even when a woman's life was in jeopardy.

Really? So we should send a guy who's beating the crap out of his wife to Family Court so they can mediate? How do you mediate between a batterer and his victim? Do you send him to counseling to teach him not to beat her up? He *knows* not to do it, and he does it anyway. My philosophy? Abusive husbands, boyfriends, fathers, and brothers should be arrested, convicted, and thrown in prison—not mediated, incarcerated.

When I became an assistant district attorney in Westchester County in 1975, it was outright blasphemy to say so, or to try to change the way "domestics" were handled. Usually, the cop would walk the husband around the block to cool off and tell the black-and-blue wife to go stay with her mom for the night.

Under my watch, in Westchester, that was going to change.

In 1978, after the law was changed in New York State, I started one of the first four Domestic Violence Units in the nation. The units were funded by the law-enforcement assistance administration of the Department of Justice. Of the initial four programs, mine was the most successful, in terms of arrests and convictions. By providing support, mental health services, and shelter, in addition to whatever she needed, a battered woman would continue with the prosecution.

One of the unit's requirements was to train cops in how to properly respond to a domestic dispute. So I trained new cops at the rookie schools, showing them pictures of women whose faces had been beaten beyond recognition and of children scalded with boiling water, and I went into police stations.

The then DA, my boss, called a meeting of all forty-three police chiefs in my county to inform them they should be making arrests in domestic violence cases. He knew full well that a letter from an ADA, especially a female, wouldn't draw a crowd. I was the only woman, as I would often be, in a room filled with cops all wrapped up in their gun belts.

I was about to get started when one of the police chiefs asked if I could get him a cup of coffee. These were tough guys—Dirty Harry types with sideburns, polyester suits, and big chips on their shoulders. If serving them coffee would keep women and children from being abused, so be it. Sooner or later, I knew I would have the upper hand, and now was not the time to fight about petty things.

I didn't ask for universal acceptance. I asked, "Milk and sugar?" Sometimes, I got acceptance along with the coffee. Mostly, I got flak. Cops in the city, and all over the state, would see me and my unit colleagues coming and say, "Here comes the Tit Patrol." Some called us the "Panty Brigade." And I never hesitated to return the favor, calling them "dicks" whenever I could.

An issue that came up a lot back in those training sessions was the cops' view that domestic violence was a lower-class problem. The thinking was pervasive because they saw more incidents in those areas. Why? There was more visibility in more crowded apartments—with more chance that the beatings could be heard. But we were about to find that women in upscale Bedford and Rye were beaten, too. It didn't matter if the woman lived in a rent-controlled apartment in Yonkers or a mansion in Scarsdale. It mattered not his chosen trade, whether he was a bus driver, lawyer, teacher, garbage collector, doctor. There are no parameters, class or otherwise. What mattered was his desire for power and control. Abuse is abuse is abuse.

Our work was cut out for us. The whole concept was new. Socially, we had been reared to believe that whatever happens in the family behind closed doors is not the business of outsiders, especially police. Judges, more often than not, reflected the mores of society. Defense attorneys exploited loopholes in these new laws.

I worked closely with Marjory Fields, then the head of the South Brooklyn Legal Services Family Law Unit (she later became a family court judge). We were constantly reworking New York's criminal procedure law and penal law. She had, and continues to have, an incredibly brilliant legal mind. She and I were like Mutt and Jeff, fighting everybody to get laws passed to increase punishment and to provide a framework for real prosecutions. We continued to work on orders of protection. Governors Hugh Carey and Mario Cuomo appointed us to draft legislation for New York State to protect battered women. Later, Governor George Pataki would make me the chair of New York State's Commission on Domestic Violence Fatality Review, also known as the Pirro Commission.

New York City in particular didn't have a stellar record of protecting battered women, or women covered by orders of protection, for that matter. In fact, the NYPD was repeatedly sued to force them to protect those women and arrest their abusers. Before those suits, most cops wouldn't take women's claims that they feared for their lives seriously. They believed women to be untruthful, and that they provoked their abusers. When I would talk to NYPD cops about domestic violence, they'd fold their arms over their chests and just stare me down. Laws can be changed with a vote, but changing a culture of violence was harder.

Sadly, that culture of violence didn't change soon enough to save Kathie Durst.

Another requirement of my unit was to train staffers in hospitals to identify domestic violence victims. We even went to medical centers to talk with doctors, nurses, social workers, anyone. It was not enough to just treat a woman who claimed to have accidentally broken her arm or hurt her stomach by falling down the stairs. Emergency room personnel had to be trained what to look for, what injuries indicated abuse, what injuries were consistent with accidents, when to call the cops, and when to offer social services to victims.

At the same time we were training cops, drafting legislation, going to hospitals, and fighting to keep the funds flowing into my domestic violence unit, Kathleen Durst, a medical student, was being battered by her husband in elite South Salem and was once treated at Jacobi Medical Center in the Bronx, where I had actually given a lecture on domestic violence. She was exactly the kind of woman I was fighting to educate and protect. It's chilling to think that, if she'd survived to graduate medical school and gone to work at a local hospital, I might have handed her one of our pamphlets about signs to look for in victims. But, of course, she would have known that information already, from personal experience.

MY EFFORTS TO LEVEL the playing field for women were not a feminist crusade. I was just a fighter. I'm not one to get caught up in shades of gray. When it comes to crime, it's black and white. And you don't dare tell me the victim asked for it. The "victim precipitated violence" excuse would send me flying. Don't give me this hogwash about background or growing up in a violent home as an excuse. You did it; you pay for it. I had to fight for that from my earliest days as an ADA to my final days as the DA.

When I first arrived in White Plains in 1975, I was Phi Beta Kappa and magna cum laude. In law school, I was on the Law Review and all that happy horseshit. I'd compare my credentials nicely against any man's. My dream was to try cases, but the bosses weren't going to let me near a trial. They tucked me away in the Appeals Bureau, to some an esoteric thinking place to review transcripts of trials, but to me a black hole of paperwork and drudgery.

Not exactly the cup of tea of someone who likes to fight.

I remember one day I went out to grab lunch with a few of my colleagues from the Appeals Bureau—all men, of course. We were walking back to the office carrying our brown bags with our sandwiches when, right in front of us, a police car went flying through a red light and smashed into a station wagon with two women and a bunch of kids inside.

The cops didn't even get out of the car to see if the women and kids in the wagon were okay. I said, "Oh, my God! Let's go check on the station wagon."

The other ADAs scoffed and said they were heading back to the office.

"What?" I couldn't believe my ears. "The cops blew through a red light. They didn't even have their siren on. There might be people hurt in there!"

The guys just shrugged and left me standing there. I went over to the women in the station wagon to see if they needed help. I gave them my contact info. "I'm a witness," I said. "If you need to, call me."

Coming to the aid of the vulnerable was ingrained in me as a kid. When I was growing up in Elmira, New York, my mom made me go across Catherine Street and wash my elderly neighbor Mrs. Fleming's hair every Saturday. Afterward, she would give me a piece of freshly made cake to eat as we sat on her big Victorian front porch. I always chose the rocker.

Looking back, I realize so much that didn't even occur to me then. One, when you get as old as Mrs. Fleming, you can't lift your arms high enough to wash your hair. Two, Mrs. Fleming may have been a covert operative of the CIA. Should anything need to be divulged from those conversations, Agent Fleming was at the ready to call Esther Ferris—my mom.

Mom and I would also go food shopping for Mrs. LaBert and then put away her groceries. Mrs. LaBert kept her yellow blinds drawn and it was always dark in her apartment.

I asked Mom, "Why is it so dark in here?"

"She's blind," Mom said. "We're her eyes."

I understood that if we didn't help, Mrs. Fleming and Mrs. LaBert wouldn't be able to maintain their dignity, let alone meet their own basic human needs. It was ingrained in me by my mom—who herself had no teacher, whose own parents left her in a foreign land—that it was my obligation and responsibility as their neighbor to do for others. That was the town I grew up in. That was my mom.

Esther was born in New York. Her dad fought in World War II and her mother was American-born as well. But, as the oldest female of four children of a father who wanted sons, she was shipped at the age of five to Lebanon to be raised by relatives along with her sisters. She had no wealth or power, nor anyone to speak for her, and was denied the benefits that America offers its citizens simply because she was a girl. Apparently, Grandpa didn't know that it was he who determined the sex of his children. I'd like to slap him with that one now. Through no fault of her own, merely because of her gender, Mom started life at a disadvantage.

None of that was lost on me. I realized that the most vulnerable people in our neighborhood, in society at large, were women, children, and the elderly. My mother taught me that through her history and her deeds. I grew up carrying my mother's baggage, gratefully. It made me strong and gave me a purpose.

Elie Wiesel once said, "We must take sides. Neutrality helps the oppressor, never the victim. Silence encourages the tormentor, never the tormented." I chose to take sides.

As a woman and a lawyer, my career would be speaking for the vulnerable. I decided to take the side of the victim.

I'm very outspoken when I think something is wrong. A cop car slamming into a wagon full of mothers and kids and the cops not even getting out? I wasn't going to let that slip.

A few days after the incident, I got a call from the secretary of Tom Facelle, the chief assistant, the number-two guy in the district attorney's office. I was summoned to his office. Facelle, scary to a young ADA by virtue of his title alone, looked like a combination of Edward G. Robinson and Peter Lorre—short, dark, brooding, intense. With a cigarette in his hand and one in the ashtray, he looked me up and down and said, "I received a call from the White Plains police department."

Oh, boy. Either the women had trumpeted that an assistant district attorney offered to help them against the police, or the police took note of the ADA doing it. He proceeded to ask me what exactly I saw and what my vantage point revealed, and was I sure of what I saw. He was razor sharp and focused, and then he asked why I got involved in the whole thing.

"So you decided to anoint yourself the one to set the moral standard for us," he said. He had an ever-so-faint smile on his face as he put out his cigarette and said, "Next time, mind your own business."

Looking back now, I understand the politics and the complaint from the police department: "You want us to help you fight crime and testify on behalf of the victims while one of yours is volunteering to testify against us."

At the time, I was just doing what I thought was the right thing.

Facelle called me in to size up the female ADA who was outspoken. He got his look, and then he sent me out.

Mind my own business. Like *that* was going to happen.

Meanwhile, back in the Appeals Bureau, I was given transcripts, transcripts, transcripts. It seemed to be official government policy to keep the little woman out of the courtroom. I remember sitting at my desk, saying to myself, "I'm *dying*. I need to fight. I need to try cases. I need to get into a courtroom."

I would go to my supervisor, Carl Lodes, and ask, "When can I get out of here and start trying cases?"

He said, "You should be grateful to have a job." It seemed to me the more I asked, the longer I stayed there. Guys were moving up quicker than I was. I remember one of my evaluations said I had a bad attitude because of my desire to get out of there. Yep. Apparently, the equal protection clause of the Fourteenth Amendment didn't apply to my circumstance. It was abundantly clear that I'd have to sneak my way into court.

Whenever I went on a sandwich run with my male counterparts, they often complained about the trials they were working, as in, "Shit, I got local court tonight," or, "Shit, I got the circuit tonight." I thought, *God, don't I wish I had local court tonight!*

The local night courts, known as "the circuit," were held after 5:00 p.m., and invariably required travel. Westchester is a large county, and the guys would have to drive for miles to get to Chappaqua or New Castle, and then miles *back* to White Plains or wherever they might live in Westchester. To them, pulling "the circuit" was a huge pain, especially on a Thursday or Friday night, date night to most of them.

Their pain was my golden ticket.

So one day, I asked a male ADA, "Are you trying any cases next week?"

He groaned. "A DWI in Yorktown." Thirty miles away.

I said, "How 'bout I try it for you."

He looked at me like I was nuts. "You?"

"I've read DWI appeals transcripts so I know what to do. I'll put your name on the file. I won't even say I did it." There were no computers back in the late seventies and not a lot of oversight, either. I could write on the files that Ronald McDonald tried the case, and no one would be the wiser. It was the disposition of the case that mattered.

No work or travel but all the credit? His eyes betrayed his excitement. "Okay, knock yourself out," he said.

And that was how I tried my first case. I happily traveled to Yorktown in my red Alfa Romeo, even picked the jury—something I'd never seen let alone done before—and I won! I remember the court clerk telling me the judge was actually amused by me and suggested I not stomp my foot when the court ruled against me. Baby steps . . .

As promised, I gave the male ADA credit. He was so pleased with the situation, he bragged about it to the other guys. Soon enough, other ADAs started asking me to try their local cases for them, and I, this little pip-squeak with the frizzy hair and horn-rimmed glasses, started winning misdemeanor cases all over the county.

And then I got another call from Tom Facelle's (aka Edward G. Robinson's) office.

"*What* are you doing?" he yelled when I walked in.

"What *ever* do you mean?" I asked. I might've batted my eyelashes.

"You're in Appeals. You. Do. Not. Have. Our. Permission. To. Try. These. Cases. What makes you think you even *know* how to try a case?"

"Well, Mr. Facelle, I learned from the best. When I wasn't doing appeals, I would go to the library and look for any trial transcript of yours. You were great in the courtroom. I even have notebooks of your best arguments."

He put the cigarette down in the ashtray. The corner of his mouth turned down to suppress a smile. "You'll try cases when we want you to try cases." I was then invited to remove myself from his office.

Tony Morosco, my boss in Appeals, was also livid. But neither one could deny my perfect record. It wasn't long after that that I was moved out of Appeals and into local courts to try cases to my heart's content.

Before long, I started trying felony cases. The same male colleagues who loved me for winning their misdemeanor cases and giving them credit now hated my guts. I was a petite, pushy female, stealing cases and glory from the big, bad alphas in polyester three-piece suits. Even after I'd been winning, I heard guys say about me, "What gives this bitch the right to try cases?"

Like most men, they looked at me and didn't know if they should be pissed off, scared, or turned on.

They were probably all of the above.

So, yes, I did get hit on as well. One guy, an investigator with a lot of attitude and slicked-back hair, sauntered up to me at the Xerox machine. "You're looking pretty good today, Jeanine," he said.

I was so naïve. I looked at him through my thick horn-rimmed glasses and chirped, "Oh, thank you!"

"You know, you ought to start getting around a little."

I suddenly got it. Even though I was prosecuting rapists, I had no idea how to handle myself in a sexual situation. Half the time, I didn't even get what was happening. I grabbed my photocopies and scurried away.

In the early eighties, my buddy Tom Facelle called me into his office again to tell me that, as a woman, I was exempt from homicide duty. I objected, saying I didn't understand why. He told me, "Women shouldn't be 'rolling' in the middle of the night on homicide duty. We can't have our women going out there."

I then proceeded to take that to the DA, Carl Vergari, and said that

I wanted to try homicides. "Women don't try homicides!" he blurted. "They can't go for the jugular."

Homicides were my glass ceiling as an ADA. I couldn't break through. After years of bashing against it to no avail, I finally elbowed my way into trying a homicide, as the chief of the Domestic Violence Unit. No woman in the history of Westchester County had ever prosecuted a homicide before.

A man named Clarence Barger strangled his wife to death. Incredibly, his sons testified on behalf of their father at the trial. I remember telling the jury that the husband wrapped his hands around the neck of his neglected wife, and squeezed, intending to kill. This was no easy feat. I asked the medical examiner how long it would take to choke the life out of her. He said, "Thirty seconds." So, in court, I looked at my watch for thirty seconds, so the jury would know just how long Barger throttled her. It was excruciating, and a most effective way to demonstrate his savagery.

I got a conviction in the Barger case and in every felony case after that. My critics have said, "She picked easy cases." Bullshit. I took only the toughest cases. There was even one time when the boss called to congratulate me after his boys had referred a case to me, thinking it couldn't be won. It was my passion to bring the jury along with me as I presented the argument, making sure they understood the pain of the victims and the ripple effect the crime had in the lives of the survivors. Prosecuting abusers like Barger isn't only about locking up the criminals. It's about bringing justice to the victims and smoothing out the ripples for the families.

After a while, I began to develop a reputation, and it seemed that I was in the paper more than Vergari himself because of cases that I tried or speeches that I gave. I was the consummate professional. I loved my job and I loved being able to settle scores. The men who beat women and thought they could get away with it, the men who killed women, the same men who said they would love and obey their wives,

were going to prison because I was determined. Governors were ap-
pointing me to committees and I was asked routinely to testify before
the NYS legislature and even the U.S. Senate.

Things started to change for me at the office. I thought that pub-
licizing the effectiveness of the Domestic Violence Unit would not
only deter batterers, but would bring victims forward. I created brochures for hospitals and police departments advising women as well as
some men of their right to prosecute crimes previously hidden behind
closed doors. They had my photo on them, giving women a face to
relate to, not a male's.

Then, in the midst of all the successes of my unit, the DA axed
us from the budget. It seemed that homicides and assaults involving
strangers were more worthy of prosecution than those involving families. Suddenly, there was no money for brochures.

I knew nothing of politics. I didn't even know who to call. But
I knew how to fight. I put together a committee of strong, like-minded
individuals who believed not only that domestic violence was a tragedy for the victims, but that the unit was a tool to be used to educate
future victims and batterers.

I made an impassioned plea before the county board of legislators
who funded the DA's budget, followed by victims willing to show pictures of themselves after a beating and by religious and mental health
personnel. After weeks of imploring every county legislator individu-
ally and discussing with the press the importance of our mission, the
Domestic Violence Unit was put back into the DA's budget. Many in
the office were none too happy with that success.

If I could do that, I knew I could one day run for DA. Step one was
to become the first woman elected to the county court bench. That
happened in 1989.

The view from the bench? It looked a lot like it had in the trenches.
Most of the male judges wanted nothing to do with me. When I asked

one for advice, he simply refused, and the others never invited me to have lunch with them.

On my first day in robes, I remember whispering to my female court clerk, "Where's the ladies' room?"

She explained that my only choices were the judges' bathroom, where my male colleagues would be using the urinals, or the public bathroom, where I would find the families of the defendants that I'd just sentenced.

To pee or not to pee? Eventually, I had to make a choice. I used the public restroom, but took off my robe before I walked in there.

To get the cops to listen to me, I gave them coffee. To get in with the ADAs, I gave them credit. To get in with the *judges*, I gave them lunch. The old adage is true: The fastest way to a man's heart, including a judge's, is through his stomach. I wooed them with food. I brought in china plates and a silver coffee urn from home, and I transformed the judges' dining room in the courthouse into a five-star restaurant. I made pasta, salads, and soups and bought dessert, staying up half the night to prepare the meal. I even threw in some cigars. After that, the judges loved me. They bought me an apron that said "Judge Jeanine."

Although I grew to love Judge Peter Rosato and Justice Nick Colabella, among others, I didn't love *being* a judge. I felt like a referee, making the calls "sustained," "overruled," and "sidebar." It felt wrong to sit up there and moderate. I was a born fighter, and I longed to be back in the trenches, solving cases and convicting scumbags. Trying cases, I was active. I was settling scores. I was in control. On the bench, I was reactive, controlled by precedent. It wasn't a good fit for me.

After only three years of my ten-year elected term on the bench, I made the decision to give up my robes in 1993. And they were beautiful robes at that. I had them custom made for me in black, navy, and brown, nothing too flashy, and lined with pink so I could turn up the edge and shock myself on a dreary, boring afternoon of testimony. I'm not exaggerating. There were judges who would literally fall asleep on the bench.

My mother, Esther, was hysterical. She thought I was turning my back on the most prestigious job I could ever hope to have. I understood where she was coming from. Mom was so proud of me as a judge. The title alone was the ultimate symbol of her daughter's success. Taking those robes off was, to her, like throwing away the American Dream. But Mom also knew me well. She knew law enforcement was in my blood. I wasn't done with it yet, not by a long shot.

I was ready for step two: run for DA. Because of the respect I had for Carl Vergari, I waited for him to retire before seeking the office. In 1993, I was elected the first female district attorney in county history. I'd come a long way from the Appeals Bureau.

I was forty-two years old, I knew I had the best job in the world, and I felt like I was just getting started. I'll never forget the morning after I was elected DA. I jumped out of bed, dancing, singing, "I'm the DA! Oh, my God!"

My real indoctrination began at midnight on January 1, 1994, with a brutal, barbaric assault on a beautiful young mother, Anne Scripps Douglas, heiress to a publishing fortune. A chronically battered wife, she was hammered in her bed by her husband, Scott Douglas. Their three-year-old daughter told the police, "Daddy gave Mommy so many boo-boos." Soon after the attack, Douglas's BMW was found abandoned on the Tappan Zee Bridge. He might've jumped, or fled with an accomplice. During the national manhunt to catch him, my office was the command center. I had multiple agencies working in concert and directed the investigation. I wasn't on the job more than three or four days and I remember one of my investigators saying to me at the time, "You're going to love this job."

"I love it already," I said. "Now get back to work." We were all energized, working together doing what we loved.

Anne lingered for five days before she died of her injuries. Three months later, after hundreds of leads, Douglas's decomposed body was found in the Bronx on the bank of the Hudson River. A suicide. Eerily, his wristwatch had stopped at midnight. Sadly, I couldn't settle that score. I didn't get to prosecute him. I'm sure he's being punished as we speak.

Being the DA *was* the best job in the world. Day in, day out, for twelve years and three terms, I leveled the playing field. I spoke (loudly) for the vulnerable and voiceless. I fought for the victims who went through hell because some dirtbag made a decision to brutalize them.

That was the easy part of the job. The hard part was the continuing annoyance of misogyny in law enforcement. I was the boss in the big office, and the alphas in polyester suits were *still* mumbling under their breath, "Do I fucking believe I'm working for a woman?"

New title, new job, same old resentment.

I TELL YOU ALL this simply to give you an idea of what it was like in 1999 when I first heard the name Durst. By then, I'd gained a national reputation fighting for domestic violence victims for over twenty years. But this case really got under my skin. Most domestic violence homicides include a body. But Kathie was never found and wasn't even given the dignity of a burial. Her family was left never knowing where she was.

Was there ever a woman who'd been silenced as definitively as Kathie Durst? She'd been wiped off the face of the earth like a gnat. Her husband and his influential family didn't lift a finger to find her. The NYPD blew it off, as if Kathie were expendable and not worth searching for. When I read her case file, I saw the telltale signs of domestic violence I'd trained so many others to recognize and report.

Kathie Durst was a battered woman. She disappeared without a trace, and no one suspected the husband? How was it even possible?

The informant, Timothy Martin, recalled that, eighteen years earlier, his sister-in-law Janet told him about a murder in a lakeside cottage in South Salem. It was a thin hook to reopen a case on. But I couldn't ignore my gut.

John O'Donnell, rugged, tall, athletic, and in-your-face, was my first choice to investigate this case. He'd been with me from the beginning. And it was a pretty wild beginning. The same day—January 1, 1994—that I took my oath of office, John O'Donnell was the investigator who responded to the "jumper" at the Tappan Zee Bridge, aka Scott Douglas. I'd trust John with my life, and knew he'd do a brilliant job on the Durst case.

I also tapped Eddie Murphy. I brought Eddie into the DA's office because he had a reputation as one of the best homicide detectives in New York City. I had to go to Albany to get a special waiver for him, since he was eyeing retirement, so that he could get a pension and also get paid by me. I didn't like the idea of double-dipping but I needed to have a deep bench for homicides. Eddie had a low-key old-cop mentality. He could beat the streets and he could read people. He had no ego, was laid-back and smart as hell. He also had a rockin' mustache that he still wears today.

The New York State Police dive team performed a grid search of Lake Truesdale in November 1999, working in eight-hour shifts. They found nothing. Honestly, I wasn't surprised. John O'Donnell searched for a meteorological report of the conditions on January 31, 1982, the night Kathie disappeared. Lake Truesdale would have been frozen solid. But it was possible the murderer could have carved a hole in the ice or stored the body until a thaw to dump later. It was worth a shot.

When that didn't pan out, the next step was to do a search of the cottage itself. Kathie's husband, Robert Durst, sold the house back in 1990, eight years after the disappearance, to Carmen and David Garceau. They'd later sold it to Gabrielle Colquitt, the owner at the time. She gave us permission to go in and search.

The Garceaus told us that when they bought the place from Durst it was in shambles, with holes in the living room floor that were covered with plywood. Had Robert cut out blood spots on the floor and done a slapdash job of repairing it? They also told us that there was a crawl space with an unhinged door on the cottage's lower level that opened up to the lake. During the last months before the sale of the house was final, the Garceaus said that Robert slept in a cot outside that creepy crawl space.

Weird, yes. Suspicious? Absolutely. We went in with cadaver dogs on loan to us from Rockland County because the state police's canine team was on another case. It would have been unusual to discover blood or tissue after all those years, but we couldn't leave any stone unturned. If the body had been stored in the crawl space, we found no evidence of it.

My team went back to the box to reinvestigate every aspect of the case that the NYPD punted back in '82.

One thing was painfully clear: There was no proof about Kathie's movements in South Salem (where she lived), Katonah (where she allegedly caught a train), or Manhattan (where she also lived and was reportedly last seen) on the night she disappeared. Her husband, Robert, supplied the entire story, and backed it up with dubious-at-best witnesses.

No one with the NYPD or New York State Police searched the cottage in South Salem at the time. Nobody checked Durst's car. There was no crime-scene preservation. There was *nothing*. The woman *vanished*, and nobody looked in the couple's home? To this day, I can't believe nobody thought to search the house of the man who said his marriage was in trouble and didn't bother to report his wife missing for five days.

The whole thing stank like the inside of that earthen, musty crawl space.

I knew he did it. I knew it from day one. I just had to connect the dots.

ON FEBRUARY 5, 1982, Robert Durst walked into the Twentieth Precinct on West Eighty-Second Street. The precinct spans an area from Harlem in the north and east to Columbia University to the west and Riverside Drive to the south and west.

Desk Sergeant Michael Struk took Durst's statement. Robert made sure Struk knew who he was dealing with by actually bringing with him an article from an old issue of *New York* magazine called "The Men Who Own New York" by Nicholas Pileggi. The article featured his father, Seymour Durst, prominently. That *New York* magazine article really got Struk's attention. The second line of the missing-persons report was that the "subject is the daughter-in-law of real-estate executive Seymour Durst."

After the hierarchy was established, Robert told Struk a story about his wife.

On the night of January 31, Kathie went to a party at her friend Gilberte Najamy's house. She returned home. She and Robert ate dinner and drank a bottle of wine at their cottage. The couple had an argument, and she decided to go back to their Riverside Drive apartment in Manhattan. Robert drove her to the Katonah station to catch the 9:17 p.m. train to the city. He drove back to South Salem and had a glass of wine at his neighbor William Mayer's house. He returned home and called Kathie around eleven. That was the last time they spoke.

He told Struk that Kathie was a heavy drinker, a drug user, unfaithful, and that she was in therapy. As to why he waited so long to report her missing, Durst said he assumed she was busy at medical school and had been sleeping over there. When he got a call from the school asking where she was, he came right in to the precinct.

On February 6, Gilberte spoke to Struk. She gave him an earful about Kathie and Robert's marriage. She told him that Kathie had retained a lawyer to get the divorce ball rolling, and that the couple often fought physically. Friends of Kathie's had seen bruises. Kathie often called her in the middle of the night to say she was afraid of Robert and that he'd threatened her with a gun. Gilberte described her last conversation with Kathie, who'd said ominously, "If something happens to me, don't let Bobby get away with it."

Struk also spoke to Jim McCormack in those first days of his investigation. Jim had a ton to say about Durst as well, that Robert had once pulled Kathie out of a Christmas party by her hair in front of her family and that the marriage was over.

On February 8, Struk searched the couple's apartment at 37 Riverside Drive, a Durst-owned building, and found nothing.

Struk interviewed the late-shift doorman/elevator man at 37 Riverside Drive, Eddie Lopez, an employee of the Durst Organization. Lopez claimed to have seen Kathie enter the building that night. Struk also said he spoke to the dean at Albert Einstein Medical School, who said Kathie had called his office to say she was sick and wasn't coming to school on that Monday, February 1. When I read that bit in the file, I nearly threw the box across the room. I was furious.

Who calls the *dean* of a medical school to say she has sniffles and won't be in?

And which dean do you call?

The dean of students?

The dean of admissions?

The dean of sniffles?

The dean of sick and hungover?

When I was in law school, I wouldn't dream of calling the dean to say I had a runny nose. Hell, the dean wouldn't even take a call from me. Why didn't Struk question it?

Would the dean even recognize Kathie's voice?

On February 9, 1982, Kathie's photo was on the front page of the *New York Post*. Gilberte Najamy had given the story to the papers to goose action on her friend's behalf. Jim McCormack called Struk and said that the druggie in the marriage was actually Robert, a huge pothead.

Struk did ask Robert where he'd been on the night in question and the days after. Michael Struk later told the *New York Post*, "Nobody really knows where the hell he was. I did take a subsequent statement in which he told me where he was every day. Some of those days were inconsistent with what we later found out. He stated that one of the days he was looking for real estate in Connecticut, and another day he took his dog to the vet. Some didn't check out later on."

Robert's whereabouts were unknown or unconfirmed.

But Kathie's whereabouts? Confirmed, because, as he told reporters, "The doorman saw her." The residents of 37 Riverside Drive weren't asked what they saw, if anything, until February 11, six days after she was reported missing, eleven days after she went missing.

In the first week after Robert walked into the precinct, all Struk had learned was that Robert and Kathie were clearly at war. According to Kathie's family and friends, Robert was an abuser, a druggie, and a cheater. According to Robert, Kathie was a druggie, a drunk, and a cheater—and asking for trouble. Struk later told Marsha Kranes of the *New York Post* that Robert thought Kathie dressed too flashy for her own good. " 'I used to tell her she dressed too nicely,' he said," recounted Struk. " 'I told her she attracted too much attention. If someone was looking for someone who looked wealthy, it would be her.

She wore diamond earrings everywhere, even to the hospital in the Bronx—not the safest place in the whole world,' he said." Not true, her family and friends insisted. Kathie was a hippie medical student, and wore casual clothes or scrubs. On the night she disappeared, she was in jeans and a down coat.

Struk would next talk to Kathie's divorce lawyer, Dale Ragus, who joined the chorus and told him that Kathie lived in fear that Robert would try to kill her for scheming to get a big divorce settlement. He also spoke to Ruth Mayer, Kathie and Robert's neighbor in Westchester, who told him that Robert once forced Kathie to get an abortion.

In *The Jinx*, Durst described that as the turning point in their marriage. Why was he so opposed to having children? He told Jarecki that he would be a jinx to his kids and a terrible father. How did he know in 1979 that he would be a jinx? Did he already know that he was evil?

Why didn't Struk ask such questions of Robert in 1982? Didn't the fact that a husband forced his wife to get an abortion bother him in the least?

The neighbors at Riverside Drive had a horrifying story as well. They told Struk that one night Kathie climbed from the balcony of her Manhattan apartment onto their balcony and banged on their window to be let in after Robert beat her.

As the NYPD's investigation continued, there were "reports" in the media that the elevator man brought a well-dressed white male, thirty-five to thirty-eight years old and 185 pounds, five-eleven, with black hair, up to the Dursts' apartment on the sixteenth floor half an hour after Kathie arrived. The police actually circulated a composite sketch of this man that contributed to the further trashing of the victim. It seemed they went to more trouble creating a sketch with a Durst employee than looking for the victim herself.

There were also "reports" that she was a drinker and a drug user.

The press hooked into these classic blame-the-victim tactics. Just call her a drunken slut and, suddenly, no one cares what happens to her. Or, if something did happen to her, maybe she had it coming.

Is it a coincidence that the person trashing the victim, the doorman, was an employee of the Durst Organization? And is it a coincidence that a second building worker who told police he thought he saw Kathie outside the building the next morning also worked for the Durst Organization?

The narrative was created by employees of the Durst Organization and by Robert Durst. But no one spoke for Kathie.

I thought back to what I was doing when Kathie disappeared in 1982. All this went down while I was spearheading awareness programs about domestic violence. How was it possible that this investigation completely escaped my notice?

I'll tell you how: Somehow, the history of Robert's abuse never made it into the public narrative. Nor would the stories from Kathie's friends about how terrified she was of him, that he'd cut her off and wouldn't pay her bills when she tried to leave him, that she'd hired a divorce lawyer and was gathering papers to prove her husband's worth to get what she felt was her fair share in a settlement.

Most disturbing: If the NYPD detectives had started at the inception of the crime, this case would have been in Westchester. As chief of the Domestic Violence Unit in 1982, I would have been the person who caught the case. Another reason I had to pursue it. I had to find her.

From what we could discern in the files, Struk bumbled around the case until April, when he received a call from famous criminal defense attorney Nicholas Scoppetta, who informed him that all communication with Durst would go through him. Robert had lawyered up. For all intents and purposes, the investigation slowed to a crawl after Struk spoke to Scoppetta.

Oh, to have been a fly on the wall in that conversation.

As far as I'm concerned, Struk ended up as nothing more than an observer who spouted the Robert Durst line that Kathie must have just run off with another man and didn't want to be found.

MEANWHILE, GILBERTE NAJAMY, KATHIE's best friend, was running an amateur investigation of her own in 1982. As DA, I've met a lot of people purporting to be "Kathie's best friend" over the years, but Gilberte stood out. Her relentless pursuit of justice knew no bounds. In fact, it almost destroyed her.

Her story of Kathie's last day differed greatly from Robert's account. As she told Struk repeatedly, on the afternoon of January 31, Gilberte was having a party for family and friends at her home in Connecticut. Kathie called her to say that she wanted to come, that Robert was in a mood and she needed to get away from him. Gilberte was delighted. She had been advising Kathie for months to leave her abusive husband, and had even helped her find a divorce lawyer. She'd have welcomed Kathie for the day or to move in permanently.

Kathie showed up at Gilberte's place, a forty-five-minute drive from South Salem, in a hooded parka and knee-high boots, in her red Mercedes, in tears. Gilberte brought her inside, gave her a glass of wine. As the party progressed, according to Gilberte, Robert called nonstop. He was furious at Kathie about something and he wanted her home, *now*. Eventually, Kathie decided it was best to leave and deal with her husband.

Gilberte said good-bye to Kathie on the porch. Kathie's last words to her were, "If anything happens to me, check it out. Bobby did it."

Even Gilberte, a woman who hated Durst and hunted him for over thirty years, refers to him as "Bobby." Most everyone calls him Bobby, including the press. I didn't and still don't. Not in a million years would I call him "Bobby." He's a serial murderer, not an innocent little kid riding his bike down the street. "Bobby" is a grown man, the epitome of cruelty and evil. Bobby, my ass.

The next night, on February 1, Kathie and Gilberte had plans to meet for dinner at the Greenwich Village restaurant the Lion's Head. Gilberte waited there for hours. She moved to a bar stool close to the door to be sure she wouldn't miss Kathie. But her friend didn't show up. That wasn't like Kathie. She didn't stand her friends up. She had impeccable manners and was so kind; she'd never in a million years do something like that.

Gilberte knew something was wrong. She called Robert Durst. He told her he assumed Kathie was in the city since he had dropped her off at the train station in Katonah Sunday night. Gilberte didn't buy that for a second. There wasn't enough time for Kathie to drive home to South Salem from the party, have dinner and drink a bottle of wine, and then drive to the Katonah station. She never would have made the 9:17 p.m. train.

To confirm her theory, Gilberte took the Metro-North from Katonah into Grand Central on Sunday nights for several weeks in a row and showed Kathie's photo to the commuters and the conductors. There were only two train cars on the 9:17. Almost all of the passengers were regulars. And it was not a crowded train. That no one noticed young, beautiful Kathie Durst in her snowy white parka and high boots could only mean one thing: She was not on that train. No one remembered seeing her.

Gilberte gave the NYPD all of this information. She was written off as an obsessed kook and essentially told to stay out of it. More sexism. Step aside, lady, and let the men handle men's business.

Instead of staying out of it, Gilberte took her investigation further. Gilberte and a couple of cohorts made clandestine weekly trips to South Salem. She would wait until the house was empty, then go through Robert Durst's trash. She discovered that he was throwing out Kathie's clothes and her schoolbooks, even her unopened mail—things a criminal might do only if he knew his wife was never coming home.

But she also found a list in Durst's handwriting, in green ink.

It read:

Town dump. Bridge. Dig. Boat. Other. Shovel or? Car truck rent.

Obviously, it was a to-do list for disposing of a body.

When Gilberte and Kathy Traystman, another of Kathie's dear friends, showed this list to Struk, he was unfazed and gave them a "so what?" response. He seemed to dismiss Gilberte's crew outright, calling them "an entourage of girls." Wow.

The first time I talked to Gilberte on the phone in 2000, three things went through my mind.

One, she was spot-on correct in her assumptions about Robert.

Two, she did an investigation that should have been done by the cops.

And three, we should all have a friend like Gilberte.

I know a bullshitter when I see one. I know a truth-teller when I see one. Gilberte Najamy was a truth-teller. She was motivated by honest emotions: fear about what happened, guilt and regret about letting Kathie go back to Robert, and love for a friend. To her dying day, Gilberte never dropped her passion for finding out what happened to her friend Kathie.

What she did to dismantle Robert's story amazes me. It is infuriating that no one in law enforcement took her seriously. Her unofficial investigation put the real cops to shame.

Gilberte and company were providing the NYPD with hard evidence of Robert's suspicious actions in the aftermath of his wife's disappearance. They ignored it. The question is why.

• • •

I wondered how Michael Struk wound up working on the investigation in the first place. To get an understanding of how the NYPD operated in the eighties, I called my friend Bernie Kerik, former commissioner of police there. "In 1982, NYPD was still spinning from the corruption investigations, the Knapp Commission, and everyone would've been on their guard," he said. "If someone walked into the Twentieth Precinct and went to the desk saying, 'My wife is missing,' he would be directed to go up to the squad room and then go up the bureau.

"As soon as the bureau found out that it was Robert Durst, there's no way that they wouldn't notify Manhattan North," he continued. "Manhattan North would notify the borough captain. There's no way that the chief of detectives wouldn't be notified by a squad commander through a file 49 'memo to chief.' It's possible that Struk just caught the case or was randomly put on the case, but, in light of the times, it would be rare for someone [on Struk's level] to direct how the case would be handled. At least a first-line supervisor, like a sergeant, would run that case."

Michael Struk was an experienced detective with some notoriety for having solved the "Murder at the Met" case, which involved the murder of a violinist at the Metropolitan Opera House. He was a smart detective. So how did he screw this up? He obviously reported to seniors in the precinct, first-grade detectives or a lieutenant. I wondered, *Was he handpicked to handle this case?* John O'Donnell thought so.

Would a man as wealthy as Robert Durst, flashing an article about his father owning half of New York City, catch just *any* person in the Twentieth Precinct? Would some husband in Harlem, complaining about a missing wife, wind up with Michael Struk as the investigator? Was he tapped for his judgment, his discretion, his loyalty?

And to whom? The department? His superiors?

I was actually stunned and horrified by Struk's work on the case. Struk seemed determined to ignore vital evidence. I was convinced he had marching orders or was so prejudiced against women that he didn't give a damn that someone's daughter, someone's sister, someone's friend was missing.

I have the utmost respect for cops, especially New York's Finest. I kept telling myself, "Give him the benefit of the doubt." But, as time went on, it seemed clear to me he had no interest in solving this case. The consensus among the cops and lieutenants quoted in the papers at the time was, "Yeah, she ran off with another guy."

How many times is a police department criticized for prioritizing cases involving the rich, beautiful, and connected? Well, Kathleen Durst was all of those things. As she was a part of the Durst family, the NYPD would have given her disappearance a high priority. And yet they gave it to Michael Struk, who kicked it around for a while until he dumped it?

Any low-level first-year Podunk, Wherever, cop would have taken the countless stories of Robert's abuse and Kathie's plan to divorce him for a large settlement to its logical conclusion. The fact is, Struk didn't do that.

Struk's bosses had to know what was going on. The press dutifully reported the line from the family spokesperson (who turned out to be future murder victim Susan Berman, Robert's BFF from UCLA), and put Kathie on the front page, dropping hints that she was a bad egg who ran off with her drug-dealing lover. Struk apparently agreed with what was in the papers, the rumors and lies fed to reporters from Robert's camp. The investigation was either unethical, corrupt, or incompetent. Maybe all three.

Eighteen years later, I saw clear as day that Struk ignored those gaping holes in Robert's story. Why didn't he search Durst's car? Why did Struk disregard the evidence hand-delivered to him by

Kathie's friends? Why wasn't *he* searching the garbage at the South Salem cottage? Why didn't *he* show Kathie's photo to train passengers? Why didn't he reach out to the Dursts and the McCormacks? Why didn't he upgrade the missing-persons investigation to what it obviously was—homicide?

For that matter, why didn't the Durst family move heaven and earth to help solve the case?

Struk could have used any one of a dozen linchpins, but he let each one slide between his fingers. He let the case die with a whimper.

Why?

Was he blind to the telltale signs of domestic violence and guided by entrenched sexism?

Did someone above Struk instruct him to leave it alone? Was that person himself pressured by one of the Five Most Powerful New Yorkers?

Or was it just that he sucked at his job?

Struk would later tell *People* magazine, "At that time, when there was a missing person without the obvious presence of foul play, you can't run a full-blown investigation."

Really? So if the criminal is smart enough to get rid of the body, he skates?

And wait: "no presence of foul play"? How about Robert's abuse? How about Kathie's telling her friends, her family, and her lawyer that she feared for her life?

Struk continued, "People take off on their spouses every day."

This was clearly not a case where a wife emptied the bank account, packed up her suitcases, and hit the road to Vegas with her secret boyfriend. Kathie didn't take any of her possessions with her. She never picked up the phone or used a credit card—ever again.

The woman wasn't missing. She was dead. Any idiot could see that.

Michael Struk retired from the NYPD and went on to consult for the TV juggernaut *Law & Order.* I may be the only person in America who's never seen *Law & Order*. I lived it; I don't need to watch it. But from the great reviews of the show, I can't imagine that the TV cops do lackluster investigations. I'll bet the victims of spousal abuse aren't written off as druggie sluts. I'll bet the abusers are arrested and convicted. And I'll bet the husbands do not get away with killing their wives.

It just made me mad, and sad. Marjory Fields and I had fought to change laws, and to make sure that police recognized domestic violence, that they didn't cover it up or ignore it, that they made reports and didn't look the other way. I thought we'd made headway in the eighties. But when I read the Durst files in 2000, I said to myself, "Nothing we said or did sank in."

I was disappointed on many levels.

Either a real cop investigated a real crime and blew it or someone above him pulled the plug on it and didn't care that a real woman was gone.

| THE DURST CASE: ONE "HOLY SHIT!" AFTER ANOTHER

Our plan in 2000 was to redo Struk's half-assed work, reinterview everyone, talk to people he'd ignored, and examine evidence that'd been overlooked. There was no way that anyone in law enforcement should have looked at this as a missing person in Manhattan.

The husband said he put her on a train?

The NYPD shrugged and said, "Guess he put her on a train!"

The husband said his wife was nutty and slutty?

The NYPD shook its head and said, "Well, that explains why she ran off."

My guys were on a mission to catch every lie Durst told the NYPD, and they did a brilliant job. Instead of ignoring the eyewitness accounts from family and friends about Robert's abusive behavior, we factored it into the timeline. My team spoke to the doorman, the elevator operator, the neighbors, the building superintendent, the dean of the medical school. Practically every interview turned up an inconsistency with Durst's story or an outright lie.

John, Eddie, and Clem would sit in the club chairs in front of my desk or on the couch by the big table in my office. Ro would bring in gallons of coffee, and we'd knock things off the list. As the months passed, I was continually gobsmacked by what O'Donnell and Murphy discovered. It was one "you're kidding me" moment after the next, such as:

• **Durst lied about reporting Kathie missing to state police.** Robert claimed he called state police himself before he went to the Twentieth Precinct in Manhattan to report Kathie missing. But my guys reinterviewed the troopers who visited South Salem and found out that Gilberte, not Robert, had made the call.

• **Durst lied about taking Kathie to the train station.** Gilberte had told the cops eighteen years ago that the timing made no sense. My guys confirmed it all. It was simply impossible for Kathie to have left Gilberte's house in Danbury at 7:30 p.m., driven forty-five minutes to South Salem, had dinner, a bottle of wine, and an argument with Robert, then driven for thirty minutes to the Katonah station to catch the train at 9:17 p.m. Gilberte's dogged investigation of the train conductor at the time was confirmed by us. No one saw Kathie on the train.

• **Durst lied about calling Kathie in Manhattan that night.** At first, Robert said he called Riverside Drive from the cottage. When police suggested they could check his phone records, he amended his story and said he called from a pay phone in a restaurant. He lied again, and said he called from a pay phone while walking his dog, Igor. The nearest pay phone was over three miles from the house. Records showed that it'd been a freezing cold, snowy night. *Really?* Durst took a six-mile round-trip walk with the dog through a blizzard at 11:00 p.m.? Igor was an Alaskan malamute, but come on. Why would anyone believe this hogwash?

• **Durst lied about having a drink with his neighbor.** My guys went door to door in South Salem, interviewing all the neighbors. No one in 1982 ever bothered to interview William Mayer to ask him, "Did Robert pop on over for a glass of wine at around ten-thirty on the night Kathie went missing?" In *The Jinx*, Durst admitted he made it up just to throw police attention away from him. Why would Durst assume no one would question his neighbor? Did he know they wouldn't check his lie? What gave him such confidence? A normal person would just assume the lie would be uncovered easily enough. But Durst was right, that entitled little shit. Eighteen years went by before John O'Donnell knocked on the Mayers' door and got the real story. Durst never came by for a drink that night or any night. Ever.

At the time of the disappearance, Ruth Mayer *was* interviewed by state troopers after Gilberte called in the missing-persons report. Ruth told a trooper named Stan Roman that Kathie and Robert fought often, that Kathie confided in her about the forced abortion—and that she'd seen a blue light shining in the lower level of the cottage shortly after Kathie went missing.

What could the mysterious blue light be? Used in combination with a chemical spray, blue light can pick up blood.

• **The doorman on Riverside Drive was unreliable at best.** The eyewitness accounts from the Durst employees at Riverside Drive were easily unraveled. Eddie Lopez was the front door and elevator operator from midnight to 8:00 a.m. He worked there for nine years. But that same Eddie Lopez told another investigator that he wasn't sure if he saw her at all.

By the time we opened the case, Lopez was dead.

Antoine Popovic, the relief elevator operator, said Kathie never came in and he didn't see her. A doorman who had said he'd seen Kathie the next morning on the street was ancient and he told my guys he honestly couldn't swear to anything. Retractions and foggy memories were typical on cold cases. Back in '82, the statements from the building employees were dubious and vague at best. We talked to every living doorman and elevator man who had worked at 37 Riverside Drive in 1982. Some confided that Lopez was an alcoholic who regularly left his post. Not one of them recalled telling the press that she'd been staggering drunk or that he'd taken a mystery man up to her apartment late that night.

How did these lies get into the papers? Susan Berman, in her role as family spokesperson, hammered away on the "confirmed" Kathie-in-Manhattan sighting to the press.

If you repeated a lie often enough, did it turn into the truth? It sure seemed to as far as the NYPD in 1982 was concerned.

• **Robert lied when he told Struk his marriage was "pretty good."** Was it pretty good for a wife to jump from her balcony to her neighbors' to escape her husband?

Was it pretty good for Kathie to hire a divorce attorney?

Was it pretty good to tell her lawyer and several friends that she feared for her life? Was it pretty good for her to go to Jacobi Medical Center to be treated for injuries?

The divorce lawyer refused to talk to my guys. She claimed all of her conversations with Kathie were protected under attorney-client privilege. She told John, "I can't give you the file."

When this was reported back to me, I said, "Kathie's dead! It's been nineteen years. When's the last time this lawyer cashed a check from Kathleen Durst?"

I called Rich Weill, a brilliant attorney, my chief assistant at the time, and said, "How can we get this file?"

He said, "If Kathie is declared dead, you've got a shot."

Kathie *had* been declared dead, but the lawyer didn't budge.

And then the lawyer died herself.

Another dead end.

• **Robert sublet Kathie's "escape" apartment on East Eighty-Sixth Street on February 4,** *one day before* **he reported her missing to the NYPD.** According to the building superintendent, Robert rented out his missing wife's haven, a nine-hundred-dollar-a-month apartment, as soon as he could. Why? The cheapskate knew she'd never come back to it, so he might as well collect rent.

• **Robert got rid of her stuff, and lied about doing so.** The super told my investigator that he fielded complaints from other residents because Durst clogged the garbage chute by dumping his wife's possessions down it. Several friends and workers who lived at the East Eighty-Sixth Street address filed an affidavit that he discarded his wife's possessions within days of reporting her missing. Robert said, in a February 1983 affidavit in Surrogate's Court, "I have not disposed of any of Kathie's belongings."

Robert Durst never worried about telling the truth, or how his actions looked to any rational, thinking person. Did he have reason to feel safe? Had the Durst name worked its magic by then? Was he reassured that Struk would never come after him? Was he just too entitled to care? Struk would live up to Robert's apparent estimation of him. "It sounds like a guy that's pissed off. It sounds like a guy who's fed up as well. You know, I mean, he could be throwing his hands up as well as saying, 'Good riddance to you' as well," Struk said on *Primetime Live* in 2001. Why would a real cop say this?

• **Kathie's call to the dean was phony or never happened at all.** I never believed this lie for a moment. No medical student was going to call the dean and say, "I feel sick today." Besides that, Robert claimed he got a call from the medical school and they said she hadn't been in classes for several days. If she had called in sick two days before, why would they call looking for her?

Apparently, the first reference in print to Kathie's calling in sick was in late February. Someone in the Durst camp created this narrative after the fact. I don't believe Kathie or anyone called the school on Monday. I believe the medical school called Robert, looking for Kathie, and that prompted Robert to meet with his brother, Douglas, and his father, Seymour, and then to report her missing. If you believe that a dean on a Monday morning is going to take a phone call from a student with a cold, you need a reality check.

John O'Donnell asked the dean himself about the famous call with Kathie. Are you sure you spoke to Kathie Durst? Could it have been another woman pretending to be Kathie? Did students often call in sick? The dean was "wishy-washy," and gave ambiguous answers like, "Well, I don't really know," and, "Well, I never thought about it." John and Eddie conducted numerous interviews with the dean and could not pin him down about whether he remembered receiving a call.

After one such interview, as Eddie and John walked back to their car in the parking lot, Eddie asked, "Hey, John. What do they call you if you graduate first in your class at medical school?"

John said, "I don't know. Doctor?"

Eddie said, "And what do they call you if you graduated *last* in your class at medical school?"

Without missing a beat, John said, "Dean!"

The man was evasive or dim . . . or maybe he was just wise to keep his mouth shut? He was the dean at Albert Einstein Medical School. Donations were coming in at *all* levels. Was he hoping for some Durst money to flow his way?

Did the Durst family send any checks to Albert Einstein in the 1980s?

• **Kathie went to the Jacobi Medical Center after one savage beating.** Ro announced that Steve Bender and Clem needed to see me about Kathie Durst. I waved them in and said, "What? Talk to me."

Clem said, "He put her in the hospital."

"Motherfucker!"

We already knew about the balcony incident, that she'd jumped from her own balcony to her neighbors' on Riverside Drive to escape Robert's rage. Gilberte told me that Kathie often called her in the middle of the night after Robert beat her. Kathie, like so many battered women, refused to go to the hospital—she was embarrassed. The feeling must have been compounded because she was a medical student.

As chilling as those accounts of abuse were, there was no medical documentation.

But a hospital visit was proof. There *was* a paper trail.

In early January, a week before she vanished, Kathie went to Jacobi Medical Center in the Bronx with bruises on her face. She told the doctors that her husband beat her. The hospital didn't contact police at the time, which infuriated me. I trained ER nurses for what to look for in domestic violence cases and how to question women who came in with injuries. It had to be done gently. Battered women were often too ashamed to admit that their husbands or boyfriends had assaulted them, or they feared a reprisal. But if a woman had the courage to come in and say, "I was beaten by my husband," the nurses and doctors were supposed to offer her referral and support services.

Why go to the ER that time, having avoided hospitals before? Did her lawyer, Dale Ragus, tell Kathie it was time for her to document her abuse to get a divorce?

This was a point of law that Marjory Fields and I would eventually rewrite. Back then, it wasn't sufficient grounds for divorce if a husband beat his wife only once. He had to repeatedly beat her and she had to have proof.

Was Kathie wisely setting up her ducks and getting his abuse on the record? Was she now memorializing the beatings so as to gather enough evidence to get a decent settlement to start her life anew?

The more important question is, why didn't Durst just divorce her? Why did he have to kill her? Our information was that Durst had turned down Kathie's attempt at a divorce settlement just three days before she disappeared. Did he kill her so he wouldn't have to give her money? Why was he so cheap? He was part of, and heir to, an organization worth hundreds of millions of dollars. The law at the time contributed to Kathie's end. The law favored the batterers. Women's rights, if they were even considered, were secondary.

• **Durst went on a field trip to destroy evidence.** One of the first things we did was a dump on the Durst Organization's telephone records at and around the time of Kathie's disappearance.
The second day after her disappearance, collect calls were made to the Durst Organization from Ship Bottom, New Jersey. When my investigators went to speak with the secretary at the Durst Organization in 2000, she indicated the only person who made collect phone calls that were accepted: Robert Durst.

And yet, in 2015, Robert claimed in *The Jinx* that he knew of other people who went to Long Beach Island in New Jersey who had a home there and were making collect calls around that time. Our investigation uncovered no such information.

Struk knew about the calls and even took a day at the beach to look into them. But that was it. No follow-up. No interviews. He let it drop.

The collect calls were placed two days after Kathie went missing, three days before Robert alerted the NYPD. We identified the location of those calls, a Laundromat. What did Robert need to have cleaned so desperately that he stopped at a coin-op Laundromat at the shore in February? Could he be washing whatever he might've used to transport body parts in the trunk? Was it seat covers, blankets?

Ship Bottom is a little town on Long Beach Island, bordering the Atlantic Ocean, mere miles from the Pine Barrens, a million-acre forested national reserve across seven counties, composing 22 percent of the entire state's land area. It's the largest expanse of forest between Virginia and Massachusetts, and has long been, according to legend and common knowledge among anyone who's ever lived in New Jersey, the mob's number one all-time favorite choice place to dump a body. (In May 2001, when Robert Durst was living in Galveston, wearing a wig and pretending to be the mute Dorothy Ciner, HBO aired an episode of *The Sopranos* called "The Pine Barrens" that featured a scene of two gangsters forcing a man to dig his own grave before they shot him there.)

In 1982, Robert had *every* reason to be familiar with the Pine Barrens, Ship Bottom, and the workings of the New Jersey mob. His main job for the Durst Organization in the seventies and eighties was to collect rent money from the wiseguys who ran the porn stores and XXX theaters in Times Square. The Dursts made their fortune there. When Ed Koch became mayor in 1978, one of his goals was to redevelop Times Square and remove the blight of drugs, porn, and prostitution from the crossroads of the world. Koch's plan was to bring in office space, legitimate retail, theaters, and restaurants, and to shut down the sleazy hotels and porn theaters. At the same time, he created an Arson Strike Force in City Hall because so many New York City landlords were abandoning buildings because of high taxes, some even torching them to collect insurance money.

Seymour Durst fought the redevelopment plan from the start, and even sued the city to stop it. He lost. And Times Square went from porn city to Disney World, a vast improvement over addicts with needles in their arms and hookers on every corner.

So Robert collected rent from those bottom-feeders, pornographers, and mobsters. Given those connections, what might he have learned?

How to kill.

How to chop up a body.

And where to dispose of the body.

Who could help us in that regard? Ironically, I had given Gilberte my private number in the event she ever needed to speak with me. She mentioned that she'd spoken with a man named Tom Brown Jr. I'd heard of Brown. He was a legendary wilderness tracker, an expert in the science and art of finding people, and he taught classes on it. He even had a bowie knife named after him. I picked up the phone and called Tom. Could he meet with members of my office?

I sent John O'Donnell and Mike Occicone, another of my criminal investigators—a good guy, quiet and low-key, who doesn't run off at the mouth and knows how to be a cop—to talk to Tom. They showed him a copy of the dig/shovel to-do list. It made perfect sense to him. He confirmed that Long Beach Island was the burial ground for many crime victims. They discussed the fact that Robert, on behalf of the Durst Organization, had worked in Times Square in the early eighties.

Development was going crazy on the Jersey Shore at the time. Speculation was rampant in a twenty- to thirty-mile area around Atlantic City. The state of New Jersey actually built a bridge, referred to as the Bridge to Nowhere, at the end of Town Road, Route 9. It was intended to go over to an island where expensive homes could be built. The Town Road was ultimately never connected, but every speculator and real-estate developer—including the Dursts—believed that was the next big thing.

So maybe the dig/shovel list—including the words "town dump" and "bridge"—that Struk said meant nothing, meant something. John would spend upward of a week with Tom in the area, poking around, looking for a burial site. Tom told John about how he searched for a body by sticking a length of bamboo into a depression in the ground and sniffing it to determine what might be buried beneath. Nothing turned up.

• **Durst was openly unfaithful—with Mia Farrow's sister.** It's fascinating that Kathie was thought to have run away with another man whose composite sketch was distributed by the New York City Police Department in 1982 when the truth is it was Robert Durst who was sleeping around. His affair with Prudence Farrow, Mia's sister, was well known at the time. She'd been the inspiration for the Beatles song "Dear Prudence." John Lennon wrote the song when Prudence accompanied the Beatles to India to study with the Maharishi Mahesh Yogi in 1968. As the story went, Prudence became so obsessed with the Maharishi, she would fall deep into meditation and refuse to come out of her little hut. Hence, "Dear Prudence, won't you come out to play?"

It should not be a surprise that Robert Durst, with his pedigree and fortune (even if he was too cheap to spend it), would be mingling with the likes of Mia Farrow's sister. We do know that he spent a lot of time at Elaine's, the Upper East Side watering hole of the literati and glitterati. He and Susan Berman went there. They partied at Studio 54, along with Liza Minnelli and Halston. It's safe to assume Prudence was in the mix as well. During the disco era, everyone had a ball. Everyone did coke (except me). And plenty of people worshiped *something*, if not the Maharishi.

I sent O'Donnell to find Prudence Farrow. He didn't locate her, but he did take a trip to Connecticut to talk to her sister, Mia Farrow.

O'Donnell knew before he got to Mia that the affair between Robert and Prudence was hot and heavy. "Like dogs," he'd later report to someone, not me. "They were wrapped around each other like dogs, man."

Normally, as DA, I was spared such details, but who knew if they might add to a profile of Durst?

O'Donnell and Murphy interviewed Mia Farrow in her home in northwestern Connecticut. "You know, boss," O'Donnell told me before he left, "I'm not all that impressed or enamored by famous people, and I kind of dread having to talk to Mia Farrow."

"Oh, get over it," I told him. But of course, I loved him for that.

When he returned, I was not surprised by what he reported.

"Got there and I could not have been more wrong, boss," he told me. "She was the most delightful and forthcoming and decent human being I think I have ever spoken to involving a homicide."

He went on to tell me that he was greeted at the door by one of her adopted children. "And she had adopted children of all different sizes, shapes, and ethnicities. Every child was articulate, gracious, and well behaved. Mia lived in an old, renovated farmhouse. It was very simple, but beautiful, tranquil," he told me. "I walked in, and the first thing I noticed over a mantel was the triangular fold of the American flag. She had a brother or some relative who was killed in Vietnam. Also, she had a picture of someone in full Marine dress blues, and I said to her, 'Who is that, if I may ask?' And she said, 'That's my father, a Marine colonel.' I figured she was just artsy-craftsy, you know, Hollywood . . ."

As sweet as all this was, I wanted to throttle him.

"What did she know about the affair?!"

"Okay, well, boss, Mia *really* didn't like Bobby. Really, from the get-go."

"Why?"

"Well, she said to me, 'I know narcissistic men.' And I'm

thinking, she's talking about Woody Allen and she's talking about Frank Sinatra. And she goes, 'I know narcissistic men and this is a narcissistic man.' "

"Interesting. What else did she say?"

"She said, 'I did not like him at all. He was not good for my sister.' Long story short, she constantly tried to discourage Prudence from seeing Bobby but it didn't work." He added that she said she'd help in any way she could, but had no direct knowledge of Kathie.

Kathie herself knew of Robert's affairs, specifically when she found Polaroid pictures of her medicine cabinet and dresser. Robert later admitted to her that he took the pictures so he could bring women into the apartment and make it appear that he was single by removing items that ostensibly belonged to Kathie and then put everything back in its place.

• **Durst had a vicious temper.** One night, Kathie's crew was clubbing with a photographer named Peter Schwartz. It was a big group and they had to split up in cabs to go back to the Dursts' for a nightcap. Kathie and Peter took a taxi alone together. Back at the apartment, Kathie and Peter were hanging out in a group with Gilberte and Kathy Traystman, among others. Robert came home, and out of nowhere, started assaulting Peter, kicking him in the face, breaking his cheekbone and jaw. Peter went to the hospital. Gilberte told me she called him the day after and asked what happened. He said he couldn't talk about it because Robert Durst made him promise to keep it quiet. Of course, some money was exchanged.

It all added up to a massive sense of entitlement. Robert did whatever he wanted, wherever. Kicking some guy in the face. Cheating on his wife. *Killing* his wife. It was all the same to him. Just one more thing to get away with.

• **The Dursts treated the McCormacks like dirt.** Robert's disrespect to the McCormacks was palpable throughout his and Kathie's marriage. Apparently, the apple didn't fall far from the tree.

In the days after Kathie's disappearance, none of the Dursts—Douglas and Thomas (Robert's brothers), Wendy (the sister), and Seymour—had reached out to the McCormacks to offer their support or to say, "Hang in there." Jim tried to rally the Dursts to help them find Kathie. On March 19, after calling the Durst offices repeatedly and being unable to get anyone on the phone, the McCormacks—Jim, his mother, Ann, and his sister Mary—were finally allowed an audience with Seymour at his home in Manhattan, almost three months after Kathie went missing. Jim hoped to get some financial backing from his in-laws to hire a private investigator and post a large reward for information. The McCormacks weren't rich. Kathie had been married to Robert for nearly a decade. Surely that counted for something?

It was weird and awkward from the moment they arrived. Seymour brought them into a sitting room. He offered them nothing to drink or eat. They asked him questions, and Seymour gave monosyllabic replies. He wasn't sympathetic, wasn't empathic. He refused to help the McCormacks search for Kathie. This was a guy who had the world at his fingertips. He could have had the human decency to say, "I'll hire the best investigators and we'll find out the truth. We'll search with dogs. We'll set up a tip line." There was *so* much that they could've done. But he wasn't willing to do *anything*. He looked at his in-laws as if they were insignificant bugs. Jim said that Seymour seemed defensive, like, "Why are you bothering me? I've got nothing to do with this."

Why would Seymour Durst be defensive about his missing daughter-in-law? Could it be that he already knew she wasn't missing?

When Robert's youngest brother, Thomas, in his early thirties at the time, walked into the room, he took one look at the McCormacks, and asked, "What's going on?"

Not a hello or "I'm sorry for what you're going through."

Seymour said, "They're trying to find out where Kathie is."

Tom frowned and said, "This meeting is over."

He opened the door and told the McCormacks to get out.

The abrupt dismissal was hostile, conspiratorial.

Was it any wonder that the McCormacks were angry? Jim was once quoted in the *Northeast News*, saying, "There were obvious discrepancies that [Struk] didn't look into. My sister Mary would seem to come up with more leads in a week than they got the whole time."

In 1983, Kathie's mom, Ann McCormack, sued Robert Durst in Surrogate's Court for half of Kathleen's estate of fifty thousand dollars, presuming that she was dead for civil purposes. Ann was going to use the money to hire PIs to search for her daughter, now that the NYPD had moved on. Robert, the heir to a $600 million fortune at that time, went to court and fought his grieving, desperate mother-in-law for what, to him, was chump change. That alone was proof of one thing: Robert Durst was a cruel, cheap son of a bitch.

During the hearing, Kathie's sister Mary brought to light even more suspicious evidence. On the night of Kathie's disappearance, Durst originally claimed she was wearing a pair of diamond earrings, two gold chains, and her wedding band. Mary would later find each piece of jewelry in a pouch in her sister's drawer.

For the hearing, the McCormacks and Kathie's divorce lawyer, Dale Ragus, filed affidavits stating that Robert physically assaulted her and that she feared for her life.

Robert filed his own affidavit saying he never touched her and that her claims of abuse were leverage to get more of his money in a divorce settlement. He said, she said. The judge sided with Durst, allowing him to keep all of Kathie's fifty thousand dollars.

• **More lives were destroyed than Kathie's.** Because of the disappearance, Jim McCormack found himself in a situation he never could have predicted, making moral and ethical decisions no one should have to face. He told me in July 2015, "Kathie and Bob were on their honeymoon across America. For me, it was single days and lots of fun. I made my first cross-country trip that year, and met Kathie and Bob in Denver, Colorado, on their way back to the East Coast. Those were happy 'in love' days for the honeymooners." Jim struggled to connect with his new brother-in-law. "[Bob had] a kind of a shyness. I hardly ever remember him laughing much. He was a hard-to-read personality," he said on the ABC News show *Vanished* about Kathie's disappearance.

When the Dursts acted as if his family didn't exist, Jim had every right to feel rage, and many thought he would act on that rage. "Soon after the disappearance, I was approached by people who were willing to kidnap Bobby, put a gun to his head, beat him up, and find out where my sister is," Jim confided to me recently. "But you don't solve one crime by committing another."

In 2000, I called Gilberte, then a caterer, into the office and interviewed her myself. She'd done all she could in '82, and nothing happened. From 1982 to 1999 when we picked up the ball, Gilberte had been virtually alone out there in search of answers and justice for Kathie. She went through some pretty rough times, turning to drugs to dull her pain. She'd been arrested six times for narcotics possession and violating her parole, and had spent time in prison. She managed to pull herself out of that downward spiral and turned a negative into a positive.

When we found her, Gilberte worked at a shelter for battered women and children. She never gave up her mission, never stopped being Kathie's best friend. Her life had been defined by Kathie's absence and the lingering questions about how she met her end.

I felt this woman's pain in my bones. It was killing her.

Some questions jumped out at me during our investigation:

• **Why didn't the press dig deeper?** Everything that was put out in public was the spin of Susan Berman, without any backup, support, or credible evidence. Why wasn't this story front-page news, for weeks on end? Why did the *New York Times* do only two stories? Imagine if real-estate developer Donald Trump's daughter-in-law disappeared, God forbid. Does anyone out there think that the presumption would be that she ran off with another guy without any evidence to support it? Or that there would be only a handful of articles written about it? It would be a front-page story for weeks.

• **Why wasn't kidnapping on the table?** I have a friend, a multimillionaire businessman, who lives in Harrison, New York. In 1979, he was kidnapped. His family had to pay a ransom to get him back. People were being kidnapped for money back then. No one considered that as a possibility. Not that the Dursts would have paid a ransom. Robert put a price on Kathie's head with a paltry ten- or fifteen-thousand-dollar reward for tips. The man was cheap even when he *knew* he wouldn't have to pay it out.

• **Why was a criminal defense attorney hired when police never even suspected foul play or suspected Robert of a crime?** Nick Scoppetta, Robert's lawyer, was a big-shot, well-known, well-regarded criminal lawyer. Why even hire him in '82? As soon as I saw his name in the files, I hit the intercom to Roseanne, "Get Nick Scoppetta on the phone."

He took my call. Everybody took a call from the DA.

After minimal niceties—I couldn't waste time on how he was doing or how he was feeling because I honestly didn't care and if I did I couldn't help him anyway—I said, "Nick, as you probably know, I'm looking at this Durst case."

He said, "Yes?" He was very quiet, very low-key. I knew I had his attention.

I said, "Nick, what can you tell me about this? Why would they hire *you*? They didn't need you." The police bought into the wife-ran-away claim—hook, line, and doughnut.

He intimated that it was about concern for Kathie and he was there to help through a difficult time.

"How difficult was it, Nick? I didn't see much in the press. Durst was never indicted. There weren't tons of people combing the woods looking for her or accusing Robert of anything."

Silence.

"Nick?"

More silence and then the "get off the phone with the DA excuse," attorney-client privilege.

Like I needed him to remind me of that. "There may be other people in danger. If this guy is a serial murderer, and I believe that he is, his brother's in trouble. His friends are in trouble," I said. "Maybe *you're* in trouble!"

I tried everything. I understood and respected the Constitution and the nature of privileged communications, but I kept pushing. "Did you call Detective Struk and congratulate him on how good a job he was doing?"

Nick didn't say a word.

"Talk to me," I said. "Just tell me if I'm on the right track?"

Silence. Then he said, "No," and hung up.

I had always respected him, but for years after that call my stomach turned every time I saw his picture in the press.

So, back to Kathie. Was Kathie a battered woman?

I'd seen thousands of them. There was no question in my mind she was. In fact, she was the classic battered woman.

Battering is not only about physical assault. It's emotional, psychological, and financial. It's about isolation and degradation. It's about demeaning and destroying the woman's self-concept. It was the classic power and control game that Robert played so well. Before she died, Kathie revealed classic battered woman's syndrome traits to her friends and in her diary pages that her brother, Jim McCormack, shared with me recently.

• **She was on a short leash.** Geraldine MacInerney, a friend of Kathie's, told Jarecki that Kathie was required to check in with Robert at all times. She asked Kathie why she always called Robert. Kathie responded, "He always wants to know where I am." She told Geraldine she didn't want to go on some outing with Robert. Geraldine asked why she didn't just not go. Kathie said, "Are you kidding? He'd kill me." Sharon McCormack confirmed this. One night around Christmas 1981, Kathie spent the night at Sharon and Jim's house. They were up until four in the morning talking. Kathie was scared that something terrible would happen to her. But before Kathie turned in, she told Sharon, "I have to call Bob." Even in the middle of the night, she felt she had to check in.

• **She feared him.** Gilberte would say for years that Kathie told her, "Promise me, if something happens, you'll check it out. I'm afraid of Bobby." Eleanor Schwank (a good friend of Kathie's), Kathy Traystman, Sharon McCormack, even her lawyer were all told by Kathie that she feared an impending death at Robert's hands.

• **It got physical.** Kathie described some of the abuse in her diary: "Spring of '79, we returned from a party. We were both drunk. We argued and he slapped me. . . . Fall of '79, we were both sober and argued about some minor issue. He punched me. I fell to the ground and hit my leg." Kathy Traystman told me in August 2015 that she saw bruises on Kathie's arms. Want proof? How about the visit to Jacobi, the bruises, the pleas to neighbors, the jumping from her balcony to a neighbor's to escape from Robert, and of course her diary?

• **She was terrorized.** Gilberte told me in May 2015 that Robert routinely woke Kathie in the middle of the night to threaten her with a gun, a scenario that one could imagine in a movie about prisoners of war. And this, from her diary, about the trip home after visiting an adoption agency in the fall of 1974: "He told me how I should act and what to say at future meetings. I disagreed and he threw a half gallon of water on my head while we were driving. I felt humiliated and cried."

• **She was controlled by her batterer.** After her forced abortion and couples counseling, Kathie wrote in her diary that Bob told their therapist that he "did not feel secure in his job financially to bring a child into this world." When Kathie confronted him with this outrageous lie, as she wrote, he said, "He was not going to allow me to make him a father."

That was when Kathie tried to change their dynamic. She decided to get her medical degree and do something for herself, by herself. Robert would admit years later he didn't like the independent Kathie. As he said in *The Jinx*, when she started medical school, their fights escalated and became more frequent, with slapping, hitting, pushing, and wrestling. He showed his egocentric, narcissistic side when he admitted that he was insulted by the way Kathie told him she was going to Gilberte's that last day. He was offended she didn't ask his permission. As if, "How dare she make a decision before he was consulted?" As he described it, "Kathie got tired of my calling all the shots, that she wanted to be independent and didn't want to be controlled all the time."

• **She had no power in the relationship.** Another chilling incident in the diary described Robert's omnipotence in their marriage and lack of respect for Kathie. In May 1976, she wrote, "The mailbox key and telephone in our NYC apartment were changed. I found out when the telephone company called me with the new number and when my mailbox key no longer fit. I questioned Bob and he said he had no idea who or why the above were changed. After one day of me thinking how bizarre this was, and persistent questioning of him, he told me someone was threatening him at work. Two days later, I removed a book on the bookshelf and Polaroid pictures of our medicine cabinet and my closet fell out, also a list of articles on our desk. I confronted him with these and he told me he was involved with a woman and would change the apartment to look as if he was single."

• **She was isolated by him.** She wasn't to talk about her life without Robert's approval. In her diary, Kathie wrote, "[Bob] insisted I never tell anyone I liked school and in particular he told me not to tell friends or family where I went to school. A few times I slipped and he became angry with me." In the spring of 1975, Robert forced Kathie to leave Westchester to move to New York City, necessitating a transfer at work. "I felt I was being forced, leaving friends."

• **She had emergency room medical treatment.** The same month she disappeared, she went to Jacobi to be treated for facial bruising.

• **She tried to get away, but it was too late.** When the violence was out of control, Gilberte got Kathie a divorce attorney and paid the retainer. The Thursday before she went missing, her lawyer, Dale Ragus, told her that Robert Durst had turned down her request for an agreement of divorce. The most dangerous period for a battered woman is after she announces her intention to leave. Seventy-five percent of homicides occur once the announcement is made. Robert Durst, having been offered a divorce settlement agreement by an attorney, knew Kathie was serious and was leaving him. Kathie did not have an escape plan and lost her life before she was able to make one.

All the pieces were falling into place. In 2001, Clem, Steve, John, Eddie, Mike from my office, and I developed a working timeline:

Sunday night, January 31: Robert Durst beats Kathie to death in the living room in South Salem. He takes her body down to the lower part of the house and dismembers it. He puts the parts in the crawl space for storage overnight.

Monday, February 1: Durst bags Kathie's remains and puts them in his car. He drives to Ship Bottom, New Jersey. He is familiar with Long Beach Island—real estate was booming in the area between New York City and Atlantic City. He drives into the Pine Barrens and disposes of the body like his Mafia pals bragged about. He goes to the Laundromat to clean his clothes, items from his car, and evidence of the crime. Mr. Cheapskate identifies his location when he calls work collect from the Pine Barrens. Then he drives back to

New York. He starts fielding increasingly panicked calls from Gilberte, eventually having Susan Berman talk to her and the McCormacks before he stops talking to anyone.

Tuesday, February 2: Durst cleans up the crime scene, using a blue light and a chemical spray to check for blood splatter.

Thursday, February 4: Durst rents out Kathie's East Eighty-Sixth Street apartment.

Friday, February 5: With all of his ducks in a row, Robert Durst walks into the Twentieth Precinct and reports his missing wife directly to Detective Struk.

The rest of his story—the nutty, slutty part—was just smoke and mirrors, his despicable way of obscuring the truth.

In our effort to punch holes in Durst's story, we were very, very careful, *very* careful, to start the interviews as far away from him as possible. That is how you do it. You're quiet about it, no fanfare. You crawl up quietly. It's no one's business. There's no point in trumpeting an investigation, allowing people to then rehearse their stories. Although evidence was mounting, there was not enough to charge. It wasn't ideal that we didn't have a body. The need for a body is not essential if there is a strong circumstantial case. But if the defendant is acquitted and you lose, there is no second trial. Game over. I wasn't going to ask the grand jury to indict him until I had sufficient proof to convict.

You only get one shot. I wasn't going to blow mine. We were steadily, quietly moving closer and closer to the truth.

| THE BECERRA LEAK

It wasn't easy to keep our investigation quiet. We had to find and reinterview everyone—the elevator operator, the dean of the medical school, the doorman, the housekeeper, the train conductor, the neighbors, the divorce lawyer, the friends, the family, *everybody*. We watched. We lay low. We created a timetable. We inched closer to the core, one interview at a time. By talking to all of those people, we figured out that Susan Berman, Robert Durst's best friend from college, was at the red-hot center of it all. She was the key. If we could get her to talk, we could nail Durst.

As in any investigation, it is important to start with generic, general-information witnesses. After that, you zero in on those closer to the person you are looking at. Everything was on track. We had gone from the periphery and were headed toward the heart of the case.

How did we know Susan was crucial to the case? We identified her as the family spokesperson who was often quoted in the press during the initial "investigation" back in '82. We'd been monitoring Robert Durst's bank accounts secretly for almost a year. In March 2000, he wrote Susan a check for twenty-five thousand dollars. Knowing how cheap he was, we found it curious at best and a payoff at worst (as we'd later learn, he called it "a gift"). If Durst was sending her money to help her out, you had to wonder, what had she done to help him out?

We put her on the board to be interviewed. Before we could do that, though, we still had a great deal of work to do.

It was my decision that the press would not be informed in any way, shape, or manner about the reopening. For a year, not one article appeared. Good. Great. Silence bought us time. Our intent, when we showed up at Susan Berman's door in Beverly Hills, was to know the answer to every question we asked, the better to test her credibility. We'd chip away at her story with what we already knew to be fact or fiction until we cracked it wide open.

In the best of all worlds, we could get Susan to admit Durst told her to tell the press about Kathie's alleged late-night visitor and her drug problems. Or that she was the one who created the false narrative that made it into the news that Kathie might have been going to the drugstore Monday morning because she had a hangover. If she told us Durst put her up to those things, we were close to his short hairs. Or she might even tell us Durst killed Kathie!

We put the wheels in motion to make this interview happen.

Because we had multiple addresses for her, even in California, it was essential to find her exact present location. We were quite sure we knew it, but we wanted the LAPD to confirm. We did not ask them to speak with her or tell them what it was about. Whenever one law-enforcement agency is about to go into the jurisdiction of another, the courtesy call is always made. Our call was a heads-up to the LAPD as well.

On or about November 8, 2000, Chief Assistant Clem Patti, after meeting with investigators as well as the ADAs assigned to the case, called a meeting in the DA's conference room adjacent to my office. Many of the players were there: members of law enforcement (NYPD, state police, my investigators) and Kathie's family and friends.

A few more bits of information came to light, including the bomb-shell that Gilberte's house had been broken into, and all her "boxes" on the case had been stolen. Kathy Traystman's house at 160 West Sixteenth Street had been burglarized as well. The thieves had taken jewelry and a TV, along with files she'd hidden in a closet with articles about the case and evidence, including the original dig/shovel to-do list. There were copies of stock transactions, financial documents, and tax returns on which, Kathie had told Kathy Traystman, Bob had forged Kathie's name. Kathie Durst gave Kathy Traystman copies of anything she wanted protected and told her, as she'd told so many others, "If anything happens to me, check Bobby."

I'd asked Clem to let me know when the meeting would be, and told Roseanne to work it into my schedule. When I walked in, I thanked everyone for coming. I thanked them for their assistance in our cold case endeavor, and indicated to them that I would spare no resource in my office's effort to solve the cold case of Kathie Durst. I also said that, although most of them knew each other, we were at a very sensi-tive point in the investigation and it was important to keep the infor-mation contained. The message was clear: Don't talk about the case.

We didn't want Berman to be aware of the case because it was always best to size up an individual in a nonadversarial setting and we certainly didn't want Durst to get a heads-up. We were all in complete agreement about this. He couldn't know.

I told them that they were in good hands, and that I'd assigned the best and the brightest in my office, as well as from other agencies—including those experts in forensics and identifying body locations—to this case. I then left the meeting to my second deputy DA Clem and homicide chief Steve. They were the fact-finders. They knew the case inside out, and their job was to find out if there were any other pieces to add so that we could tie everything together before our effort to talk to Susan Berman.

From my perspective, things looked tight.

Little did I know what was coming.

On Saturday, November 11, 2000, articles about the case appeared simultaneously in the *New York Times* and the *New York Daily News*. Both articles spoke of the work of the state police and the tip that led to the case being reopened. There was no mention of the task force of people from my office—the chief assistant, the chief of homicide, the chief of investigations, the chief investigator, the two senior investigators, as well as other investigators—who were working on this case. According to the articles, the DA's office didn't exist. How could the papers print articles about an investigation and not mention where it was coming from or where it was centered?

The articles had it all. That we searched the lake, the cottage, and the crawl space. That we were reinterviewing the elevator man, the doorman, the South Salem neighbors, the Albert Einstein dean, and Detective Struk. Whoever talked to the *Times* and the *News* gave away the store.

The worst part: Durst was referred to as a "suspect."

Saturday mornings were generally reserved for my kids. Kiki was fifteen and Alex was eleven. The lunacy was predictable. Theater, hockey, haircuts, and a bottle of arsenic reserved for me at the end of the day. I remember David Hebert called me at home and said, "Take a look at the *Times*." He directed me to page A-20 (not the front page).

I read the headline and my blood ran cold: DISAPPEARANCE UNDER SCRUTINY AFTER EIGHTEEN YEARS.

"Oh, my God!" I screamed.

David said, "Can you believe this?"

I read the article, my blood boiling. "Did you get a call on this at all?"

"Judge, you know I would have told you if I did." Then he said, "It gets better. Get the *Daily News*."

I jumped into the car to go buy one. I didn't have one fast enough to get to the deli down the street. And there it was, an article on page 8 with the headline, COPS SHAKE THE DUST OFF '82 DURST CASE.

"Son of a bitch!"

Whoever talked to the press compromised our case!

And get this: Years later, in a Galveston courtroom, I would be the one accused of putting Durst's name back in headlines. Right. I leaked the news that screwed the investigation I'd spent a fortune on and had been obsessed with for a year, just to make sure my office and my name didn't get in it.

It wasn't about credit. If I wanted credit for the DA's office, I would have called Charles Bagli at the *New York Times* myself. I could have picked up the phone any day of the week and gotten headlines. Our every directive was to keep the investigation under wraps, to make sure an essential witness did not get a heads-up, could not rehearse or reach out for even more money from Durst to keep her quiet.

Douglas Durst gave Bagli a quote: "Robert Durst continues to maintain his innocence." Not exactly a strong defense of his big brother.

Robert gave the *News* a statement about the reopening of the investigation: "I know nothing about it, but I would not have any comment."

Two weeks later, *People* magazine gave the case the full treatment, with photos of Kathie.

I was furious. Again, no mention of my office. Some said I was upset because I wasn't in the article. Like I needed more exposure in *People*? I'd already been named one of their 50 Most Beautiful. I didn't need to see my name in there. I needed this case NOT to be in *People* magazine.

Now, what—or who—was the common denominator in all three articles? Only one member of law enforcement is mentioned by name in all three articles: Joe Becerra. But he wasn't just mentioned. He was actually quoted.

It doesn't take Woodward and Bernstein or a rocket scientist to conclude that he was behind the articles. Joe put himself smack dab at the center of the investigation as if he were single-handedly running it. He ran his mouth on the eve of our biggest interview yet.

A man with a reputation for being a notorious media suck-up, Hollywood Joe Becerra had the connections to coordinate the *Times* and *Daily News* articles appearing on the same day. If one paper had gone first, I might've believed that one dedicated reporter had found us out. That two papers covered it simultaneously proved that one person had given the information to both outlets at the same time.

Even if the *Times* and the *Daily News* had snatched the story out of thin air or from some other big-mouth at the same time, Becerra actually went on the record with both reporters. Hollywood Joe couldn't resist getting his name in the *Times*, the *Daily News*, and *People* magazine. And, as if the world should thank him and him alone, he stood out, the lone cop for whom we should all be grateful. At the very least, he did interviews with reporters, without state police approval or our approval. And to make matters worse, he didn't even bother to give us a heads-up that he'd done it. He knew, as did everyone else on the team, the danger zone we were in.

In direct disregard of our effort, he blabbed. You can't have one member of a team going rogue. I'd worked with hundreds of state troopers for over twenty-five years, and this was the first time a police investigator had taken it upon himself to reveal specific details of a major case investigation. He alone decided to release facts that were not in the public domain. He betrayed his fellow law-enforcement officers and prosecutors and put others at risk.

Why did he do it? I can only assume his actions were motivated by ego, that he did it for credit and to get his name out there.

Now secrecy wasn't possible. Becerra had tipped our hand. Sure enough, Durst lawyered up. We never got near him.

Susan Berman would have her back up now, too. We hadn't spoken to her yet. Now she'd know everything. She could prepare and get her story straight with Durst. She could run.

I kept trying to figure out how we could get past this new problem that was wreaking havoc on the investigation. I'd made it abundantly clear that *not* talking to the media was the strategy. We weren't really looking for more witnesses at that point. We were looking to talk to only one in particular. Not only that, Becerra knew full well that Susan Berman could only be approached cold. She couldn't have the benefit of a warm-up or a rehearsal.

Members of my staff were deflated, but not because our office wasn't mentioned. As professionals, they understood the peril that they, the case, and the potential witness were in.

Of course I confronted Joe about what he'd done. He blamed the leak on a civilian, the one person who had carried the torch to find Kathie for eighteen years, Gilberte Najamy, and accused her of taking money from the press. He said we should never trust her again.

I never trusted *him* again.

As he was talking, I thought to myself, *Really? So what if she talked? What about you? You gave it the law-enforcement confirmation. You were quoted in the articles. Why wouldn't you give us or the supervisors a heads-up?*

I'd already spoken to Gilberte about that. Her name was in the articles, too. She swore she'd just been interviewed and had called no one. But she wasn't in law enforcement and she had already been the most vocal firebrand about Kathie since the day she disappeared. Any reporter would automatically go to her for quotes. She was not informed about every step of our investigation. That information could only have come from the inside.

Besides which, Gilberte wasn't under a code of silence. She was a regular person, a private citizen. She could say whatever she wanted. But Becerra was a member of law enforcement and *was* under a code of silence, and he happily violated it.

He didn't have to do it. He would always have been the trooper who caught the initial informant. He was the one who said, "Can we look at this again?" It was a great contribution to the investigation.

At that point, I could have said, "Thanks for the tip, Joe, now get back in your squad car and patrol the highway." But I didn't. I decided to let him stay on the team. I brought him into the center of an intelligent, well-honed, long-term prosecutorial investigation. Why wasn't that enough? He repaid that generosity by stabbing me, the team, and the office in the back.

He wanted to be at the center of the action. I had heard that Hollywood Joe was a Lothario among the secretaries. But when he started hanging around my front office, I was uncomfortable. I then found out why. He started dating the woman in charge of my schedule who was working with Ro.

I'd locked horns with this type of man as a young female assistant DA, when I was one of the few. I'd run into cops and witnesses who, upon meeting me, would say, "I want to talk to a man, not a woman." But all that changed when I became DA. I became accustomed to being treated with the respect I'd earned. After the leak, Joe seemed uncomfortable being admonished by a woman.

I thought to myself, *He'd listen to a man, though.* I picked up the phone and called the state police superintendent, Jim McMahon, Joe's boss. I explained the situation and said, "Jim, I don't want this guy running his mouth ever again about this case. Now Durst has been identified as a suspect." In the coming weeks, I would need to mitigate that in the press. I said in a dozen interviews, "I'm not ruling him in as a suspect and I'm not ruling him out. *I don't know.* When I believe he's a suspect, I'll tell you."

Superintendent McMahon, too, was concerned about what Becerra had done. Troopers were like marines, trained weapons who took orders and didn't speak unless spoken to. There was a loose cannon in his ranks.

"You want him off the case?" asked McMahon.

I thought for a moment but said, "No." I knew he might have insight that could be valuable one day. I'd keep my enemy close, but I had to get a muzzle on him. "But I do want some people monitoring him."

McMahon agreed, and he assigned two more high-level troopers to my office above Joe to watch him and keep him in line. In effect, he inserted two layers over Becerra: Eddie Lloyd and Domenic Chimento.

Hollywood Joe has no one to blame but himself.

For better or worse, the story was out and I had to deal with the consequences. Durst had lawyered up and gone off the grid. By now, Susan knew we were coming. We continued to monitor Durst's bank accounts and saw that, on November 21, he sent Berman *another* check for twenty-five thousand dollars. My investigators started calling witnesses who would be in contact with Susan to find out what she knew.

Chief assistant Frank Donohue died of cancer on December 15. We knew he was sick, but we never thought he would die. He was that tough. Frank was a mentor to me. Because of him I learned chain of command and I ran my office with a quasi-military vibe. Frank taught me that.

Frank's passing was a huge loss to the office and to me personally. The annual office Christmas party that year was a somber affair. Usually, it was a blowout. Not this year. Frank was gone. No one really wanted to be there. But we showed up anyway and tried to comfort one another.

I was sitting at one of the tables when the person next to me excused himself. Joe Becerra saw an opening and quickly took the empty chair next to me. I was annoyed, but I wasn't going to make a big deal of it.

I said, "Hey, Joey. How are you?"

After his usual perfunctory compliment on my appearance, he

said, "Judge, there's someone who wants to talk to you outside of the office."

My bodyguards made eye contact with me. They read me like a book and were at the ready to haul him away as soon as I gave them an indication.

I said, "Who?"

He said, "Michael Kennedy."

Michael Kennedy was a lawyer retained by the Durst family trust. Fans of *The Jinx* will remember him as the man who pleaded with Robert to turn himself in after he'd jumped bail in Texas, saying, "Robert, please come home. You have loved ones who care about you here in New York." More like the Dursts wanted to find him so they could kill him themselves.

Hollywood Joe Becerra wanted to worm his way back into my good graces by connecting me with him? "*Why* would I want to meet with Michael Kennedy?"

"Well, he wants to talk to you. He wants to have a meeting. So, I could arrange it for you somewhere out of the office . . ."

Becerra was trying to make himself important again. There was no reason for me to meet with Kennedy.

"Joey, why are you bringing this to me?" I asked. Any discussion should always go through the team, through the investigators and the lawyers, to be discussed, analyzed, and *then* brought to me for my information and input. How was it that he was even in contact with a Durst lawyer? Why was a member of the investigative team talking to Kennedy? Why would a trooper be engaging in any conversations with an attorney at all?

"I thought you'd want to . . ."

He thought I'd forgive him for what he'd done if he screwed things up even more?

I thought to myself, *Do I let this guy even know what I'm thinking?* I knew there was no way, but should I tell him? I did.

The answer was no. He sat there, crestfallen, with a painted-on smile. I turned around and talked to the person on my other side. He didn't know what to do next. He probably got up and went looking for another female to boost his ego.

Becerra had a reputation for jumping in front of every camera he saw. He threw a monkey wrench into my case for a turn in the spotlight. He tried to blame someone else for his mistake. And he was *still* trying to be my friend?

Unbelievable.

As difficult as the holidays were for me that year, they were a lot worse for Susan Berman.

Thank God I didn't have friends like Robert Durst.

| GOOD NEWS, BAD NEWS

In 1982, Susan Berman was living on Beekman Place, partying at Elaine's and Studio 54, basking in her newfound fame as the author of *Easy Street: The True Story of a Mob Family*, her just-published memoir. The book—about growing up as the only daughter of David Berman, aka "Davie the Jew," a '40s and '50s gangster who murdered and kidnapped at Bugsy Siegel's behest—was a hit. Reportedly, she got $350,000 for the movie rights.

Good for her. Berman's life thus far hadn't been easy. One year after her father died (ironically, nonviolently, on the operating table), when she was twelve, her depressive, often institutionalized mother committed suicide by swallowing a handful of pills. Despite losing both parents young, Berman scratched out a life for herself. She graduated from UCLA (where she met Robert in the late 1960s) and got her masters in journalism from Berkeley. As legend has it, Susan and Robert became fast friends, sniffing out immediately that they shared a childhood of wealth, privilege, tragedy, mental illness, and, no doubt, extreme loneliness.

In 1983, after the original investigation was closed and Berman's role as Durst family spokesperson was done, she left New York and moved across the country to California. No one can say for sure, but I wonder if one of the reasons Berman moved was to put some distance between herself and the NYPD. She and Robert stayed in touch. When Susan married a younger man named Mister Margulies at the Bel-Air Hotel in June 1984, Robert gave away the bride. The marriage lasted a year. Margulies died of a heroin overdose a year later.

Tragedy clung to this woman. When Susan Berman hit my radar in 2000 and I read about her history, I found her to be an interesting character. Her once-promising journalism and publishing career had crumbled. She had no children of her own, although the son and daughter, Sareb and Mella, of her ex-boyfriend Paul Kaufman preferred to stay with her when she and their father broke up. She couldn't get any of her screenwriting projects off the ground. Apparently, she was a hypochondriac, an extreme neurotic, and desperately broke.

When Susan reached out to Robert to get that first twenty-five-thousand-dollar check in March 2000 to buy a new car, she had a hard time locating her supposed best friend. We had a tough time locating him, too. Robert was a hard man to find, intentionally. He had homes in Connecticut, New Orleans, Houston, and Trinidad, a quiet town in Northern California. Since he quit the Durst Organization in 1994, he'd been buying houses and floating between them, slipping on and off the grid. The man didn't like to be pinned down. Postleak, in November 2000, Durst turned himself into the invisible man (actually, he was the invisible *woman*). We had no idea where he was.

But we knew where Susan was. Susan had moved several times during her fifteen years in Los Angeles. We had previous addresses for her in West Hollywood and Brentwood, and her current location at 1527 Benedict Canyon in Beverly Hills. We were putting out feelers to confirm our information and smooth the way for our guys to go to Los Angeles to talk to her. And then the leak happened. Fucking Becerra.

We believed Susan Berman knew a lot more than she'd said publicly about Kathie's movements on the night in question, and, quite possibly, Kathie's current whereabouts. She certainly knew a lot about Robert's actions and his state of mind. After Kathie's disappearance, Susan was the only friend he spoke to for weeks. She'd been his filter. The team had spent the better part of a year compiling enough evidence to shake the foundation of his house of lies. Susan Berman spoon-fed selective narratives to the media about Kathie that they ran with, and the NYPD picked up on. Irrespective of what Susan had done, my goal was to solve Kathie's case. If she helped me do that, I could forgive all of her transgressions.

In late December 2000, we were ready. John O'Donnell called the LAPD and told them we would be coming out to talk to Susan. In advance of the trip, he asked if the LAPD could drive by her house to make sure she was still there. We suspected she might have rabbited, too, given the Becerra leak. No surprise Robert Durst had written her a second check for twenty-five thousand dollars around Thanksgiving, certainly enough money to allow her to run and hide from us. It was reasonable to assume that the two of them were in touch by phone. If we could find her, we could find him. Susan was probably nervous. Given her personality, I bet she was chewing her nails off, one by one. In *The Jinx*, Robert confirmed that she thought the police were coming when he told Jarecki that Susan said the LAPD had reached out to her. I have never known that to be the case. Susan had kept her mouth shut in '82, but she had been on Easy Street at the time. She'd seen eighteen years of rough road since then.

Could Robert still trust her?

On January 5, 2000, Clem Patti and John O'Donnell came into my office.

"I've got good news," said Clem. "And bad news."

I groaned. "What's the good news?"

"We found Susan Berman."

"What's the bad news?"

"She's dead."

I yelled, "Son of a bitch!"

He beat us to her.

On Christmas Eve, neighbors of Susan's on Benedict Canyon called the cops. Her three wirehaired terriers were barking incessantly around the ramshackle bungalow. When the cops arrived, they found the rear door open, and Susan's body in a pool of blood with macabre dog paw prints in blood around the body. She'd been shot once in the back of the head with a nine-millimeter. No sign of forced entry. Nothing was stolen from the house. Nothing was amiss, except for, you know, a corpse on the floor. To some, the murder looked like an old-school mob hit, something like her father might've done back in the '50s.

Before Clem told me the particulars, I knew Durst had done it.

Within six weeks of the press leak, he'd silenced her. Whatever she knew, it must have been explosive.

I was afraid to ask, "Where is Durst?"

"Unknown."

"Get on a plane to L.A.," I said. "Give them whatever they need."

John O'Donnell and Joe Becerra flew to California that day.

THE FIRST TIME I spoke on the record about the Durst case was on January 6, 2000, two weeks after the murder of Susan Berman. I held a press conference. My battle gear didn't change—a simple solid Armani suit and Manolo Blahniks. When I tried cases, I always wore a red suit for my opening statement. I wanted their attention. But for summation? Always black, to remind the jurors of the solemnity of the occasion. Press conferences were somewhere in the middle.

My battle dress was carefully considered and devised to create a certain effect. Authority. Impeccability. Gravity. My style was intended to project competence and confidence in my gestures, words, and actions.

When I spoke to reporters, I connected the dots between Kathie Durst's disappearance and Susan Berman's murder. The usual bashing about my being a well-dressed woman in the spotlight was not far behind.

As a woman in power, a younger and supposedly attractive woman, I wasn't exactly the norm. There will always be questions leveled at those outside the norm, or anyone who pushes a new agenda. My agenda was to level the playing field, whether it was for victims of hate crimes, battered women, or child victims of Internet pedophiles. I was the first DA in the nation to nail a pedophile who flew from Washington State to kidnap a young girl in Mamaroneck. I used my bully pulpit to nab scumbags who hurt women and raped children. And I was pilloried for it.

People in public life have critics—especially women in power. Just by virtue of my doing my job, negative attention was focused on me. It didn't bother me, except when that noise overwhelmed my goals. I focused on my purpose. My purpose was to find and catch Robert Durst. Sometimes, not everyone in the audience could get over the fact that I was on TV and could hear what I was actually saying. My attempt to link Durst to Berman's murder was one of those times.

A ton of my media coverage was about my ton of media coverage. Just one example: In a 1998 article in *New York* magazine called "Pirro Mania," the opening scene was about a press conference I was invited to by the police commissioner of New York for catching a serial rapist who'd attacked fifty-one women across the city and in Westchester. Instead of talking about the arrest or my office's contribution to it, the writer, Kevin Gray, described my makeup, how short my skirt was, and my "gym-toned" thighs. How the heck did he know? Later that day, he tagged along to watch a lecture I gave about domestic violence, child abuse, and elder abuse. The reason I agreed to the article in the first place was to get that information to the public. Gray called my talk a "spiel," and wrote, "Her gutsy voice peppers the room with images of penetration, penises, and vaginas."

I was raising awareness about violent crimes against the most vulnerable members of society, and the reporter wrote about makeup, skirts, legs, and vaginas.

Writing me off as a grandstander was an easy narrative to sell to misogynists and morons. The voters in Westchester saw through the sexism. They elected me, reelected me, and reelected me again. They understood that I'd do whatever I had to do, even if it meant taking jabs from jerkoffs, to get the job done.

I wasn't about to remain silent when I was pursuing a goal on behalf of a victim. The cacophony and the criticism didn't matter. What mattered was leveling the playing field. The small minds around me were obsessed with other things. That was their issue, not mine.

Okay, rant over.

I started doing interviews about the case for papers and TV. I brought Becerra into my office to do *48 Hours* with me to prevent him from going rogue again. I made sure to be vague, and said things like, "Berman knew Robert and Kathleen Durst. We believe she may have stayed in touch with Robert throughout Kathleen's disappearance and afterward. We were interested in talking to her and were working toward making that happen. We were extremely disappointed when we heard what had happened to her."

Whoever I was speaking to would inevitably ask, "Is there a connection between Susan Berman's death and Kathie Durst's disappearance?"

"We're not ruling it in and we're not ruling it out," I said.

I was very careful not to say that Durst was a suspect. I had no power to do so. It was up to the Los Angeles DA to make that call. At no point did I ever—*ever*—say that Robert Durst was a suspect in either case, or that I was going to indict him for Kathie's murder, or that we had any evidence linking the two crimes, or any knowledge of the LAPD's investigation that could lead to an arrest. Didn't happen.

Why hit that point so hard? Bear with me. It becomes important later on, when the story gets to Galveston, Texas.

IN EARLY 2001, THE media were going crazy about Durst. They couldn't get enough of it—wealthy husband, missing wife, dead friend with mob links shot execution style. Outlets invited anyone and everyone tangentially connected to the case or the principals on television. A lot of people used Susan Berman's murder to get their fifteen minutes of fame.

One of them was a woman named Ellen Strauss, a lawyer and, she claimed, a dear old friend of Kathie's from college.

Strauss carved her niche as the self-appointed chief critic of how I, the Westchester DA, had mangled the investigation. She told any journalist who'd listen that if I'd only done my job and rushed to interview Susan Berman *when she told me to*, Susan would be alive today. Strauss started using the phrase, "What was she waiting for? Godot?"

After Durst's Galveston acquittal in 2003, she told Phil Reisman of the *Journal News*: "Here's my feelings about Jeanine. You can write it all down because I don't care if you quote me. Jeanine is a shameless self-promoter. She's been blowing smoke for two years . . . she put the whole series of events in motion."

Strauss claims that she and Kathie were friends at Western Connecticut State College in Danbury. As she would tell the *Houston Chronicle* after *The Jinx* aired, they shared "that feeling you have when you meet someone. We both had the same values. I wanted to set up a storefront legal firm and save the world. She wanted to be a doctor and take care of children."

It might be true that they went to the same college, and that they had altruistic visions of their futures. The rest of Strauss's claim appears to be complete hogwash.

This past spring, I went to Yale–New Haven Hospital to speak with Gilberte Najamy. She wasn't doing so well and was struggling with infections and liver and heart disease. Sadly, she did, in fact, die of her illnesses on July 26, 2015. My conversation with her on May 15, 2015, was her last recorded statement on the Kathleen Durst case. On her deathbed—and she knew she was severely ill, with nothing to lose and no reason to hold back—she discussed her final thoughts, including her feelings about Ellen Strauss.

According to Gilberte, who met Kathie in a college chemistry class, Kathie and Strauss never met each other at Western Connecticut. Not once. "Ellen Strauss did not know Kathie when she was alive," Gilberte said emphatically.

Gilberte told me that it was she herself who originally introduced Kathie to Ellen Strauss over the phone. "Ellen had one telephone conversation with Kathie at my request in 1981. Kathie wanted legal advice. I said, 'Well, you can talk to my friend Ellen and see what this divorce is going to involve.'" Strauss had just graduated from the Franklin Pierce Law Center in Concord, New Hampshire, and was in no position to give expert legal advice to anyone, let alone a desperate battered woman going up against a wealthy family with unlimited resources. But Gilberte was just trying to help. So she arrranged the call.

I was stunned. Strauss latched on to the Durst case from the beginning, and has described her twenty-year accumulation of documents and reports about it as her "life's work," inspired by her close, intimate friendship with Kathie. And now Gilberte was telling me, on her deathbed, that Ellen and Kathie's entire personal interaction was exactly *one* phone conversation? That the self-described close friendship *did not exist*? That Strauss's "life's work" was based on an epic lie?

Just to be clear, I asked Gilberte again, "Ellen said that she was a friend of Kathie's from college. That's not true?"

"Ellen Strauss *did not know her in college*," she confirmed. "They spoke only once, over the phone when I introduced them. *They never met in person*."

Yet Strauss had repeatedly claimed that Kathie told her, as she told others, "If anything happens to me, don't let Bobby get away with it."

Gilberte listened in on their one brief conversation. Kathie had been guarded, not divulging too many details about her marriage, just asking about how to initiate a divorce. But then, "after the disappearance," said Gilberte, "Ellen became obsessed and was convinced that she was going to solve the case."

Kathie's brother, Jim, confirmed this. "Ellen Strauss was Kathie's best friend *after* the fact. Her name didn't come up until after Kathie disappeared. Ellen was not with Kathie and Gilberte the last night she went missing."

One of Gilberte and Kathie's friends from college triple-confirmed this. She said, "Kathie, Gilberte, and I were very close. As far as I know, Kathie never met Ellen Strauss in college or after."

So was this great Ellen-Kathie friendship a figment of Ellen Strauss's imagination?

The reams of information about the case she claimed to have personally collected over the years, in particular between 1982 and 2000? If it was so important, why didn't she provide this information to the grieving McCormack family when something could have been done? Why not give it to the Dursts, who had the wherewithal to find Kathie? Why didn't she give it to the Westchester DA in 1982? Where was it? Why did she wait eighteen years to criticize the one person who decided this was worth looking into?

"She took notes about what I told her," said Gilberte. "I asked her to because if something happened to me, somebody needs to know. Ellen took down everything I said about what I'd found out. All of the information she's been talking about is stuff I gave her."

Strauss claimed to have been with Gilberte every step of the way, to have gone through Durst's trash with her. To that point, Gilberte said, "Ellen has a problem with her memory. She clearly said to me that she had a career and she couldn't risk getting caught, so she didn't want to be involved in the actual evidence-gathering."

Ellen Strauss is one of the wannabes in the Durst theater of the absurd.

She has told reporters that I could barely give the grieving family a minute of my time. As if she had any idea what it was like to run a highly successful prosecutor's office with a staff of people who were determined to provide the energy, resources, and empathy that a case needed. I had my fact-finders in that room: Clem, Steve, John. They would be the ones to write the reports of the information and follow up on leads or inconsistencies.

At the time, when Strauss trashed me in the press, I ignored it. There was nothing to gain from paying heed to a self-important hanger-on like Ellen Strauss.

Since *The Jinx* aired, Strauss has been stretching her fifteen minutes, appearing on various TV shows, going on about her friendship with Kathie, and, shocker, trashing me. She's still trotting out that "Godot" line.

It was lame back in 2000.

Ellen Strauss recently said on *Nancy Grace*, "I had phone conversations with the detectives, and they told me that they—the prosecutor's office—didn't want to cut any checks to fly out to California. They didn't get interested in [Berman] until after she was dead. And Pirro went on television and she said to the general public, meaning me, we didn't know how the police worked. They liked to work from the periphery and go inward. Well, I said, 'Go right to Susan, do it now.' "

Really? You told *me* what to do? I wasn't doing everything in my power to set up an interview with a key witness—clearing it with L.A., going after all her friends to get their stories, tracking her movements, researching her, all the detail and double-checking of an investigation on the highest level that this fraud knows *nothing* about—on a case I'd been working for over a year? Didn't want to cut checks to fly to L.A.? We don't cut checks for travel. She has no clue about what we do.

What had Ellen Strauss done to prevent Susan Berman's murder?

She called Joe Becerra with Berman's address in Beverly Hills.

Did this ditz think she could get information off the Internet that the DA's office couldn't? Did she think we didn't know where Susan Berman lived?

Ellen Strauss got her name in the papers. If she weren't talking about me, no one—*no one*—would give a crap what came out of her mouth.

A LOT OF PEOPLE wonder why Durst didn't cut up Susan's body, as he would later do to Morris Black, and had previously, presumably, done to his wife. One theory was that he refrained out of respect and because he genuinely loved her.

Love? If he loved her, he wouldn't have shot her in the head.

There were three reasons Robert Durst didn't dismember Susan Berman:

1. He wanted police to assume she'd been executed mob-style. Everyone knows that a shot to the back of the head is classic Vito Corleone MO.
2. Los Angeles wasn't his milieu, so to speak. It wasn't his home, his apartment, his private space, making it more difficult for him so he didn't feel comfortable doing it.
3. He didn't have time. As we eventually found out, he had to get to the San Francisco airport for a ten-o'clock flight to New York that night.

As soon as John and Joe arrived in L.A., John visited the crime scene. He said there was still coagulated blood and pieces of her gray matter on the floor. It was not wiped down. There was a possibility of collecting and interpreting forensic evidence. John connected with Detective Paul Coulter and other L.A. detectives, telling them about Durst and opening up a two-way flow of information. The LAPD was skeptical that the murder of Susan Berman was connected with a nineteen-year-old cold case about a missing person in Westchester. They were looking at a possible mob connection or at Berman's on-again, off-again boyfriend/manager Nyle Brenner.

On January 11, 2001, Jonathan Bandler of the *Journal News* reported, "Los Angeles Police said yesterday that they were skeptical about whether the execution-style slaying of a writer there last month was connected to the 1982 disappearance of Kathleen Durst. Nevertheless, investigators from the Westchester DA's office were in Los Angeles yesterday to see if it could stir up any new leads. . . . Los Angeles Police Detective Ron Phillips, a supervisor of the West Los Angeles Homicide Unit that is handling the Berman case, said Tuesday night that the cases were not connected. The Department spokesman reiterated that."

My team certainly tried to convince them otherwise. One thing my team and the LAPD agreed on was that Susan must have known her killer. Forensics proved that she'd invited the Devil inside and trusted him enough to turn her back to him. John talked to a cop at the crime scene who told him that, assessing the trajectory of the entry wound and how she was struck, Susan had been bent over when she was shot. When they removed her body, there may have been a paper towel or a tissue underneath her with dog mess on it. This lends itself to the theory that she had bent over to clean up some dog poop when her executioner struck.

A major point of contention was whether Susan knew our case had been reopened. It had been in the *New York Times*! Robert was like a brother to her. Of course she knew. In *The Jinx*, her friend, the novelist Julie Smith, later confirmed it. She asked Susan about the article, and Susan told her back then, "I don't want to talk about that. They're out to get Bobby."

Durst told Jarecki that he contacted Susan and that Susan said, "Bobby, this is terrible for you. I hate that you have to go through this." Durst claimed Susan said the L.A. police contacted her and they wanted to talk to her about Kathie's disappearance.

So Durst and Julie Smith both said Susan knew, but my office did *not* tell the L.A. police to talk to Susan about Kathie. We would *not* have had another agency do an interrogation in a case that we had meticulously and fastidiously studied for over a year. They wouldn't know where to start on our case. As a courtesy, we notify another police agency when we are in their jurisdiction or are heading their way.

L.A. was contacted *only* for the purpose of locating Susan so that I could send out John O'Donnell and Joe Becerra to question her using the vast amount of information that they had garnered. L.A.

did not know why we wanted to talk to her, which might explain why they thought New York's case had nothing to do with theirs. So they concluded early on that it was probably a mob hit because of Susan's father or that her manager killed her, neither of which feeds into the idea that she was killed because we were coming out to talk to her.

The headlines—from the *New York Times*, A WITNESS POLICE HOPE COULD SOLVE '82 MYSTERY KILLED; from the *Los Angeles Times*, POLICE HOPED TO QUESTION WRITER WHO WAS KILLED; from the *New York Post*, SLAIN WRITER FACED QUIZ OVER MISSING WOMAN—were more in tune with what was happening and what was needed.

But the fact is, there was no stone left unturned in the investigation. Susan would have known the investigation would lead to her. Kim Lankford says she and Susan had a conversation about being interviewed by law enforcement. She told Jarecki that Susan was excited about a new project that would "blow the socks off" something big. Was she so desperate for money that she'd reveal what she knew about Kathie and betray her close old friend, a man who was like a brother to her?

More important, Robert knew the police were coming for her.

According to Robert in *The Jinx*, Susan told him, "The police want to talk to me. I'm just going to talk to them. Is that all right?" He replied, "Do whatever you want."

The Berman case didn't get far and quieted down quickly.

To me, the key was the cadaver note, which was shared with us by L.A. No progress there, either. I have used handwriting experts many times. To me, the most credible handwriting exemplars are not the ones where you sit down with a suspect and ask him to write certain words. He knows how he wrote them, and if he's got half a brain, he'll write them differently this time. Handwriting exemplars are not that valuable. What is valuable is writing that already exists, and is known to be the suspect's, to compare to the evidence in question. But at the time L.A. wasn't collecting or looking at Durst's handwriting anyway.

I kept calling L.A. to see if there were any breaks in the case. In 2002, I called Bill Bratton, who had just become chief of the Los Angeles Police Department. I had worked with him when he was police commissioner in New York City. I made a friendly call and said, "Bill, you've got to look at this case again."

He was the consummate professional, the consummate cop, so when he said, "Of course," I knew we had a second shot at Durst.

Before we even knew Susan was dead, she was buried. She was laid to rest on January 2, placed next to her father in the mausoleum at Home of Peace Cemetery in Los Angeles.

Robert did not attend the funeral.

Her memorial service was at the Los Angeles branch of the Writers' Guild the following week.

And although Robert was in Los Angeles at the time, he did not attend the service. What does that tell you? Why would he be in L.A. at the exact time of her service and not attend? He knew it would be a bad idea.

Anyone as seasoned as Durst in the art of human disappearance knows that the police are looking at anyone and everyone at such a service. Plus, any news outlet would have killed to get a shot of Durst at Berman's memorial.

It's interesting, though, that Durst would connect with Susan's adoptive son, Sareb Kaufman, that week. You meet with the adoptive son but don't go to the service? Was Durst just trying to find out from Sareb the kinds of questions police were asking? Sareb had stayed loyal to Robert, despite the field day the press was having about his stepmother's murder and its possible connection to Robert. Instead of being suspicious, even a tiny bit, he rewarded Robert with Susan's most treasured possession.

In her will, she left Robert her father's silver medallion and key chain. David Berman's name had been engraved on them. Robert accepted the gift from Sareb, left Los Angeles, and completely dropped off the radar.

A few months later, he resurfaced in my neck of the woods in a bizarre and eerie way.

On April 12, four months after Susan's murder, Gabrielle Colquitt saw a man standing on the dock by the lake at her cottage in South Salem, staring wistfully at the water. Colquitt recognized him as Robert Durst and called us in a complete panic.

The date was significant. It was Robert's birthday, as well as his wedding anniversary.

O'Donnell remembered that Colquitt was *hysterical*, like, "He's here! He's here! He's outside! *He's here!*" By the time John arrived, though, Durst had driven off in his Saab to God knows where.

"Boss, you're not going to believe this one," John reported to me later, and told me about Durst's trespassing on his old stomping grounds.

"Oh, I believe it," I said. "*Every* criminal returns to the scene of the crime! That son of a bitch!"

| "I HAVE A DOG NAMED CODY"

I was in Midtown Manhattan on the morning of 9/11, coming out of an early meeting. I remember it was a sunny day, and thinking what a beautiful blue the sky was. John Orfei and James O'Donnell (no relation to John or Rosie) were on my security detail that day. Chief Mike Duffy, John's boss, called him to say that we needed to return to Westchester.

John said, "Boss, we have to go back. There's something wrong."

I said, "What's wrong?" I was not interested in returning.

John then reported to Chief Duffy that I wasn't interested in returning.

My investigators and I always had an interesting relationship. Even though we were mutual caring, we were often at odds. They were cops. They carried guns. They had a sixth sense about things. But I was the boss. I was more of an independent free-agent type, not at all interested in being told what to do.

John told me, "Boss, a plane hit the World Trade Center."

It didn't sink in that it might be terrorists. I thought, "Some idiot flew into the building." I could see a gray cloud downtown. At that point, my brain didn't go to terrorism. The chief then said, "Just throw her in the car and get her the hell out of there."

I said, "Okay. Let's go."

We got into my police vehicle and headed north on the FDR Drive back to White Plains. John was listening to the police radio on the way. When we arrived at the office, I went to the investigators' squad room where everyone was watching a television. By then, the second building was hit. We were all numb, wondering who would do this. I remember saying, "This is Pearl Harbor all over again!"

The sense of helplessness that we all had was overwhelming. I thought about my family and thanked God none of them were in the city.

And then I heard the news that the Pentagon had been hit. I screamed, "Kiki is there!" My sixteen-year-old daughter, Cristine, was in Washington, D.C., touring the Pentagon with her class that day. Someone came into the room with a very somber face, telling me that Scott Nelson, the headmaster from Rye Country Day, was on the phone. My heart dropped. I didn't want to pick it up.

I did and said, "Hi, Scott."

"Jeanine, I need your help," he said. "Some parents are upset. We need to know where the kids are and whether we can get them home tonight. Can you find out what's going on?"

"Let me try, I'll get back to you." At the time, Rudy Giuliani was mayor of New York. Bernie Kerik, the police commissioner of New York, was someone who, like Bratton, I'd worked with as DA. He was also a dear friend. I asked James O'Donnell to try to get through to Kerik. He was able to do so and brought the phone to me. At the time, Bernie was walking through hell.

I said, "Bernie, I know you don't have time for this, but my daughter and her class are at the Pentagon . . ."

I didn't even finish my sentence.

He said, "I'll get back to you." That was Bernie. A great guy and a 9/11 hero.

About an hour later, he called. "Everybody is okay," he said, "but there is no way they're coming home tonight." I immediately reported the news to Scott.

By afternoon, my office was fielding hundreds of calls from distraught and panicked citizens. Meanwhile, New York City law enforcement arrived in my White Plains office en masse. I'd set up a state-of-the-art high-intensity drug trafficking area (HIDTA) program with advanced-intelligence technology. The NYPD traveled to White Plains to use our center because their lines were down in the city. Dozens of officers, squad cars with lights blazing, and vans with more electronics streamed to our building. They set up at my office and stayed for weeks. I got to know a number of the investigators, and some of them would wind up working for me.

Many families in Westchester County were ravaged by the terror attacks at the World Trade Center. We lost a total of 123 people, including thirty-one mostly young investment bankers at Cantor Fitzgerald and fifteen Westchester firefighters. And that didn't include the hundreds of victims who were raised here, still had family and roots here, but had moved to the city for an education, a job, or both. Too many husbands and wives, brothers and sisters, sons and daughters were gone. One minute they had everything to live for, and the next they had vanished into thin air in an act of senseless violence.

I walked Ground Zero within twenty-four hours with Governor George Pataki, his wife, Libby, state troopers, and my friend Christy Ferrer, whose husband, Neil, had just gotten a new job at the World Trade Center. The governor had appointed him as director of the Port Authority. As we walked through the ashes, Christy had a stack of photos of Neil that she handed out to people, hoping that someone had seen him. Libby Pataki, Christy, and I visited hospitals, hoping to find him. It was not to be.

I remember the soot on my shoes. I wore a pantsuit that day. I remember how dirty it felt to walk through the debris. At the time

I didn't think we could be walking on the perished bodies of those innocent victims of terrorism.

I brought in staff from my victim/witness program to work with the families of those who'd been killed. Along with our collective shock and sorrow, logistics had to be dealt with. Many Westchester residents ride the train to their jobs in the city. But first, they parked their cars in the various commuter lots. It was painful to see the ghost cars whose owners would never be returning. Permission was needed to remove those cars. I gave the okay.

As a former judge, I was friends with the Surrogate's Court judge. Many of the spouses who started coming into my office needed information and quick access to victims' bank accounts. Some of the family members knew *nothing* about finances. They didn't know how to pay the mortgage or access their savings to pay for groceries. Along with their loss, I felt they shouldn't have to worry about such mundane things. We short-circuited the paperwork and the endless appearances it would have taken to probate wills.

When the idea occurred to me that these families needed somewhere to go to get answers, I knew what I had to do. On the Saturday after 9/11, I called everyone into the office, starting with Anne Marie Corbalis, my public affairs director. She had been getting her hair frosted in Yonkers. I told her she had to come in. A half hour later, she showed up at the office with her hair still wet. She never resented the hours we kept. She chuckled, quoting her colorist, who asked her, "Who the hell do you work for?" as she ran out of the salon. Most of the staff wasn't surprised at all to be called in on a Saturday, but the colorist was put out.

We worked day and night to accommodate those devastated by 9/11. Mary Ann Walsh also worked for me in the Office of Public Affairs. Her dad had been a murder victim and, knowing what we needed, she brought in mental health workers and bereavement counselors and set them up in the conference room next to my office. She had the 9/11 victims' assistance unit up and connected to those who had suffered losses.

The families of these homicide victims wanted closure, but they didn't have bodies to bury or even proof that their loved ones were dead. Forensics could bring closure; DNA was the key. I organized a system for victims to bring toothbrushes, hairbrushes, anything we could use to match DNA with remains found at Ground Zero.

The bereaved came through our halls seven days a week. The grief was overwhelming. I watched them grow more and more depressed, thinner, and frailer. I remember one woman to whom I said, "You're too thin. You need to eat." I gave her whatever health bars I was eating at the time. She wasn't hungry.

Virtually no one in the New York area was unaffected by what the terrorists did to us. Eddie Murphy's brother Ray was an FDNY lieutenant with Ladder Company J. He was missing, and Eddie went off the Durst case for a period of time. In fact, 9/11 put the brakes on almost everything.

September 11, 2001, was the first day in years I didn't think about Robert Durst. A month later, he came roaring back into my life in a big way.

On the morning of October 11, 2001, now chief assistant Clem Patti walked into my office, as he did every morning, to discuss any big cases that had arisen overnight. What wasn't usual was the look on his face—part bug-eyed, part "holy shit." Clem was always hyper, but today he was intensely so.

Anything could have come out of his mouth. Another terrorist attack? Another anthrax mailing somewhere?

"You're not going to believe this," he said.

"What?" I yelled. I was anxious because I knew he was.

"Durst killed his neighbor."

I eyeballed him for less than a second.

"*WHAT?*" *Robert Durst?*

Clem chuckled. "Durst killed his neighbor. It's confirmed. He was arrested."

"SON OF A BITCH."

I knew what Durst was, I knew he was a killer. But still. *Really?* He killed his neighbor? I cooled my jets, or tried to, while Clem briefed me on what he knew so far.

"Durst was living in Galveston, Texas."

Galveston? I knew Galveston only from the Glen Campbell song ("Galveston, oh, Galveston"), but otherwise, nothing. Is it an island? Did rhinestone cowboys ride horses there?

"He chopped the guy up."

WHAT?

"And he already posted bail."

Of course he did.

It was only nine months since Susan Berman had been executed. Because of 9/11, Robert Durst had hardly been at the top of anyone's priority list.

My own world had been turned upside down, too. I was in the last month of a tough reelection campaign for DA. I suspended the campaign for three weeks after 9/11, out of deference to those who lost loved ones, but now it was back in full swing with lots of catching up to do. My opponent, Tony Castro, was a bare-knuckle-tactics kind of guy, a Bronx assistant DA with no political experience, but he knew how to operate. I was used to rough-and-tumble elections and the inevitable sexism that came with them. In my first race for DA, in 1993, my opponent, Mike Cherkasky, a father of three whose wife was pregnant, made an issue of my being a woman. After all, how could a mother of two be able to put in the necessary hours?

I ovulated, so I therefore couldn't work late? I was forced to hold a press conference to announce to the people of Westchester that

I had household help and a husband to care for my kids if I had to work late. I won huge and became the first woman to be elected DA in Westchester County history. To this day, Cherkasky thanks me for beating him, because he says if he had stayed in government, he'd never be making the money he makes now. Happy to help, Mike.

My third time running brought a whole new level of crazy.

Have I mentioned that my then husband was in a federal prison?

It took guts to seek a third term as the chief law-enforcement officer with Al away. I hoped voters would see me as a strong DA, an independent woman, and more than just an appendage of the man to whom I was married.

Castro, as everyone expected, made Al's conviction for tax evasion his central campaign issue, to no avail. The voters rejected it. My record of success as a DA was well established. Of course I took some hits. I'm a big girl, I get it. Politics is a blood sport, especially in New York. And I have the scars to prove it.

In any event, that's what life was like for me the day I learned Robert Durst had dismembered his neighbor: in the midst of a tough campaign, raising two kids with an absent father, grieving with the survivors of 9/11, and handling the regular duties of an office that prosecuted tens of thousands of cases a year.

"Everybody's here, boss," said Clem, referring to the team of investigators on *our* Durst case. "Can I bring them all in?"

"Sure," I said.

I stepped out from behind my huge desk to join my staff at the conference table, where everyone was gathering. I yelled to Ro to bring out some coffee. I always liked to feed my staff. I have this mother thing. We sat at the conference table in my office. I first made eye contact with John O'Donnell. He shook his head. They were all shaking their heads. Clem kept chuckling.

"Can you believe this son of a bitch?" I said.

And for a moment, they all relaxed. I saw a few welcome grins. But then it was down to business.

We kicked it around, the little bit we knew.

"Look," I told them, "I'm not worried about the Texas case. It's Texas, they're probably going to kill him. Isn't Texas where they have the hanging immediately after the arrest?"

My staff was used to me. Someone laughed.

"I don't care whether they hang him in the village square or shoot him and charge his family for the cost of the bullet. What I want is peace and closure for Kathleen's family. They deserve to know what happened to her. And *I* need to know."

"Yes, Boss," they pretty much said in unison.

"And I don't want any quick plea deal by some smart-ass defense attorney, saying, 'If you don't give us the death penalty, we'll give you x, y, or z.' *I* want to be the x, the y, and the z. I want to be in the deal if any deal is going to be made down there."

I wasn't even thinking of prosecuting that roach. I was thinking of putting Kathie to rest, and giving Ann McCormack, then eighty-seven, some kind of peace. She deserved to know what happened to her daughter, and where the remains might be.

Now the question was whether to go to Galveston. My instincts told me there were things I could learn about Durst and things I could tell authorities there. There was no question L.A. would send someone; the gun used to kill Morris Black was a .22 semiautomatic. Susan had been killed with a nine-millimeter—the same type of gun found in the car when Durst was arrested in Galveston.

We don't know how Kathie was killed, but we do know that Susan Berman and Morris Black were killed with semiautomatics. Curiously, whenever Durst was on the run, and later arrested, he was always in possession of revolvers, in both Pennsylvania and in New Orleans. Why? Robert Durst is not stupid. He learns along the way. Revolvers "keep the brass"—which explains why in many organized crime cases,

.22 revolvers are used. Unlike an automatic, where the shell casing is ejected and falls on the floor, the revolver shell casing stays in the cylinder. It's less evidence at the crime scene.

I needed to sit with the Galveston DA and talk to him about Kathie. The McCormacks had been waiting twenty years for answers and Durst was finally on the ropes—or about to be hanged with one. And I wanted to eyeball Durst. I wanted to size him up. I wanted to see for myself what made this man tick. His arraignment was scheduled for Tuesday, October 16, five days away.

I was jumping out of the chair, ready to make a run for the airport. "I've got to get down there. John O'Donnell, you're coming with me."

But I also knew that I'd take a political hit if I went. If I left the office to go to Galveston on a case I was not prosecuting, Castro would make hay of it. The only upside of leaving town was that he'd lay off Al for a couple days.

I looked at David Hebert, my most trusted confidant.

"What do you think?"

"Judge, you don't have any choice. You have to go." All my detectives called me Boss, but David always called me Judge because he first worked for me when I was a county judge.

I buzzed Ro and said, "Call Pat D'Imperio [my chief financial officer] and get me a flight to Galveston, Texas. And one for John O'Donnell." I weighed whether to include Becerra. As disgusted as I still was with him for the leak, the case was more important. I said, "After that, get Superintendent McMahon on the phone so Becerra can join us." He okayed Becerra and added state trooper Domenic Chimento, paying their way since we couldn't because of liability issues.

On Monday, October 15, the day before Durst's arraignment, we flew into George H. W. Bush Airport in Houston. It was already 4:00 p.m. when we landed. And we had a lot to do.

While we waited at the baggage carousel, I checked in with Ro, as

I always did if I was out of the office for more than three and a half minutes.

"David needs to speak to you," she said, in that tone of voice that made me wonder, *What now?* She put me through to his line.

"Press calls," said David. "Lots of press calls. 'Did you go? Why did you go? If she didn't go, why didn't she go?' "

"Tell them I went to a damn rodeo," I replied, though I knew he wouldn't.

I dropped my phone back into my Chanel bag and looked up to see O'Donnell walking toward me with an enormous cop in khaki pants and a buzz cut. You can always tell a plainclothes detective, even in Texas, even if he's wearing shit-kicker boots like this guy was. I thought, *Who cuts their hair like that?*

"Boss," said O'Donnell, "this is the lead detective on the case, Cody Cazalas."

"Your name is *Cody*?" I blurted.

"Yes, ma'am."

I was stunned. Nobody had called me ma'am before. But I skipped right by that. "I love that name! I have a dog named Cody!" I said.

He didn't take the offense that one might, and I certainly didn't intend any. He just kind of looked at me. Looked *down* at me. He was a good foot taller. He smiled, amused.

We all walked out of the airport together and toward a dark blue van in the parking lot.

"I got a van to drive us to Galveston," said Detective Cody.

O'Donnell muttered what I was thinking. "Looks like a school bus." In big letters, DARE—for Drug Abuse Resistance Education— was painted on the side in red.

I climbed in, almost broke a heel. The van had bench seats. I sat in one behind Cody, who was driving. I was a little antsy on the ride, bumping along (did they not have shock absorbers in Texas?). It was not quite what I was accustomed to in New York, in my black super-duper Tahoe with a fax machine in the back and phones in every corner. We were going as slow as molasses through Houston. I wanted to get to Galveston before dark. Hell, I wanted to get there before Christmas. But Detective Cody was in no rush. No siree. I leaned forward to eyeball the speedometer. Forty-five miles per hour? *You've got to be kidding me.*

"Does this THING go any faster?" I asked loudly.

Cody didn't skip a beat.

"Ma'am," he replied, "you mind reachin' around and grabbin' me a beer from that cooler in the back?"

O'Donnell tried hard not to laugh.

I actually turned around, wondering if there really was a cooler of beer in the back. Shame on me.

Now Cody was shooting the shit with O'Donnell. He was telling him that Texas passed another law saying you couldn't drink and drive. (I forgot to ask, "What happened to the first law?") And that just recently, Cody said, "They made it illegal for a passenger to drink."

"Huh," said O'Donnell.

"Next thing the state's going to say," deadpanned Cody, "is that you can't drive and shoot your gun out the truck window."

"You can do that down here?" I asked, shocked, horrified. Terrified.

"Gotcha," said Cody, and the boys were now laughing their asses off.

Southern charm? I started laughing, too, and decided that, apart from Robert Durst, maybe Texas wasn't so bad.

WE WENT STRAIGHT TO Galveston Bay off Channelview Road where, two weeks before, on the Sunday evening of September 30, a thirteen-year-old boy out fishing with his father came across the headless, limbless torso of seventy-one-year-old Morris Black washed up on the rocks. It was a gruesome thing for anyone to come across, let alone a kid. We got there just before sunset, about the same time the boy found Morris.

We got out and walked along a concrete bulkhead. Cody steered us to the rocks where the torso was discovered.

"Watch your step, ma'am," said Cody.

He showed us where the garbage bags had been bobbing in the shallow waters by the pier, about eighty feet from the torso. Morris's legs were in separate bags. His arms were in a third bag. The cops didn't have to look far or long for the body parts. The idiot dumped his dismembered friend while the tide was coming in.

"That's how we knew right away," said Cody, "that we probably weren't looking at a homegrown killer." No one who grew up in Galveston would be so stupid as to dump a body at low tide. "And anybody with any sense," he continued, "wouldn't have left them in bags." Bags float. "Now if he just threw the body parts in, even in a short time, marine life could eat on them. We got big fish that could grab an arm and take it anywhere."

"You okay, ma'am?" He was referring to my heels. We were walking along large granite boulders that made up the bulkhead. Next time, I'd wear flats.

With the sun setting, and the water splashing against the rocks, we talked about Morris's missing head. Even then, Detective Cody was pretty certain of two things: One, that Durst did not dump the head in the bay; he deposited it somewhere else. (Very soon, Cody would have a damn good theory about where.) And two, if they ever did find the head, there'd be a bullet in it, and the bullet would have entered from the back, as Susan's did.

From the bay, we went to the apartment house at 2213 Avenue K, where Durst and Black lived across the hall from each other in the only two apartments on the first floor. They each paid three hundred dollars a month in rent. Going from the bay to the apartments was precisely what Cody had done two weeks ago, because Durst had left him directions.

Wrapped around one of Morris's legs in one of the trash bags was a newspaper, stamped with the home delivery address of the building we were standing in.

Also in the bag of limbs? A receipt from Chalmers hardware store for trash bags and a drop cloth, also a price tag for a paring knife and the cardboard cover from a new $5.99 bow saw. The receipt was dated September 28, two days before Morris's body parts were found. Interspersed were tens of individual Metamucil packets, all of which came from the same box as identified by the lot number.

The wood-framed house at 2213 Avenue K was somewhat shabby, but you could tell that, once, it'd been cute. There was something very sweet about Galveston, despite how some parts, like any other city, were run-down.

"Before we go in, come around here," said Cody. He wanted to show us what he did first, which was check the trash can in the alley behind the house. There, he said, he'd "hit pay dirt." In Durst's trash can, he found a .22 caliber pistol plus two clips of ammunition. One bullet was missing. The empty shell casing was in the garbage, too. Also in the trash: the box that the black trash bags came in, packaging for a four-inch paring knife, a bloody sock, an eviction notice for a man named Morris Black in Apartment One, and a receipt from a local optometrist for one Robert Durst in Apartment Two. This was the first time Cody had read the name Robert Durst.

Cody started to tell us about how he asked the landlord who Robert Durst was, and almost magically, the landlord appeared. Klaus Dillman, a bandana on his head, was a bit of an odd duck. But hey, it's Galveston! There was also a no-bullshit charm to the guy. He told us what he'd told Cody two weeks ago—that he had never heard of

Robert Durst "before all this," that the person who rented Apartment Two was a mute woman by the name of "Dorothy Ciner." Dillman explained that a man had called earlier to inquire about renting an apartment, saying he was calling on behalf of Dorothy Ciner. When Dillman actually met "Dorothy," she wrote that a man would be coming around periodically because she traveled but still needed her plants watered. She even paid up front in full.

This was the previous fall, shortly *before* Susan Berman was murdered.

Dillman took us inside. We went to Durst's apartment first, just inside the front door and to the right. The cops had taken anything that might have evidentiary value. A mattress remained on the floor. It was what you'd expect for three hundred dollars a month, the kind of apartment a student or two to be living in. Two frying pans sat on the stove. But most striking was the linoleum floor, already carved up by Galveston's forensic guys. Of course, the blood from the body he chopped up would seep through that linoleum, $3.99 tarp or not. Even two weeks later, we could see the stains from Morris's blood under the patches of flooring the cops had removed.

Morris's apartment, which Dillman showed us next, was even creepier. According to the forensics experts who processed the place, what was most stunning was that Morris's own fingerprints were not in the apartment. The walls, the cabinets, the doorknobs seemed to have been scrubbed clean. All of his clothes were gone.

Morris wasn't exactly a fashion plate, but still: Why get rid of all of his clothes?

I felt a chill down my spine. In the early days after Kathie "disappeared," there was a great deal of evidence that Robert had been throwing out her clothes and personal belongings. Gilberte found some of Kathie's clothes in the trash cans outside the house in South Salem. A maintenance man at one of the apartments Robert and

Kathie owned in Manhattan complained that Robert had thrown so much stuff in the trash chute, including clothes and medical school books, that it got clogged.

Cody would later discover that Robert paid a woman to clean both apartments, including the walls.

The saddest parts of Morris's apartment were the clues to how he lived. Durst hadn't bothered to clean out the kitchen cabinets while scrubbing down the walls. The man apparently lived on canned peaches, Fig Newtons, and Spaghetti-O's.

Our next stop was at Chalmers, the hardware store where Durst bought the garbage bags, tarp, and saw. We walked there from the apartment. I said to John O'Donnell, "Wow, it's quiet, isn't it?" There was no one around. The evening was clear. The streets were lined with really old trees. "Would you like to live down here?"

John was a hunter, and said, "Not enough deer." I later found out that there were never any deer in Galveston. Bambi refused to travel to places that averaged ninety degrees in the summer.

We walked into Chalmers and Cody showed us the kind of saw Durst purchased. I said, "Oh, my God." If you're not aware, a bow saw is shaped like a bow (I'm not talking a bow on a present), with a curved side and a straight side with sharp, serrated teeth. I don't think I'd ever seen one before. When I heard "saw," I pictured something a lumberjack or a carpenter would use. I don't know from saws. But Durst did. Why would he even know what a bow saw was? It's not like he was a lumberjack or a carpenter. Or a butcher, for that matter. Why pick that particular type, unless he'd had experience using it?

Had he used one on Kathie?

Our tour continued. Next, Cody showed us where Durst got a haircut and had dinner—the same day he'd dismembered the body. I would have loved to find one of Durst's classic agenda lists for that day in green ink: "Kill. Dismember. Haircut. Dinner." What kind of cold-hearted animal could saw off a leg and then go get a haircut? There was never any doubt in my mind. The man was evil. Pure and simple.

It was close to 9:00 p.m. when Cody drove us toward our hotel. On the short ride there, he told us how the arrest went down. It started to become clear to me that this cop knew what he was doing. He went to the eye doctor's office with the receipt he found in the trash, told them he was looking for one Robert Durst, and said that if he came in to pick up his glasses, to please call him. It was a long shot. Why would a man who had just dismembered his neighbor and dumped a torso and limbs in Galveston Bay, having already moved out of his apartment, and surely suspecting that the cops were on his trail, pick up his glasses?

A friend of mine with bad eyesight and thick spectacles loves this part of the story. "I totally get it," he said. "It's not easy to function without a good pair of glasses."

But surely Durst could have gone to a LensCrafters or whatever in a different town for another pair?

The reason: he'd left a deposit on the glasses and Durst was a cheapskate. He was always the guy who forgot to bring his wallet to a restaurant. Who cut Kathie off from his credit cards when she wanted to leave him. Who called collect from Ship Bottom. This was a man who would rather risk arrest than forfeit a fifty-dollar deposit on a pair of specs. Cody was shocked when he got the call from the optometrist's office that Durst showed up for his appointment. Cody drove over and saw Durst when he drove right by him. He called a traffic unit to knock him down on a traffic violation because he noticed the inspection sticker had expired, but continued to follow him until they showed up and pulled him over. Lights and siren on, guns out. Traffic told him to get out of the car and handcuffed him.

In plain view in the rear window of his SUV—the bow saw.

He was then taken before a judge, who ultimately set bail at $300,000—$250,000 for murder and $50,000 for the illegal possession of marijuana.

Cody spent a great deal of time with Durst during the booking process. Mugshots, fingernail scrapings, processing DNA. Cody would later say there was something different, off, about Robert. His conclusion: this was one creepy little bastard.

Robert asked him, "What should I do?"

Cody replied, "I don't know. Do you have $300,000?"

"Well, not on me," he said. Cody could tell by his demeanor and tone that this guy might very well have the money.

Within twenty-four hours, the full amount arrived via wire transfer, and Durst was out on bail. Free as a vulture.

What to make of all those clues he left behind? It seemed as if he *wanted* to get caught.

On the face of it, he did make a lot of mistakes. Not weighing down the bag with Black's body parts. Putting a newspaper with his address in the bags. Throwing out guns in the garbage outside his home. Coming back to Galveston to get his glasses.

To him, they weren't mistakes. They were just pushing the envelope, which he got off on. He'd leave a trail of bread crumbs, but would anyone follow it? Would he get caught, or would he dance away on that edge *again*? He's a guy who likes to fly close to the sun on waxy wings, like Icarus. But Durst, when he fell to Earth, usually bounced. Testing the system was a game to him, one he loved playing. I get the sense that he doesn't have a lot of friends. So he plays games with the police to keep himself amused.

Like, "If I steal this sandwich . . ."

Or "If I use a fake ID . . ."

Or "If I put on a wig . . ."

Or "If I appear on an HBO documentary . . ."

Does his predilection for playing dangerous games make him crazy?

Yes. Crazy like a fucked-up fox (no relation to Fox News).

WE CHECKED INTO OUR hotel and then went to dinner at Gaido's, a popular seafood restaurant overlooking the Gulf of Mexico. We traded stories with our southern brothers in arms. Lots of laughs, good food. It was a good time. I remember the guys in Texas were very interested in 9/11, asking, "How bad was it? What did you see?" I liked all the guys and got along well with them. The vibe was positive. John and I were relieved Durst had finally been caught. Cody did an excellent job of collecting evidence and nabbing him. I wouldn't call that dinner a celebration, but a few beers were lifted.

After dinner at Gaido's, I had a beer at the hotel bar with John and a few others. One nightcap was enough for me. It'd been a long day. I said good night and excused myself and proceeded to the elevator.

All of a sudden, Joe Becerra appeared. I looked up and there he was. It was just the two of us in the elevator. As I would with any guy in a small space, I moved away. It was awkward, and I was uncomfortable, to say the least.

I pushed the button for my floor. The door closed, and he took a giant step closer to me. And another. "You want to get a drink or something?" He looked me up and down.

There was no question in my mind what he wanted.

The thought of it made the hair on the back of my neck stand up.

My skin crawled. I knew his reputation. He had a lot of success smooth-talking the panties off secretaries and lonely Hamptons socialites. For me, his charm was nothing but smarm. And to top it off, this guy was a low-level investigator coming on to the chief law-enforcement officer. The gall was stunning. Here I was, married, with an impeccable reputation. To make a move on me was the height of arrogance and delusion.

Starting in law school and for decades after, there was only one previous time that a man had been inappropriate. It was a judge. I was an ADA. He commented on my legs at sidebar. In response to my rude reply, he banged his gavel and dismissed the case I was prosecuting.

For a while, I was often the only woman in rooms full of men. As I progressed, I was the only woman in rooms full of men with guns. I was never threatened or intimidated by them. There was always a line of respect. It was earned and warranted. For Becerra to cross that line was amazing and insulting. Although I was infuriated and disgusted, as with the incident with the judge, I said nothing about it. I understood what it was like working with men. I knew how they thought, and how they were wired. But I would not and will not step aside from my goals to address petty, pathetic sexual advances. I wasn't interested, I didn't have time for it. I wasn't going to be distracted from why I was there. I just thought to myself, *What an asshole.*

Make believe it never happened, and try never to be alone with him again.

I said, "I don't think so, Joey."

The door opened on my floor, and I walked out of the elevator.

Nowadays, I'd say to Joe, "Keep it in your pants."

So, for those keeping score, in one year, I had shot Joe down both professionally and personally. No wonder he gunned for me in the press.

It was a classic male move to try to deflate my power. If a woman was sexualized at work, then she was no longer an authority figure.

His pathetic attempts to run the case, to control me, to bring me down to a person-to-person level were inappropriate. I'm not better than anyone else, but when I was the DA, and you were working on a case for me, you did not ever cross that line.

The next morning, I didn't even address the elevator incident. As previously planned, we all met up in the lobby to go to breakfast. Becerra was in a suit and tie. I wore a pantsuit and flats. I hardly ever wore pants. But I figured, Texas. Dirt. Horseshit. Cactus. Tumbleweeds. I'd nearly broken my ankle in heels yesterday. The rest of the guys were dressed casually.

"Why are you all dolled up?" I remember asking him.

He said something like, "Why aren't you in a dress? We all like looking at your legs."

I gave him a withering look and said, "Really, Joey?"

After our breakfast, we headed over to the courthouse for the arraignment. Joe was walking ahead of us. I was moving pretty fast, too. I was finally going to see Durst in the flesh. As we came around a corner of the building of the courthouse, cameras and photographers were all over the place. It was a wall of press. I said to myself, "Son of a bitch."

No wonder Joe was all decked out. He knew the press was going to be there (for all I know, he tipped them off). I was supposed to be the media savvy one, and dressing up for a press event hadn't occurred to me.

We went into the courthouse and I met with the DA at the time, Michael Guarino, telling him about my desire to give Kathie Durst's family some peace. I said, "This family needs to know where the body is." I explained that her mom was over eighty years old. "Any deal you cut, any plea, please include us. We'll help you. I'll give you whatever you need on this guy."

Guarino was a well-respected district attorney, recognized as one of the best DAs in Galveston County history. He was attentive, respectful, and agreed to include us if any deal were to be made.

I took a seat in the courtroom, in the front row on a wooden bench, swinging my foot, checking my watch, waiting for Durst to appear for his hearing. I was anxious to finally eyeball him. Fifteen minutes went by. A half hour. An hour.

He never showed.

Durst blew off his arraignment. I was more than surprised that the Texas guys were shocked that a guy would forfeit that much bail. They had no idea.

For Robert Durst, three hundred thousand dollars was lunch money.

We waited for another hour. Durst's court-appointed lawyer in Galveston couldn't get hold of his client. It became clear to everyone present that there would be no hearing.

My flight was scheduled to leave, so John asked Cody if he could take me to the airport. He said, "Sorry, I have to stay and testify."

John asked, "Where are you testifying?"

"In the grand jury."

I said, "*Today?*"

And indeed he did. Before lunch, the Galveston DA indicted Durst for murder. It was that fast. They might drive slowly in Texas, but they indict like lightning. They understood that if Durst were found in another state, Texas would need an indictment to extradite him back.

I said, "Whoa! Texas justice! I'm glad I got down here before the hanging!"

I remember Cody looking at me as if I was a wack job. I would catch that look from him many times over the years. His idea of a proper lady doesn't match up with my New York, no-nonsense, in-your-face personality, but he's gotten used to me. Or maybe I've grown on him.

We talked a little bit before we went our separate ways. I remember saying, "Are you going to catch this guy?"

Looking down at me he said, "Have no fear. We'll get him!"

I had a vision of Cody in a ten-gallon hat, with a gun belt and six-shooters, galloping on a horse, lassoing Durst as the prairie dust made a cloud around him.

I liked the vision, and clung to it all the way back to New York.

| DEBRAH LEE CHARATAN, QUEEN FOR A DAY

In October 2001, I was just back from Texas. John O'Donnell remained in Galveston to work with Cody Cazalas.

A call came in to the Galveston police department from a retired NYPD officer working for an investment bank. He said that one Debrah Lee Charatan had come into the bank to wire a $180,000 bond to Texas. As soon as he spotted the Durst name on the wire, he picked up the phone and called Cody Cazalas. John was in the office with Cody at the time and spoke with the quick-thinking retired NYPD officer. Then he called my chief investigator, Casey Quinn, to identify the person who wired the money.

Casey had Roseanne patch both him and John O'Donnell to my phone.

I was in Manhattan in the backseat of my black Tahoe, shuffling through a stack of files as usual. I answered my phone. John said, "Boss, we found Robert Durst's wife."

My heart stopped. They found the body? I said, "Where?"

He said, "She's living in New York City."

Kathie was alive? I said, "What do you mean?"

He said, "He's got *another* wife—Debrah Lee Charatan. She's the one who bailed him out of Galveston. They got married in December 2000."

My head was reeling. Who in her right mind would marry Robert Durst? Was he legally allowed to marry if he wasn't divorced from Kathie?

We'd learn soon enough that Robert was, in fact, divorced, and had been for quite some time.

In New York, you can get a divorce on abandonment grounds even if one spouse is absent—if you jump through a few hoops. First, you have to make an effort to find the spouse through channels, such as the DMV, the Board of Elections, or just a Google search. If a search came up empty, you would then publish a summons that said, essentially, "Attention, spouse, wherever you are! I'm going to divorce you." The only specifications about where your notice appeared in print? The publication had to be available in the area you believed your spouse was living (or, in Durst's case, not living). If a normal person used this law to get a divorce in an upstanding way, he'd place the summons in the *Daily News*, a well-read paper the spouse might actually read. Robert Durst's notices appeared in the *Westchester Law Journal*. Never heard of it? Exactly. His objective was to adhere to the letter of the law in the sneakiest possible way.

He ran the notice for three consecutive weeks and waited the requisite thirty days for her to respond.

Robert Durst knew that wasn't going to happen. Why? *Because he murdered her.*

Next, Robert took his proof of publication, and an affidavit that said Kathie didn't reply to his summonses, to Westchester Supreme Court Justice Matthew Coppola, who signed the divorce decree in June 1990.

A secret divorce.

Followed by a secret marriage.

What the hell was going on?

I asked Surrogate's Court Judge Rennie Roth, "Is it bigamy?"

She looked into the question and concluded, "It's not bigamy." An uncontested divorce by publication was completely legal. In Durst's case, it was also devious. No one except Robert's lawyers, the judge, and, presumably, Debrah Lee Charatan knew that he'd gotten divorced. Not the Durst family. Not the McCormack family. *No one had a clue* that Robert divorced Kathie in June 1990, or that he'd married Debrah in December 2000.

"I'm already in the city. Where is she?" I asked from the backseat of the Tahoe, my paperwork instantly forgotten.

John gave me the address in Manhattan of Debrah Lee Charatan Realty, Inc., on Madison Avenue.

"I'm going to talk to her *right now*," I said to John on the phone.

John said, "No, no, no. We'll do it."

I responded, "No, I'm doing the interview." Again the push-pull DA-investigator thing. What was John going to do? Tell me I couldn't talk to Debrah? I was the Boss. And I had to meet this woman.

I said, "James, change of plans. Take me to the East Side."

Investigator James O'Donnell was driving. Chief Quinn dispatched investigators Bob Jackman and Pat Sturino to interview her alongside me.

When we arrived at her Madison Avenue office, a pretty receptionist smiled at us.

I said, "Debrah Lee Charatan, please."

"And you are?"

"Jeanine Pirro."

She might not have recognized my face, but the name clicked. Her eyes got big. "One minute," she said, and went through a door into the rear of the office suite. She came back a minute later and said, "I'm sorry. She can't see you. You don't have an appointment." Years later, this same receptionist would corner me at a charity event at Lincoln Center. "Don't you remember me?" she asked, and we had a nice dishy conversation.

But that day, she was not my friend.

"Well, you tell her she can talk to me now or she can come to the grand jury," I said, which was my number-one favorite threat. On cue, James whipped out his badge. It was a law-enforcement bully move—and it never failed.

The receptionist went back in again, and two minutes later, she came out and said, "Follow me."

We were brought to a large, sunny office. The woman behind an impressive desk said, "I'm Debrah Lee Charatan."

"Are you married to Robert Durst?"

In her gravelly smoker's voice, she answered, "Yes."

I have a firm handshake to begin with, but I would have made sure I had one that day. I took one look at her and knew two things. One, she was not a woman you could mess with. And two, she was my kind of broad. She was impeccably dressed in high-end designer clothes. Great jewelry. She was fit and obviously worked out. Here's a woman who spends a lot on clothes and lifestyle. Money is very important to her. She oozed confidence and was, as I'd realize quickly, sharp as a whip.

"Did you try to withdraw $1.8 million from his bank account the day of his arraignment?" While we were cooling our heels in the Galveston courtroom, Debrah was in New York, trying to withdraw a truckload of cash. The accounts were frozen, though. We knew a tall, thin woman had tried to get at his money, but we weren't sure who.

"Yes."

I eyeballed her; she eyeballed me. It was just bizarre to be standing in front of my nemesis's *wife*. If Debrah Lee Charatan and I had happened to meet in the 1980s at a restaurant like Elaine's or Michael's, and were introduced by mutual friends (Al was a real-estate lawyer and was part of that crowd), I could see talking to her over a cocktail and thinking, *This is one smart cookie.* She was attractive, stylish, an unapologetically ambitious woman who'd made a success of herself despite her modest upbringing. We actually had a lot in common.

But we weren't meeting under pleasant circumstances.

She was married to the man I believed murdered two women and one senior citizen. Why do it? Why marry *him*? Robert didn't make a move unless he had a damned good reason, so their secret marriage had to serve a larger purpose. Knowing him, and getting to know her, I concluded that reason could only be one thing: *money*. It sure as hell wasn't *love*.

"When did you marry Robert?" I asked.

"Last year," she replied.

Last year, meaning 2000? Instantly, I thought, *Susan Berman*, who'd been murdered in December 2000. "Do you remember the date?"

"No."

"You don't remember the day you got married?"

She said, "Not really." She didn't even try to sound enamored of her new husband.

She was giving me the runaround while two men with guns stood behind me. This woman had seriously big, clanging balls.

But so did I. "Why don't you get your calendar and we'll take a look?" I asked.

Debrah called in the receptionist/assistant to get her calendar. She came back with the leather-bound book. Debrah flipped through it and said, "We got married on December 11."

Twelve days before Susan Berman was murdered.

I said, "Were any people at the wedding?"

"It was a small ceremony." I'll say it was small. As my team later discovered, Robert and Debrah had the smallest ceremony ever—and super-romantic. She'd opened a phone book and picked a rabbi, one

Robert I. Summers. He arrived at 1500 Broadway, an office building in Times Square, and performed a fifteen-minute ceremony in
a conference room. Robert gave her a $78,000 ring. It might sound
like a lot. But consider that Durst received $3 million a year from his
trust. If you used the one-month-salary rule, Durst should have spent
$250,000 on the ring. The betrothed couple next went to a lawyer's
office, and he signed over his power of attorney to her, giving her control of his vast fortune. Durst would himself describe the union to his
sister, Wendy, as a "marriage of convenience. I had to have Debrah to
write my checks. I was setting myself up to be a fugitive."

I said to her, "You do realize that Robert Durst is a dangerous man."

"He's not dangerous at all. If he came home, I'd open the door." He
was on the lam at the time, having jumped bail in Galveston.

Clearly, Debrah didn't scare easily. I would find out that she grew
up a butcher's daughter in Howard Beach, Queens. Her parents were
among the few Polish Holocaust survivors—her father lost a foot on
a landmine during the war—so you can only imagine how tough *they*
were. Their daughter came with a survivor's instinct preinstalled. It
was in her blood.

"Do you have kids?" I asked.

"A son."

"Would you let Robert in if your son was home?"

"I didn't get custody," she said.

Her first marriage, to attorney Bradley Berger, ended in 1985. The
divorce, and the custody battle for her then five-year-old son, was
brutal. Her husband got full custody. (You just know there's a crazy
story there.) After losing numerous appeals, Debrah didn't visit or
speak to her son for fifteen years. She was also estranged from her
mother and siblings. Her father had died.

"Let's back up for a second. How'd you meet Robert?" I asked her.
"*When* did you meet him?"

"Oh, I've known him for years," she said.

Indeed, they had. As it turned out, they met at the Rainbow Room at a real-estate-industry party in December 1988. I can totally understand why Robert Durst would have zeroed in on her at that event. She was sixteen years his junior, striking and elegant with an unmistakably hard edge. But she was having a rough time. She was buried under lawsuits and legal bills, recently divorced. Her first firm, Bach Realty, Inc., had been an all-female firm founded in 1980. It was, initially, a huge success, with annual billings of $200 million. Her ultimate dream, as she described it to *Harper's Bazaar* in 1984, was to become "the female Harry Helmsley." (Good thing she didn't say "the female Seymour Durst" or it never would have worked with Robert.) Charatan was obsessed with money and fame. In a profile called "Money Dearest" for *Manhattan Inc.* magazine in the mid-eighties, she was quoted as saying, "If I couldn't be a star, I wouldn't be happy."

By the late eighties, her star had fallen. The Labor Department was investigating her on three cases, and at least four lawsuits were filed against her by ex-employees. They used words like "tyrannical," "greedy," "hawk," and "shark" to describe their former boss. Susan Berman's friend Kim Lankford called Debrah a "barracuda."

So many predators in this crowd.

One burned Bach employee, Ronda Rogovin, told *Newsday* at the time, "I was the top saleswoman there for the last three years in a row. [Charatan] fired me the day I was due for a check. That's her usual pattern." Debrah lost most of the suits and had to pay hundreds of thousands in fines and commissions. The firm never recovered and dissolved in 1987.

In 2015, I spoke to some Bach Realty women for my Fox News show. They characterized Debrah as a woman who'd lie, cheat, steal, and do anything for money.

Enter Robert, her savior, in 1988. Somehow, he overcame his chronic cheapness and gallantly paid off her lawyers. He showered her with Durst Organization perks like car-service vouchers. Practically overnight, she went from down-and-out to riding in style and living large. In 1990, two years into their relationship, Charatan moved into Durst's Fifth Avenue apartment.

After altruistic, naïve Kathleen, Robert must have seen Debrah as appealingly ruthless and savvy. His murky past (he was suspected of having killed his wife) and personality quirks—routinely burping, farting, urinating, and smoking pot in public—wouldn't faze her. She could handle him.

For her part, Debrah must have looked at Robert and seen dollar signs.

Their romance didn't last long. She moved out after a year of living together. But their friendship was forever. Robert would turn to Debrah when he needed help with his family. In 1994, Seymour gave the keys to the company to Douglas, not Robert. Debrah was there to hold his hand. When Seymour had a stroke in 1995, Debrah convinced Robert to visit his dying father in the hospital. She couldn't convince him to go to the funeral, though. Robert cut ties with the Dursts. If his brothers or sister needed to get in touch with him, they went through Debrah.

Between 1995 and 2000, Debrah was the only person in New York who had a bead on him. She was, it seemed, the only person in the world he trusted—including Susan Berman.

I said, "You know, his wife is missing. Susan Berman was murdered. And he chopped up a guy in Texas."

She said, "Yeah. I'm not afraid of him at all."

"What'd you do for Christmas?" I asked. Susan was killed on December 23.

She said, "We don't celebrate Christmas."

"What'd you do for Hanukkah?"

"I don't really remember."

I said, "What'd you do for New Year's Eve?"

"I was probably in the Hamptons. He was wherever."

"You don't know where your husband spent New Year's Eve, and you'd only been married for a few weeks?"

She shrugged.

"Where did you go on your honeymoon?"

"We didn't go on a honeymoon," she replied.

"Well, that's weird," I said. "It's not like he didn't have the money to afford it."

"Look," she said. "I'm a businesswoman. I have a business to run. I have a lot of other things going on."

"Okay," I said. She got me there. "So you get married, you don't go on a honeymoon, you don't spend Hanukkah or New Year's together. Are you guys living together? Did you consummate the marriage?"

Before she could answer that gruesome question, a man came into the room. He introduced himself. "Steve Rabinowitz. She's represented by counsel. No more questions." The receptionist must have called in the lawyer. It didn't take him long to get there.

With Rabinowitz there, the flash-your-badge routine wouldn't work.

I tried to schmooze Rabinowitz a little bit. He was a decent guy, a former Manhattan prosecutor. "She's got nothing to hide. Why does she need a lawyer?" I asked. "Just talk to me. I just want to get some dates."

Nothing doing. Rabinowitz started making noises about asking us to leave.

I could tell by Debrah's voice that she was a smoker. I was a smoker then, too. I said, "Where can we have a cigarette?"

Apparently, she was jonesing for one, and she took me out onto the fire escape to light up. The two of us—in our skirts and heels—climbed out the window. I tried to get more out of her. I asked again about their living situation and their intimate relationship, but she danced around the details. From her expressions, though, it was obvious that she wasn't a real wife and theirs wasn't a real marriage. She was a front, a beard.

"Forget about Kathie and Susan," I said. "At the very least, your husband chopped up a man. Police who saw the body believe it wasn't the first time. You're dealing with a very hardened person here. Aren't you afraid of him?"

She blew out smoke. "Absolutely not."

"I don't get it," I said. "Why would you stay with Robert after what he's done?"

"You're a stand-up woman," she said. "You stood by your man."

It was one of those moments in time where you're kind of depersonalized. You come out of yourself and you look down at these two women talking on the fire escape.

She was equating my loyalty to Al, the father of my children, with her loyalty to Robert Durst?

I said, "My husband never laid his hand on me or anybody else." For the record, I stayed with Al because I believe in family. I'm old-fashioned that way. Al was a great father, a great provider, and a decent, wonderful man. There was a difference between an accountant's screwup and dismembering a human.

"Well, I'm not afraid of him and I'll take him back."

I think she was comfortable talking to me and would have gone further. But by the time we finished our cigarettes, her lawyer had gotten paper. "She's done talking," he said.

The conversation had reached an end, unless I could pull a fast one. "She's a material witness in Galveston," I replied. "We get one day with her or we charge her with hindering prosecution and send her to Texas."

"Spousal privilege."

Let me break into the story to explain what spousal privilege is. People think it means you can't be forced to say anything bad about your husband. If he stole the cookies from the cookie jar, you wouldn't be compelled to tell the judge you found him with chocolate on his fingers. No. Spousal immunity has to do with *testimony*. If Debrah actually saw Robert do something, she cannot deny it or rely on privilege to protect herself or him. What is protected: what he *says* to her about what he's done.

That's why it's called "testimonial immunity."

I've said it before, and I'll say it again: Everybody thinks they're a fucking genius because they watch *Law & Order*.

Including Durst. I believe he married her to protect his assets and so she couldn't say what she knew about Kathie, Susan, and Morris Black. The only thing she didn't have to reveal was what he said to her. But they'd been pals for a long time. She must have *seen* something. If Debrah had any insight into what happened with Kathie or Susan based on what she'd seen, she could have been compelled to testify or plead the fifth.

Steve Rabinowitz and I worked out a deal. He wanted "Queen for a Day" immunity. Nothing she said *that day* could be used to prosecute her.

I agreed and went back and forth with my office, getting the paperwork done. It took about thirty minutes and a lot of faxing to get it together. Debrah agreed and signed the agreement. We all sat back down in her office and I said, "Okay, when was the last time you spoke with him?"

Rabinowitz said, "Spousal privilege."

You could have blown me over with a feather.

I said, "Prove it." I wanted to see a marriage license before I took that on faith.

Debrah produced the marriage certificate. It was legitimate. My team would get their hands on the durable power of attorney she and Durst signed that same day, too, also legit.

I said, "Without saying what he told you, when's the last time you spoke to him?"

"A few days ago."

"Where did he call you from?"

"I don't know."

"Give me your phone numbers." We would get the records and find out where he'd placed the call.

We went over the details about the wedding. The rabbi's assistant had been the only witness. No family, no friends. It had all the passion of a business meeting, which was what it was.

I asked, "Do you have normal sex with your husband?" The consummation question. This time, she had to answer.

"We've been together for a long time," she said.

Vague. I repeated the question.

"We never really lived together, but we've been together for thirteen years."

I took a different tack. "Do you have a sister? Any good friends, really good friends? I have a really good friend, Connie Cappelli. She knows everything about me." I hoped to get the name of someone else we could interview, or make her feel as if she could confide in me like a friend.

She said, "My sister and I don't talk."

"Well, isn't there someone in your life who would know where you were? And whether he was with you? Or who might have said to you, 'Why aren't you with your husband at Hanukkah and New Year's?' Or didn't you tell anyone about the marriage?"

She said, "It really wasn't anyone's business."

Debrah Lee Charatan was in our sights, and I would not forget how she'd helped him get out of jail in Texas. I walked out of her office feeling that Debrah was a very hard woman. I hoped for her sake she was as tough as she needed to be to survive in Durst's orbit.

I believed then that Debrah Lee Charatan knew what Robert did to Kathie.

I also believed that she didn't care what had happened to Susan Berman.

In fact, sources would say that the two women didn't get along. I understood why the hippie California writer and the fashionable New York broker weren't the best of friends.

But Susan had been very close to Robert once. Both Kathie and Susan died because Robert's love turned on its head. Debrah Lee Charatan would be wise to remember that.

He married her because he needed someone to watch and control his money if he got arrested for the murder he was already planning to commit in California. Whatever she got in return for protecting him was worth it to her. Susan Berman must have thought the same thing.

If Debrah Lee Charatan were a vault, she'd be Fort Knox. Her secrets, and Robert's, were safe.

For the time being.

| ROBERT DURST, FUGITIVE

Durst or his mouthpieces once described my reopening of the investigation of Kathie's disappearance as a "witch hunt." After Durst jumped bail on October 16, 2001 (as he said in *The Jinx*, "Good-bye, $250,000. Good-bye, jail. I'm out!"), the witch hunt was upgraded to a nationwide manhunt. The dragnet was on.

Durst had been on the run for the better part of a week before I even got down to Texas. If I had known of his arrest before bail was set, I would have warned the DA in Galveston of his enormous resources so he could ask the court to simply remand him.

While all of us were in Galveston, Durst was actually holed up in a Residence Inn in Mobile, Alabama. The day he failed to show up for his arraignment, he rented a blood-red '96 Chevy Corsica, paying in cash and using Morris Black's driver's license on the paperwork.

Over the course of the next five weeks, Durst went on an exhausting road trip.

Tips flowed in from all over. A former neighbor spotted Durst in Northern California. A landlord in New Orleans called police to say that "Diane Winn," the mute woman he'd been renting to, might have been Durst in another wig. Cody went to New Orleans and confirmed that Winn was in fact Durst. Robert cleaned out that apartment—one of his many—well before Cody got to it. He left behind some old utility bills; a VHS of *Vanished*, the ABC show about Kathie's disappearance; Diane Winn's wig (which was partially burned); and the silver medallion and key chain with David Berman's name engraved in them that was bequeathed to him by Susan and given to him by Sareb. He discarded Susan Berman's most treasured possession like garbage. That's how much he cared about his best friend's memory.

I have to give Robert Durst credit for his ability to disappear himself. I underestimated his talent for staying off the radar screen. It would come out eventually that he'd rented apartments in New Orleans; Miami; San Francisco; Dallas; Ridgefield, Connecticut; and Belmont, New York. He lived well in some places, and in squalor in others—even in the same town. He stayed at the luxury San Luis Resort in Galveston when he wasn't at the flophouse on Avenue K.

The guy likes to keep his options open.

He eluded the FBI for forty-five days. But then, in Bethlehem, Pennsylvania, his cheapness got the best of him. Ironically, the day Durst was arrested he was featured on *America's Most Wanted*. The show had flown Cody to Washington, D.C., for a live broadcast and tip line. Durst was arrested while Cody was on the air.

Ro buzzed that Clem and John had some Durst news. Walking in, John said, "You won't believe this."

"What?" I asked.

"Durst got arrested in Pennsylvania for stealing a sandwich."

Before I could make a declarative statement, John said, "I got odds, Boss. What's it going to be today? 'Fuckin A' or 'son of a bitch'?"

He and Clem grinned at me, waiting for me to respond.

"MOTHERFUCKER!" I screamed. "You both lose."

I told Ro to call James and tell him to get ready to take me to Pennsylvania. (And, no, I did not select him as my driver so that I could say "Home, James.")

The next day, the team—investigator O'Donnell, troopers Becerra and Chimento, and forensic investigator Thomas Martin—headed west to Pennsylvania. It took three hours to get there.

Along the way, we got more details by phone about what happened and how the fugitive who eluded an FBI dragnet for six weeks was brought down.

On November 30, 2001, a week after Thanksgiving, Durst went into a Wegmans supermarket in Bethlehem. He looked like any other disheveled old man in a windbreaker and sneakers, but kind of weird, with a shaved head and eyebrows. He took a few Band-Aids out of a box, put some in his pocket, unwrapped one, and stuck it under his nose, Hitler-mustache style. He grabbed a newspaper and selected a chicken salad sandwich on a roll. He concealed the sandwich in the newspaper. Then he shuffled out of the store without paying. Total boosted merchandise: $9.18.

Store security guard Kay Millimaci stopped him in the parking lot. She asked for ID and Robert said he had identification in his glove box and that he would go to his vehicle and get it. Instinct warned her not to go to the car with Durst, and to bring him back to the store to wait for the police. Good call. Later, when the car was searched, a loaded .38 was found in the glove box. Cody is certain that, had Millimaci gone to the car with Robert, he would have tried to shoot his way out of there.

Dean Brenner, the arresting officer, showed up and asked Durst some questions.

Brenner: "Why did you steal the sandwich?"

Durst: "I don't know. I'm an asshole." Finally Durst speaks the truth.

Brenner: "Where are you from?"

Durst: "New York."

Brenner: "Why are you in the Lehigh Valley?"

Durst: "I'm visiting my daughter at Lehigh University."

Of course, Robert did not have a daughter. It was just another of his lies.

Brenner explained that, since Robert was from out of state, he had to be brought down to the station to pay his fine. So he handcuffed him and searched him for weapons, finding $523 in his pocket. Brenner took Durst to the Colonial Regional Police Headquarters. Durst gave Brenner his Social Security number, a different one than he'd given to Millimaci at Wegmans. Brenner phoned in the info to Northampton County dispatch and, in moments, got a call back asking for verification. From the police report by Brenner: "Dispatch then told me that Robert Durst was wanted in Galveston, Texas, for murder. I asked him, 'When was the last time you were in Texas?' The color ran from his face and with a dead stare, he replied only, 'I want a lawyer.' "

Durst didn't show much emotion, except when he got out of his chair and banged his head against the wall. Another smart move on his part.

If I were on the lam, avoiding a murder warrant, and was arrested for stealing a sandwich, I'd probably bang my head against the wall, too.

So why did Durst give his real name and number?

He'd lived in five different states and routinely, comfortably, used dozens of aliases. But he just loved to scatter those bread crumbs.

Pennsylvania police sealed the car and impounded it. Since it was a Texas case there would be no unsealing or execution of the search warrant until Cody and Lieutenant Walter Braun arrived from Texas. They did so on December 5. Both my office and the New York State Police offered to help process the evidence so the Texans wouldn't have to bring cameras and search equipment. I remember the day—there were people all over, Pennsylvania cops, New York cops, Texas cops, the media. The media, however, were kept at bay and not allowed near the garage. Like everything else in this case, the anticipation was building. What might be in that red Corsica that was rented from Rent-A-Wreck in Alabama, using the license of a dead man? Everybody was ready for anything. It was a treasure trove of proof that Robert Durst was a devious, diabolical, dangerous man. Cody took one hundred photographs of evidence.

Here is some of what was found:

• **Guns and ammo.** Two .38 caliber revolvers and a box of bullets were in the glove compartment.

• **Pot.** Robert Durst goes nowhere without his weed, putting peace-loving potheads to shame. He had a baggie with over two ounces and, as always, a few rolled joints.

• **Smokes.** His ever-present Marlboro Lights.

• **Cash.** Along with the $523 in his pocket, Durst had $36,800 in $100 bills—enough to buy five thousand chicken salad sandwiches!—in envelopes in the trunk. The police dog got a hit on the cash, a positive reaction for drugs.

• **A spiral notebook.** He must have sat in that car, making his lists and scribbling his notes with his green pens for hours at a time. Some choice excerpts: "I live to eat. The other things are just to get thru the day." Interesting, since Metamucil packets were found in Galveston, Citrucil in Pennsylvania, and also a note to buy syrup of ipecac (induces vomiting)—either this guy has some weird gastro-intestinal problem or he was worried about his figure. More disturbing was the note written in green ink: "What DD is doing to me, puts me in the same place, as what Kathy did to me." Putting aside the ominous threat to DD (Douglas), Robert misspelled his own wife's nickname! It's Kathie, not Kathy. But, as we know from "Beverley," spelling wasn't Robert's forte. Or maybe he is dyslexic.

• **Green pens.** As always, lots of them.

• **A calendar.** It was a formatted page in the spiral notebook. He'd circled in green ink the dates November 11, 2000 (the day of the press
leak), the 13th (when he called Susan Berman in California about
the coverage), the 15th (when he rented the apartment on Avenue K
as Dorothy Ciner's friend), December 8, 2001 (three days before
the wedding to Debrah; did he have a meeting with lawyers about
power of attorney, perhaps?), the 23rd (the day Susan was murdered),
and July 25 (the day ABC aired *Vanished*). All green-letter days,
for sure.

• **Stolen IDs.** He had Morris Black's driver's license and Medicare
card, and a Fleet Bank Visa under the name Emilio Vignoni.

• **Real IDs.** He had his own driver's license, an American Express
Platinum card, and a Bank of America Visa card with his real name.

• **Photos.** Tons of them from childhood, shots of Kathie, wedding
pictures, and—the best one—an awesome photo of Debrah Lee
Charatan with big eighties hair. It must have been from around the
time they met.

• **Hotel receipts and stationery.** He kept all his receipts . . . for tax
purposes? He kept random notes, many of them just scribbles.

• **Names, addresses, and phone numbers.** Among the names and addresses we found: Peter Schwartz (the photographer Robert assaulted
in the eighties) in Stratford, directions to "exit 105 Garden State
Parkway," phone numbers for "Arthur," "Mich." Were they dealers?
Pimps? We had no idea.

• **Flight information.** An old trip, in April 2001, between Susan's and
Morris's murders. I guess he wasn't really on the run.

• **Pages from a self-help book.** It's a book called *You Mean I'm Not Lazy, Stupid or Crazy?! A Self-Help Book for Adults with Attention Deficit Disorder*, by Kate Kelly and Peggy Ramundo, originally published in 1995. He'd circled passages of the book, including the lines, "The grown-up ADDer often has trouble working steadily on the job," "The adult with ADD . . . is so distractible that she isn't *with her feelings* long enough to deal with her emotions. Unable to process emotions very well and blaming the world for problems, she might experience explosive outbursts or depressive episodes," and "arguments with spouses and coworkers and yelling matches with children can become a way of life for some ADDers. The short fuse that causes temper tantrums in childhood can now create problems of intensified negative interpersonal relationships." The paragraph about adult ADDers and impulsive spending and financial hardship? He scratched that one out. He was circling what might apply to him and crossing out what obviously didn't.

• **The most disturbing piece of evidence we found:** A note written on a notepad from the Hilton Garden Inn in Danbury, Connecticut, in green ink, of course, with the address of the Center for Women and Families on Fairfield Avenue—Gilberte Najamy's workplace— and her personal cell phone number. Cody believes he was waiting for his chance to kill her. "There's no doubt in my mind he was going to try to kill her," he told me recently. "I guess he never got a good chance to shoot at her. But he stayed at that hotel for a week waiting for the opportunity."

He wrote a "like" list in the spiral notebook with names and contact info for people he did not want to kill, including Emilio Vignoni, his sister Wendy Durst Kreeger, Teresa Joan Something-stein (his script was almost illegible), Greg Press (some PR person?), Diane Leonard, Delly, Lu. We knew some of the players, but most would have to be tracked down. Fortunately, he'd supplied their phone numbers.

I found out years later that he'd also penned a "hate" list. It had three names on it.

1. Jeanine Pirro
2. Douglas Durst
3. Gilberte Najamy

What we did *not* find:

- Morris Black's head.
- A map to Kathleen Durst's remains.
- A signed confession.

When we pieced together his travelogue, it was clear that he'd visited old haunts. The guy couldn't resist returning to the scene of the crime(s).

He went to the Jersey Shore—to Atlantic City, only a few miles from Ship Bottom and the Pine Barrens, where Kathie's remains are most likely located.

He spent a week in Danbury, Connecticut, where Kathie spent part of her last night alive and where Gilberte currently worked.

He'd paid a visit to his brother Douglas's Katonah home, even drove up the driveway in his Chevy and looked in the window. He left without firing a shot.

It stands to reason that he swung by my home in nearby Harrison, too. Cops from my town were doing regular drive-bys. Al hired investigators to trail the kids to and from school and to patrol our property at night. He was always more worried about me than I was about myself. At the office, I was surrounded by law enforcement at all times. I'd faced death threats as an everyday part of the job for decades. A prisoner I'd put away mailed me a drawing of my face covered in blood. (I still have that one.) A man who had threatened to throw his chair at me as I was cross-examining him was threatened with removal by the court. That was unnecessary since I got him removed to state prison for twenty-five years. My window had been shot at years earlier when I was prosecuting a Rastafarian for shooting and killing his wife and then placing her in an oven while their children slept in the next room. I wasn't shaking in my Louboutins about Robert Durst on the lam. I was armed to the teeth. I had gates, a security system, cameras, and guns all over the house. If Durst had driven up my driveway in his Chevy, I would have grabbed my Mossberg pump-action twelve-gauge shotgun and blown his head off.

His last stop in this trip down memory lane was in Bethlehem, Pennsylvania, where he attended college at Lehigh University back in the sixties. And that was where he got a strong craving for a chicken salad sandwich.

How could a smart man be so stupid, stealing that sandwich?

Simple: Robert the millionaire was a cheapskate.

In a taped phone conversation with Debrah Lee Charatan while Durst cooled his heels in the Pennsylvania prison, he told her he stole the sandwich because he was trying to stay within his two-hundred-dollar-per-day budget. "I was renting cars at face value and I was living for two months," he told her. "That's why I got into shoplifting, trying to stretch my money. If I just hadn't done any of that shit . . . That's why I'm in jail, because I started counting my money."

I've often wondered, besides driving and thinking about his "likes" and "hates," what was he doing during those weeks on the run? He'd originally fled with, as he told Debrah on the prison tapes, "five envelopes each with $9,500 in it," or a total of $47,500. In less than two months on the lam, Robert spent $10,000. He was staying at inexpensive hotels. The Chevy rental was paid for with $2,500 in cash. So what did he drop thousands of dollars on? Gas. Food. Ipecac. And we don't know what else he stole. We know he bought a razor to shave his head and eyebrows. I wonder, was he alone all that time? Could he have been pushing the envelope as usual, and burning through his money on hookers who could potentially ID him? Did he get off on that?

While he was in prison in Pennsylvania, Durst's phone conversations were recorded. He often spoke to Debrah about Douglas. In one such call, she said, "[Douglas] screwed you out of everything, your birthright, the entire Durst Organization . . . He took it from you. He could have done it with you. But no, he took it from you." She fanned the flames of Robert's hatred, for sure.

Debrah Lee Charatan is a dangerous woman. No wonder she wasn't afraid of Robert. You wouldn't want to tackle her in the pots and pans section of aisle five in Walmart.

In another of his taped conversations, she referred to Robert's heavily armed visit to Douglas's home in Katonah, and then said, "Douglas knew you were planning suicide." As if he drove to his brother's house with guns to shoot *himself* out of spite?

I don't believe Robert intended to kill himself for a second. But—he *would* rather die than let his family get his money. So he married this woman to keep his cash out of his hated brother Douglas's hands and to spin his criminal actions into a pathetic cry for help.

Robert replied, "I screwed up."

There has been a lot of speculation about what she meant by the suicide comment. I believe Debrah was sending a coded warning to Robert that Douglas knew Robert was gunning for him. Robert's "I screwed up" was an expression of regret, because now he knew he'd never get as close to his sibling again.

In fact, Douglas hired bodyguards after that incident.

I was criticized for going to Texas. Why should my trip to Pennsylvania be any different? Reporters and pundits asked, "What's she even doing there? This has nothing to do with her cold case."

It was climb-the-walls infuriating that people didn't understand that it was all connected. What Durst did in Los Angeles, Galveston, and Bethlehem were related to what he'd done in Westchester in 1982. One day, I'd prove it. But, in the meantime, I had to see the evidence for myself, and go through it piece by piece. I needed to be there to offer insight and share information with law enforcement in other states.

They didn't know Robert Durst like I did. But they were learning.

We banded together on this case. Texas, California, New York, and Pennsylvania were working together. Texas was tracking evidence. We were watching the money. Pennsylvania was recording prison phone calls. Los Angeles was interviewing witnesses. We all wanted this guy. No one more than me.

I take that back. Cody wanted him as much as I did. He tracked down every lead, tirelessly, without complaint. He probably logged as many miles as Durst did during those six weeks of cross-country investigating. I came to think of Cody as the moral core of the whole investigation. He pushed and pushed and never lost faith or hope. Cody and I banged the Durst drum the loudest, and the longest.

I always knew that, eventually, we would find out what happened to Kathie.

• • •

I started thinking about Durst's defense. How was he going to try to get away from a murder he admitted committing? The pop psychology book pages in the Chevy hinted at an insanity defense. During his time on the lam, he was probably turning it over in his mind, wondering, *How can I prove I'm crazy?*

The family photos—which he hadn't been in possession of when arrested in Galveston, Texas—hinted at a sympathy ploy, like, "Look how much I love my family and friends! I carry around their pictures!" So what? That had nothing to do with his fleeing from Galveston, evading arrest for weeks, plus all the evidence of his longer-term plans to go off the grid.

He married Debrah to protect his money before he killed Susan.

He rented or bought all those apartments, including the Galveston one, before the L.A. murder as well.

To me, all the signs pointed to premeditation. He'd been plotting for months how he'd get away with Berman's murder before he committed it. And then, after he murdered Black, he continued to plot and scheme to get away with that one, too.

He'd need a miracle to pull it off. He dismembered a body and jumped bail. It looked bad, no matter how many self-help books he studied.

With Debrah's help, Durst hired a triumvirate of Texas swagger, some local big guns, to represent him. Collectively, their fees were $1.8 million—a mere pittance for the price of freedom.

Dick DeGuerin, a criminal defense attorney from Houston, had defended David Koresh, the cult leader in Waco, and would go on to defend Tom DeLay for money laundering. He was a good old boy with a Texas accent and a ten-gallon ego.

Michael Ramsey from Dallas had just unsuccessfully defended

Kenneth Lay of the Enron Corporation. He tended to take on the corporate clients accused of fraud and conspiracy to the detriment of the little guy. He had a reputation for loving a fight.

Chip Lewis, also from Houston, was a trial lawyer and former prosecutor. He was younger than the other two, but I didn't make any assumptions about his competence.

Michael Kennedy was out. Debrah hated him. As she ranted on the prison tapes, he didn't have Robert's interests at heart—only those of the Durst Organization. Ultimately, he was kept on, but as an impotent spectator, not an active defender.

A good wife, Debrah went to Northampton County Prison in Pennsylvania to meet with Robert and his freshly hired Texas legal eagles to talk strategy on the Morris Black murder.

A few days later, at the request of Durst's defense, the judge who'd been assigned the case in Galveston, one Susan Criss, issued a gag order on me and the DA in Pennsylvania. We were banned from speaking to the press about our cases.

Outrageous! Since when can a judge silence out-of-state DAs who are doing their jobs? Who was this judge?

But the ADAs in my office suggested that we lie low and let the Texas prosecutors do their jobs, after which Durst would be locked up for ninety-nine years if not immediately dragged to the closest hangin' tree. So I lay low.

I didn't like it, though. This judge had *no* legal authority to gag me or anyone else. At the very least, there was no notice or a hearing or evidence that what I, or anyone, might say on the record was relevant material to an upcoming murder trial in Texas. This judge was shooting from the hip and she did it at the behest of the defense. There was no basis for the gag order. For a judge in Texas to think that she can just deprive somebody of her First Amendment right of free speech is ridiculous. The woman wasn't in Texas. She was in Lalaland.

I couldn't talk, but I could certainly write. I sent Susan Criss a letter.

December 7, 2001

Dear Judge Criss:

I was just advised that Your Honor issued an order prohibiting me, as well as every member of my office, from making any public statements regarding Robert Durst in the disappearance of his wife twenty years ago.

Quite frankly, this order mystifies me. Neither my office nor I was served with any motion papers requesting this relief. I am neither a party nor a participant in the criminal matter before you. And I know of no authority that grants to a Texas state court the power to control the free expression of an individual in another state, particularly one seeking public cooperation in a "cold case."

Moreover, while I have made public statements regarding our New York investigation, long before it is even alleged that Robert Durst beheaded and dismembered a senior citizen in your county, I have said virtually nothing about the substance of the Texas case. Even were I within your jurisdiction, which I am not, the defendant could not make any showing of statements on my part regarding the Texas case sufficient to warrant such a dramatic restriction of my right of expression.

I am investigating the disappearance of a young medical student who was gravely concerned about her own safety prior to her disappearance. In addition to using ordinary police methods, it is essential that I am able to appeal to members of the public who might possess information regarding the fate of Kathleen Durst. Given the passage of time, these individuals may be living far away from Westchester County. Your Honor's order not only is unauthorized and unjustified; it also has

*attempted to foreclose a significant investigatory option that should
remain open to me, particularly in view of the age of New York's case.*

*It is my sincere hope that Your Honor will reconsider the wisdom of
this order in light of the above.*

> *Very yours truly,*
> *Jeanine Pirro*

I cc'd Michael Guarino and John Morganelli, the DAs in Galveston County and Northampton County, respectively, as well as Dick DeGuerin, who wasn't gagged himself. He held numerous press conferences before the trial.

The stern letter didn't work. Judge Criss refused to lift the ban.

Durst hadn't even been extradited back to Texas for this trial, and as opposed to focusing on her case in her own county, this judge was concerned with my case, an investigation seventeen hundred miles away and long before Durst killed Morris Black.

So why did she do it?

She did it because Dick DeGuerin asked her to.

From the beginning, I suspected that he would get whatever he wanted.

I'd never heard of the guy before he started calling me a grandstander. What was going on in the Lone Star State? I know they think they've got a separate republic in Texas, but they still have the Constitution down there, don't they? But apparently, DeGuerin was well known in Texas. Was Criss trying to ingratiate herself to people with deep pockets to secure her next election? (In the years after the trial, DeGuerin and Chip Lewis would both give money to Susan Criss's reelection campaigns.)

I acceded to the request so as not to create a side issue. In contrast, District Attorney John Morganelli, also gagged, trumpeted in the Galveston papers, "I'm not following the order. . . . A judge in Texas can't make an order that has any power to apply to anyone outside of Texas. If members of the media want to call me and ask me, I'm going to feel free to talk to them." So that DA wouldn't follow the gag order and he wasn't "slammed," but yours truly continued to be: PIRRO SLAMMED BY DURST LAWYER, reported the *New York Daily News* at the time.

DeGuerin made another pretrial motion requesting that the judge order that I come to Texas to reveal under oath my evidence about Kathie's disappearance. DeGuerin argued it was time for me to "put up or shut up"—or both!—about Kathie's case, claiming that I was hounding Durst. "The evidence in this case is going to be complex enough without Ms. Pirro running for governor," he told the *Daily News*.

Wait a minute. This guy is calling New York newspapers, badmouthing me, and I'm not allowed to talk about my own case. Smart.

In response, Rich Weill, the chief assistant in my office, filed an affidavit that read, "It is obvious that counsel DeGuerin's agenda is to switch the focus from the evidence against his client in the brutal murder, beheading, and dismemberment of a senior citizen to the bizarre claim that the district attorney 'made him do it.' "

Then Galveston District Attorney Kurt Sistrunk argued on my behalf. Judge Criss rightly denied DeGuerin's motion, but spewed that I had come close to violating her gag order: "I don't want her investigation to interfere with Mr. Durst's right to have a fair trial."

Really? Since when is the district attorney, who is obligated to investigate and prosecute crime within her jurisdiction, required to cease and desist using the name of a suspect by a judge seventeen hundred miles away so that the defendant can get a fair trial in that judge's courtroom?

Hey, Judge. Stay in your own lane and worry about yourself.

As if there wasn't enough insanity in the air, barring the prison tapes of Debrah and Robert hashing out his defense and how he should act, how he should look, and whether his defense would interfere with her cash flow was, out-and-out, crazy. DeGuerin knew the tapes incriminated Durst. He successfully blocked the jury from hearing them.

But that wasn't enough for him. He had to lasso me into the fray. Since the tapes were leaked, DeGuerin tried to connect me to the leak. Again, he wanted me ordered to Texas to explain how the press got hold of those tapes. He told the *Daily News,* "I'll bet $1,000 right now where it came from."

I remember hitting the ceiling. I never possessed those tapes! I read about them in the *New York Post* like everyone else did. But if I did have them, you can bet DeGuerin's thousand dollars that I would have fought tooth and nail to get them admitted into evidence. The tapes were that important. You can never have too much evidence, even in Texas. Although the Texas prosecutors tried, Judge Criss denied that request and hid from the jury the creation of the narrative that clearly incriminated Durst.

David Hebert gave the classic reply to the press about DeGuerin's bet. "A fool and his money are soon parted," he said.

The Texas big hat was casting roles, with yours truly as the Devil. Of course, every story needs an antagonist. So let's try some role reversal. Take a woman in law enforcement who spent her career fighting for the underdog, crusading for the silent victims of crime, and make her the villain. And the guy who chopped up a human body better than my butcher Tommy at A&P? Let's make him the victim.

The fact that I was doing the job I was elected to do, that prosecutors all over the country were doing—dusting off and trying to solve cold cases with the advancements in forensics and DNA—was of little note. He would have been happier if the little woman quietly sat behind her desk and waited for murderers to just turn themselves in. Instead, according to DeGuerin, I was on a witch hunt, and was thus cast as the Wicked Witch. He was good.

The truth? *He* was the media hog. I was not.

On January 25, two months after his Wegmans arrest, Durst went to court in Northampton County to be officially released on gun and pot charges so that he could be sent to Texas to face murder charges. I met with John Morganelli, the Northampton County DA. Morganelli was a no-bullshit kind of guy. We bonded over our fury at the so-called gag order. He told me and a group of reporters that he was glad to get Durst out of his state. The Galveston County sheriff's office was represented to escort Durst back to the Lone Star State. Cody was there and prepared to testify in the event Durst fought extradition to Texas.

Before the hearing, John O'Donnell and I waited in the hallway of the courthouse for Durst to be brought in.

I was finally going to get to eyeball the bastard.

Tons of people were lined up against the walls—police, reporters, ADAs. They started murmuring at the far end of the hallway and I knew Durst was on the move. He was surrounded by police. Durst was very short and the cops around him were very tall. Even in my heels, I was no giant. I stood on my tiptoes.

He got closer to me, and I craned my neck to catch a glimpse.

He was a small, beady-eyed nothing. The chains were standard operating procedure, but it seemed like overkill given his escorts and his size.

I said to myself, *What a wimp!* This little man, this schlep in glasses with a shuffling gait, killed his wife, killed his friend, dismembered his neighbor, evaded law enforcement for weeks? How could this elf be a monster? I couldn't believe he could lift a bow saw, let alone use one to hack up a body.

I thought, *If it came to it, I could probably take him.*

He was totally focused on just looking forward. No eye contact—and I was so ready to give him a big smile to unsettle him. I later learned that he'd been coached by Debrah to show nothing, to put on a poker face. I don't think it was a challenge for him. I got the feeling he was bored by the whole situation. Boredom was the mask of entitlement and arrogance.

He thought he would get away with anything, because so far, he had.

In the courtroom, I sat right behind Durst. Once I'd recovered from the initial shock of just how tiny he was, I could get a better read on him.

He was fidgety, twitchy. His hair had partially grown back, but it was patchy and sparse. He looked around with flat, dead eyes, and I remember thinking, "How does he even pass for human?"

Gilberte was in the back row. She hadn't been in the same room with him since before Kathie disappeared, and had been dying to ask him one question for the last twenty years. When the hearing was over, she got her chance. I watched as he walked down the aisle right by Gilberte.

She yelled, "Tell me what you did to Kathie."

He paused and stared at her. His beady eyes showed nothing, no feeling, no remorse, not even recognition. And then he moved along.

I thought, *He's the Devil walking.* Not because he was radiating malevolence, but because any one of us could walk by this little old man on the street and have no idea of the violence he was capable of.

Undercover evil. Anonymous evil. Evil you thought of as a friend that crept up on you from behind and shot you in the head. Evil that got a haircut after dismembering a human being with a saw. Evil that wouldn't let a family put their beloved daughter to rest in peace.

I felt a chill as he turned away from Gilberte. I can still feel it.

AFTER MORRIS BLACK'S MURDER, the LAPD was suddenly looking at Durst for Susan Berman.

Took them long enough!

They'd been barking up the wrong tree on their case for nearly a year and hadn't come close to indicting anyone. Now they were calling me for help. Texas was calling. I was so determined to solve all of our cases that I put together a task force of detectives from New York, Texas, and California.

My office, state police, Paul Coulter from Los Angeles, and Texas investigators met in White Plains and brainstormed, looking for similarities, looking for common denominators. In the past year, Coulter had been digging a bit into Durst, running credit card and phone records, tracking Durst's movements.

Eddie Murphy gets credit for putting Robert Durst in California in December 2000. He discovered that Durst took a United flight from New York, stopping in San Francisco, and ending in Eureka, California, on December 14, ten days before Susan's murder. Five days later, on December 19, Durst got his Ford Explorer out of long-term airport parking. Murphy next tracked him to a flight from San Francisco to New York at 10:00 p.m. on December 23, twelve or so hours after the murder. There was no evidence Durst had been in Los Angeles on December 23, unfortunately. But it was possible. He had enough time.

Our investigation took many turns. One was a trip to Homer, Louisiana. In the summer of 2002, we received a letter from an inmate who said that Robert Durst told him where Kathie was buried. I immediately sent John to interview this inmate. John flew to Dallas, then to Shreveport, then to Homer, Louisiana. In the meantime, I called the district attorney, James Bullers, and told him that the inmate said he met Durst when Durst was on the run after killing Morris Black and that he was willing to say where Kathie was buried in exchange for being removed from the Louisiana prison system and brought to New York.

The DA said, "Are you kidding? This guy stole my motor home! He ain't going anywhere!" As serious as the case was, there were times when we all got a chuckle or two. This was one of them.

After I suppressed a laugh, it was clear to me that that motor home was very important to Bullers. But, in the end, it mattered not, since there was very little information that could be corroborated.

John O'Donnell came back and said, "Boss, he talks a good game but he's full of shit."

To which I responded, "I hope the crawfish was at least good. And what makes this idiot think the New York prisons are better than Louisiana?"

We spent a lot of time on the cadaver note. For months, Los Angeles had been trying to get a match on the cadaver letter with samples from Nyle Brenner, Susan Berman's manager, but they couldn't make it happen. Of course not! Brenner didn't write it. But I knew who did.

When John told me about the note—I hadn't been in the meeting that day—I had one question about it. "Was the note written in green ink?"

John said, "Yes, Boss."

"Of course it was."

We were hanging on to hope about the cadaver letter because, as Robert Durst would say in *The Jinx*, "Only the killer could have written it." Now all we had to do was get a handwriting match, and it would be enough evidence to indict him.

God knows, we tried.

Handwriting analysis is as much an art as a science. It isn't exact, like DNA (although don't tell the O.J. jury that). The LAPD handwriting expert opined that, based on the Robert Durst exemplars—he'd been forced to produce handwriting samples while awaiting trial in Galveston—it was not a definite match. It was "highly probable" that it was his writing, but the evidence was inconclusive.

Could Robert Durst have disguised his handwriting? Of course. He knew what the issue was and what the damning evidence was. He knew exactly what he shouldn't write like. He put on wigs. He would put on a style of printing, too. By doing so, he created an almost insurmountable hurdle for the prosecution in the Susan Berman case. We didn't have the evidence to prove beyond a reasonable doubt that this guy wrote the note, or killed the woman, to a unanimous jury of twelve.

The inconclusive handwriting analysis was a get-out-of-jail-free card for Durst.

When Paul Coulter was in New York, I kept saying, "Paul, there's more. You know there's more."

He didn't believe there was. "Not according to the handwriting experts."

I said, "Who the fuck are your handwriting experts?" Not that I had any reason to question them, but I was convinced Durst wrote the note. Why couldn't there be a match?

The *Jinx* team came up against the same problem we did. Unlike the tristate task force, Jarecki and Smerling had a far wider collection of samples—including the rental application where Durst described his job as "chief botanist" in block letters.

Where did they get all of their samples?

I have no idea where they got them, or countless other documents, recordings, videos, and photos. Jarecki and Smerling were able to amass documents we in law enforcement couldn't get.

It helped that Durst was on board for the first few years of the project. He gave the producers a lot of material to work with. Every photo and document he turned over to them was a risk. He must have known that. But taking crazy risks, dancing on the edge of discovery, was his comfort zone.

I have a pet theory about the misspelling of "Beverly." Robert and Susan met while they were students at UCLA. Later, Susan went to Berkeley College for a masters in journalism. Robert likely wrote letters to Susan while she was at Berkeley.

Berkeley.

Beverley.

You can almost see how he'd get used to writing "Berkeley," associated that word with Susan, and then misspelled "Beverley" when he wrote to her at her new address. For all we know, he misspelled it on purpose, like an "in" joke with her, and then forgot or didn't think to correct the spelling when he wrote the cadaver note.

That note would prove to be the first time Durst pushed the envelope—quite literally—too far.

But it took fifteen years for anyone to prove it.

| JEANINE PY-RO, THE DA, MADE ME DO IT

The Durst defense playbook:

A trial is a simple retelling of a story.

The courtroom is the theater.

The voir dire is when you get your ticket.

The opening statement is when the curtain goes up.

And, of course, like any script, it is worthless without an actor who is believable, portraying the image, exhibiting the emotion, and connecting with the jury.

The pretrial motions are the rehearsals where the evidence gets tested and the lawyers find out what they have to work with.

On March 28, 2002, Dick DeGuerin changed Durst's plea from "not guilty" to "not guilty by reason of self-defense or accident."

Really? I thought to myself. *Interesting. This guy DeGuerin knows the other guy is dead and can't speak for himself, so self-defense is probably a smart move.* But it told me that Durst would have to take the stand to make the self-defense or accident argument. How could this guy take the stand when there was so much out there that implicated him in so many questionable situations? A defendant doesn't have to be convicted of something for a prosecutor to cross-examine him about it, but, with all the skeletons in this guy's closet, he'd have to be an amazing actor to get the jury to believe him, not the truth. And I wasn't sure that Durst could be rehearsed so well that he would be prepared for the inevitable tough cross-examination regarding his past.

Little did I know that DeGuerin and company were the best directors, producers, and puppeteers that money could buy.

I was also fascinated by the choice not to go the insanity route. Personally, I don't think the insanity defense has *any* place in a criminal courtroom. The whole concept is crazy. Either the criminal did it or he didn't do it. Save that psychological mumbo jumbo for sentencing. Having prosecuted more than my share of insanity defense murder cases, I know that juries rarely buy it. In more than 80 percent of cases, the strategy fails.

But, then again, this case was so bizarre that it lent itself to that defense.

Durst had seen a shrink after his mother jumped off the roof of their family home when he was seven years old. He had tried primal scream therapy back in the 1980s. He had taken enough psychology classes to believe that he could self-diagnose. The pages from the ADD book found in the trunk of Durst's car in Pennsylvania and his highlighting of diagnoses—in green ink, of course—that he felt applied to him indicated that he intended to use some psychiatric defense.

In fact, the ADD book may have been his first attempt to see if he fit into "crazy." What better case to use an insanity defense than in one where the defendant chops up some guy like a side of beef?

That was nixed. Debrah Lee Charatan Durst and DeGuerin got the idea to go with self-defense instead. Debrah Lee was one smart cookie, even smarter than Robert and his lawyers. She understood that insanity, even if it got Robert off, would be the end of her Chanel suits and mansion in the Hamptons. If Robert were found incompetent, as she told him in the Pennsylvania prison tapes that were leaked to Andrea Peyser of the *New York Post*, then their marriage and his signing over power of attorney to her would be invalidated. That was why she threatened to divorce Robert if he retained Michael Kennedy as his lawyer, since Kennedy would've gone the insanity route, which would have boomeranged the Durst trust back to his family. "I'm not going to stay here and watch this. I can't handle it. I won't stand by you if you stick with Kennedy," she raged on the prison tapes.

As she shrewdly reasoned, "Michael Kennedy's allegiance is to Douglas. First, he was going to say you're incompetent. Then he was going to say you're insane. That would mean your decisions, like giving me power of attorney . . . it's not good. What he doesn't want is for me to get any of the trust money. Since I'm not your wife, since you were incompetent at the time, means that they are the only ones who can make your decisions. So they will take all your money and they will become the guardians of it."

Lady Macbeth had nothing on Debrah Lee Charatan Durst.

Durst did as his wife commanded and hired the Texas good old boys. It was the smart move for anyone who had seen Michael Kennedy so unconvincingly ask Robert to come home on television when he was on the run because his family missed him. "Robert, if you see this or hear this, please come home. You have loved ones who care about you here in New York. Your family is solidly, unifiedly behind you. The trust has the wherewithal to pay for your legal defense."

Yeah, right. Robert had embarrassed and humiliated his family. He was skipped over to run the empire precisely *because* they despised him, a move that, per the *New York Times*' Charles Bagli, was one of biblical proportions. Dangling that carrot and leading with their wealth was the way the Dursts worked.

So, how would Durst's self-defense strategy unfold? As I would later come to understand, it began, bafflingly, with the gag order that sought to prevent me from "running her mouth," as DeGuerin put it. He threw a dozen pretrial motions at Susan Criss, the judge, both to shut me up and to bring me to Texas to testify. Either he couldn't make up his mind as to which way to go or he was employing a rather common strategy: throw everything at the wall, aka Judge Criss, and see what sticks.

Before the trial began, DeGuerin, Ramsey, and Lewis actually tested their scripts on shadow juries and mock trials. They used jury selection experts, the courtroom equivalent of casting agents.

There are trial attorneys who swear that cases are won or lost on jury selection. With the right jury composed of citizens who particularly connect to your theory of the case, you win. With jurors who, for whatever reason, do not relate to your themes, you don't. I am not sure I subscribe to this theory, but the Durst defense definitely got their money's worth from their jury selection consultants.

No doubt the consultants came up with a profile of a good Durst juror—someone who is impressed by wealth, someone who relates to an idiosyncratic personality. And what about someone who might be receptive and predisposed to the "DA made me do it" argument, someone who is disinclined to respect a woman in power doing her job?

It is in this realm that prosecutors who work for the government are at a disadvantage. We don't have the money to hire jury consultants. Defense attorneys can pretty much do whatever they want. And, with Durst's money, the prosecution was clearly outgunned.

The truth of this is reflected in a CNN interview after *The Jinx* aired. Twelve years after the verdict, juror Deborah Warren commented on how "brilliant" the defense was, "fighting for him, when the DA only had two people sitting over there fighting for this case," intimating that, if it were such an important case and they were convinced of Durst's guilt, they'd have more than two people sitting there. For the record, juror extraordinaire, Robert Durst is rich and famous, able to pay the likes of DeGuerin, Ramsey, and Lewis, along with a whole entourage, to show up in court every day. As prosecutors, we don't have that luxury because we work for you and are paid for by you, not by Robert Durst.

I didn't go to Galveston for the trial. What for? Far be it from me to accommodate the Texas big hat. But the media inquiries were constant. David Hebert and Anne Marie Corbalis in public affairs were called for my response every time DeGuerin took a shot at me. Suffice it to say, what came out of my mouth was never relayed to the media.

Opening arguments started on September 22, 2003, almost two years to the day after Morris Black was shot in the head and his body chopped up into pieces and thrown into the bay in your big black plastic everyday garbage bags. I have always believed that opening statements are critical. Although they are not evidence, they set the tone, send a message, and give that jury, fresh and anxious to hear what the case is about, a road map to their conclusion.

Trial attorneys know this, no one more so than DeGuerin and company. When they opened, the die was cast. Their case depended on the jury believing that Morris Black was a violent, terroristic man who posed a dangerous threat to poor Bobby, that I was the Wicked Witch on a hunt to destroy an innocent man for my own gain, and that poor Bobby was a harmless lamb about to be slaughtered by me.

That afternoon, Ro buzzed that David and Anne Marie needed to see me.

"Judge, you're not going to believe this one," said David, walking in. "The defense's opening statement was all about *you*."

"What? How?" What on earth did I have to do with Morris Black?

I got my hands on a transcript of DeGuerin's opening.

It started with classic blame-the-victim stuff. Morris Black as a "violent, dangerous, threatening, unpredictable old man" who "frightened children" and "carried a stick."

Then he characterized Robert as the guy who got the short end of the stick, the scion of a wealthy New York real-estate family "worth billions—that's with a 'B'—of dollars" that gave his crown to his duplicitous younger brother, and the victim of an investigation after his wife fell off the face of the earth. "The investigation went nowhere, although there was a lot of press about it," DeGuerin said.

Not true, I thought. *An astonishing lack of press in 1982 was more like it.*

And then, the truly, mind-bendingly surreal part. And I quote:

Twenty years later, almost twenty years later, an ambitious, politically ambitious lady, district attorney from Westchester County, announced to the public that she was reopening the disappearance of Kathie Durst and that Bob Durst was the person they were centering on. The media went into a frenzy.

The New York tabloids carried front-page articles. These are the same kind of newspapers that report when Elvis is sighted. That report when some movie star has a baby by space aliens. That's the kind of news they report. That's the kind of sensationalism. But what it did to Bob Durst was it caused him to want to get away and not be Bob Durst, to hide from that horrible investigation based on no evidence whatsoever. And a lawyer hired by the Durst Organization told Bob Durst that Janine [sic] Pirro, the politically ambitious DA who you may have seen on one of the talk shows—we call them "scream shows" where everyone screams at each other and everyone takes positions. She is on Larry King Live *probably tonight.*

The lawyer hired by the Durst Organization told Bob, "With no evidence whatsoever, Bob, she can have you indicted and thrown in jail with a million-dollar bond placed on you." And it so scared him that he left New York and he came to Galveston, and he disguised himself as a woman. And he took the name Dorothy Ciner, the girl that he had gone to the high school with. And he bought a wig and signed the lease. And that's all true. And he began living in Galveston across the hall from Morris Black, out of the frying pan and into the fire.

Bob liked Galveston. His life began to return to normal from having paparazzi follow him around in New York and taking his picture every time you walked out of his apartment building, with banner headlines screaming that he was guilty of Kathie Durst's disappearance.

Let's deconstruct this opening statement bit by bit.

"Politically ambitious LADY"? He might as well have said "Dragon LADY." It's sexist bait. Pure woman hate.

"Announced to the public that she was reopening the disappearance of Kathie Durst and that Bob Durst was the person they were centering on." Really, Dick? I was never mentioned in any of the articles that first broke the reopening of the case, let alone had I announced that I was centering on Robert Durst. In fact, I didn't speak to the press until after Susan Berman was killed.

"The New York tabloids carried front-page articles." Well, that's not true, either.

The kind of papers that "report when some movie star has a baby by space aliens." There were stories about the case in the *New York Times* and the *Daily News*. Do you really believe that the *New York Times* is on a par with supermarket tabloids? *I was not even mentioned in those articles!*

Trusty trooper Joe Becerra's name and quotes, however, were all over them. November 11 *Daily News*, November 11 *New York Times*. And *People* magazine on December 4, again, with not a mention of me but repeated quotes from Becerra. I know you do your homework, Dick. So when the facts didn't fit into your make-believe narrative, you just substituted my name for the trooper's.

And "scream shows"? Talk about trashing! I appeared on network news shows—*48 Hours, Nightline, 60 Minutes, Today, Good Morning America*—never *Jerry Springer*.

"Paparazzi following him . . . banner headlines." Dick, a teaser on the front page is not a banner headline.

DeGuerin's first act was a classic "the victim deserved to die" defense. After all, he had it coming. Morris Black was a vicious, violent old man, who yelled at children and assaulted a man twice his size for no reason. Hey, Dick? It's because the larger man was threatening your client, who was mumbling and twitching. And, as is always the case in this kind of defense, the unlucky, dead, chopped-up senior citizen was six feet under with no way to respond. No corroborating witnesses would be called by the defense. Could it be there were none to call?

I was stunned. I hounded Durst out of New York and forced him to kill a man and chop him up? But it wasn't just the words. It was the venom, the way DeGuerin mentioned my name, emphasizing the first syllable—*Py*-ro—with his southern accent that made it clear I was despicable. He insinuated to those Texan jurors that I was *Eye*-talian. (FYI: I'm actually of Lebanese descent, although at the time I was married to an Italian.)

I always heard, "The Devil made me do it." Never "The DA made me do it"!

It had to be the nuttiest, gutsiest defense in the history of crazy.

"Oh, my God!" I said. I remember saying to David and Anne Marie, "Call the DA to let him know that he could easily rebut the claim." But, having tried many murder cases, I told them to wait until the end of the day when prosecutors had gotten out of court and regrouped a bit. I then suggested that John O'Donnell call Cody, since he was the lead investigator, to tell him about the misrepresentations that were being made.

I knew it was not my place to get involved in that trial, but did DA Kurt Sistrunk and ADA Joel Bennett know that Durst was not hounded out of New York, that, in fact, he flew back and forth to New York several times during this period when he wanted to "disappear"? And the paparazzi chasing him? Where were those photos?

Clem Patti theorized that the Texas prosecutors probably assumed that it was nothing more than rhetoric, that it was collateral, meaning not something that they'd need to rebut because it had no bearing on whether Durst killed Black and would make no difference to the jury. Of course he was right.

But, in my gut, I knew it went to the heart of their defense. Because I chased him out of New York, no one would believe he killed in self-defense, and that he had *no choice* but to chop up the body.

DeGuerin was actually creating a pattern of behavior for Durst. He fled to Texas because he was hounded by me. He had to then flee Texas, not because he wanted to get away with murder, but because this is his pattern.

I was unaccustomed to taking a punch without hitting back, or at least defending myself. I called Sistrunk later that night, and said, "I understand they made me an issue down there. What the defense is saying can be contradicted by newspapers and airline tickets. I don't want to be a distraction, but, with your permission, I'd like to send my investigators to present the facts."

John O'Donnell was champing at the bit to go. He wanted to set the record straight also.

DA Sistrunk declined the offer.

I understood. These guys were in the middle of a trial. Plus, you don't second-guess another DA. They were in the courtroom every day. I wasn't. But, given the calls seeking responses from my office based on the goings-on in that Texas courtroom, it sure didn't feel that way.

Stepping back, most prosecutors would see the case as a "slam dunk"—open and shut. Why wouldn't they? Cody had more than just done his homework. He lived this case. He knew *everything* about the case, meticulously cataloguing every piece of evidence and recording every interview.

But, then again, Durst admitted to butchering the body, dumping the parts, and fleeing using Morris Black's ID. So maybe all the drama and Durst's defense carping about Dragon Lady Jeanine was irrelevant. It *was* irrelevant, to the prosecutors. But they had brains.

But to the jurors? They ate it up.

An ambitious, telegenic, *ethnic* New York woman with a powerful job? That turned out to be more terrifying to them than a serial murderer who dismembered his neighbor with an axe and bow saw and then casually went for dinner and a haircut.

I couldn't believe what was happening down there. I hit the ceiling every time they came in and gave me an update. There was talk of storing a scaffold in my office closet so they could peel me off the ceiling every time the press called with another shot.

The trial was entertainment. The defense's smoke-and-mirrors approach in that Texas courtroom had *nothing* to do with truth and justice. They pumped the smoke so thick, the jurors couldn't see through it.

Every aspect of the defense was staged.

Defense production expenses included costumes—DeGuerin's good old boy suit, boots; Durst's extra baggy suit that made him look meek.

The defense's staging of the Durst/Black struggle for the gun—with the lawyers as understudies in court—was as dark, rehearsed, and choreographed as Shakespearean theater. So perfect. If you've ever been in an actual fight, an actual life-or-death struggle, with your adrenaline flowing, you couldn't possibly remember every twist and turn. But then again, since the jurors and experts didn't have Morris Black's head to examine, thanks to Robert Durst, who could deny their version?

I found it fascinating and infuriating that one of the jurors would later describe the defense as "[they] told us their story and stuck to it."

"Their story." Damn right about that.

The puppet makers put on the best theater Galveston had ever seen.

Meanwhile, I saw much evidence that Judge Criss was completely out of her depth. According to ADA Joel Bennett, whom I spoke to recently, "A lot of our strategy was knowing the judge as well as we knew the law. We didn't make objections that we knew were going to be overruled by the judge. Why object and call attention to disputed issues?"

When the prosecution finished their case, the defense was asked if they intended to present their first witness. The name Robert Durst was spoken and a deafening silence befell the courtroom. For the record, most defendants do not take the stand, especially as the first witness. I know a bit about criminal law and procedure, having tried murder, rape, and violent felony cases as an assistant DA for more than a decade and then sitting on felony cases as a county judge for years in Westchester.

Remember the scaffolding in my closet? They had to take it out—two, three times a week—to peel me off the ceiling.

The scaffold takedowns occurred when:

• **Durst's testimony began with his childhood.** "Is your mother alive?" "Is your father alive?" "How old were you when your mother died?" "Were you present when she died?" "How did she die?"

WHAT? Is this a courtroom or Robert Durst on *This Is Your Life*?

Most judges are prepared for the "life story" line of questioning because all defendants want a sad story put before the jury. But it usually runs for a minute or two and then it's on to the issues at hand. The defendant's life story is not relevant, even if he is rich.

Questions like these are irrelevant, immaterial, and superfluous.

Okay, so he was a sixty-year-old orphan. His mother died fifty-three years earlier! What does that have to do with the killing and dismemberment on September 28, 2001?

Sympathy for the butcher?

Look, *everybody's* got a story. The issue before that jury was not whether Durst's mom jumped off a roof. The issue was, "What happened on the day that Morris Black died?" Can you imagine an inner-city defendant being allowed to say "My mom was a crack addict fifty-three years ago, so feel sorry for me because I chopped up my friend in the hood"?

But it didn't end there, Durst had a domineering father. "Even in the seventies, was the Durst family business, the Durst Organization, one of the most powerful entities in New York?" asked DeGuerin.

Who gives a damn? Should the scales of justice tip based on the number of coins in your pocket?

Poor Robert testified he wasn't interested in his family's business, but he was the obedient son who sold his health food store in Vermont to return to New York to go along with his father's wishes. That the judge would allow this testimony about Mommy and Daddy, which had nothing to do with Morris Black, is mind-boggling.

I thought to myself, *Maybe the defendant will argue some psychological trauma that affected his actions in the case.* Nowhere did DeGuerin make a connection between the violent death of the defendant's mother and his behavior on the day that he killed Morris Black. More smoke and mirrors.

But then I thought, *Well, maybe he wants to argue that he runs away from bad situations to explain his fleeing.* But surely Susan Criss would never allow it. She would have to instruct the jury that flight after a crime indicated "consciousness of guilt"—a charge that is given to jurors across this country all the time.

The trip down Durst's silver-spooned memory lane didn't stop there, either. Durst's family photos came into evidence. Robert was such a sensitive, sweet, caring human being, as DeGuerin said, he carried around photos of when he was seven and eight years old in a bathing suit, pictures of his first girlfriend, his not-yet-dead wife and their not-yet-dead dog on their wedding day (yes, the dog was in the wedding picture). DeGuerin said those personal photos identified what mattered to Robert. Poor Robert, he had been dealt such a bad hand that his only solace was in the pictures he carried around.

But put the photos in evidence? Really? Evidence of what? A wedding? You bozos. He killed them all! They weren't "what mattered" to Robert. The dead wife and dead dog pictures were trophies, memorabilia. Like a pedophile, Robert carried them around to remember his conquests.

Can you imagine a gangbanger from the projects charged with murdering and dismembering a neighbor being allowed to bring in family pictures of his youth and his family members, one of whom he probably killed?

A trial is about *evidence*. The judge determines the admissibility of evidence. If the evidence is relevant and material, it comes in. If it's not, it doesn't. I would never allow any defendant on trial in my courtroom to bring in a photo of his wedding day thirty years earlier. Not even if he murdered his wife.

When I was a judge, if I saw things that needed to be addressed, I wouldn't wait for the prosecution or the defense to object. I would say, "You're *not* doing that! That's irrelevant. You cannot do that. Come up to the bench and explain your proffer and I might allow it, subject to connection." If I had a slow DA or defense attorney, either way, it was my job to see justice done. It's about fairness for *both* sides. Honestly, that was why I disliked being a judge. I preferred to take a side and fight for it. But, as a judge, you're the ringleader of the circus. You have to control the clowns, even if the other side doesn't object.

• **And Asperger's?** In the defense's opening statement, co-counsel Mike Ramsey picked up where DeGuerin left off and talked about Durst's "bizarre, strange behavior," such as renting a three-hundred-dollar dump in Galveston instead of escaping *Py*-ro by flying to Europe or China. "We will prove beyond a shadow of a doubt that he suffers from Asperger's," he said. "It means that he is susceptible to a kind of panic state, that trauma in and of itself brings on a panic state in that kind of personality. It's the kind of personality that runs from trouble rather than trying to solve problems."

Hey, Mike. I'd say *most* people run from trouble. Does that mean we all have Asperger's? Criminals in particular run from their crimes.

"Panic state"? The guy *killed* somebody, chopped him up with experienced precision, and then calmly went out to get dinner and a haircut. That's some panic. My guess, Mike? The only guy panicked was the old man who was beaten up before he was shot and dismembered.

This mysterious condition, Asperger's, turns you into Jack the Ripper? What law school did you go to?

Maybe I'm wrong, but how about you prove it? Bring in a psychiatrist. Bring in a therapist. Hell, bring in Dorothy Ciner. Bring in *anyone*. You can't throw out psychiatric theories without backing them up. Joel Bennett told me recently, "Actually, all three of Durst's team of mental health doctors the jury was promised to hear from were in the courtroom to hear all of his testimony. After hearing it, none took the stand." That says it all.

As a judge, I would not have let that giant leap slip by. When testimony ended, I would have called up both sides and, directing my remarks to the defense, I would say, "You said in your opening statement that your client had Asperger's, and, as a result of that condition, he was panicked and detached. You didn't call a doctor to confirm that Durst has Asperger's. You didn't have a doctor explain the condition." Then I'd look at the DA and say, "Counselor, would you like to make a motion to strike that from the jury's consideration?"

Joel Bennett recalls that Criss stated the opening was not evidence. There was nothing to strike.

Wrong! If defense attorneys can say whatever they want and thread unsupported claims throughout the trial, then juries can acquit based on openings and not facts.

On the witness stand, Robert described in detail the struggle over the gun that led to Black getting shot. But when the prosecution asked him about the details of the dismemberment, he said, repeatedly, "I don't remember."

Asperger's strikes again! Conveniently for the defense, the condition, they claimed, affected his memory, too. Ramsey, who must've spent many a night around the campfire studying the *Diagnostic and Statistical Manual of Mental Disorders*, claimed he fell into a "dissociative state" after the murder that "amounts to an out-of-body experience. A fog descends upon the mind. You're able to pick up *parts* of things that occurred." Where the hell did that come from?

Strike it! Since they never called a doctor to say anything about Robert's susceptibility to a dissociative state, I would have stricken from the testimony the lawyer's explanation for Durst's spotty memory. The jury should have been instructed that there was no evidence that his memory was faulty due to any specific psychiatric condition. Translation: His stream of "I don't remember"s on cross-examination was nothing but obfuscation.

• **And the victim, Morris Black, aka violent cranky-pants.**

Did the defense offer a witness to say that Black was prone to fits of rage? No.

Police reports about violent attacks? No.

The defense said that the guy was a schemer and a cheap bastard. In truth, he was a charitable man who had his own program to give away free glasses to the needy! Ironically, it was Durst's return to Galveston to retrieve a pair of discounted eyeglasses—in spite of his wealth—that led to Cody making his arrest. So, Mike, who's the cheap bastard?

Any decent judge would have told the jury, "You cannot consider any unproven claims about Black's character."

Meanwhile, Robert got to sit in the courtroom in his oversize suits, acting innocent and sad.

Yes, the system is always stacked against the victim. The jury gets to see the defendant every day. If it's hot in the courtroom, they feel the heat together. If it's cold, they shiver together. They share some emotions and experiences. They might laugh together at something funny. There's an inevitable human connection. The defendant is always seated and submissive. The jury might get to like the guy, despite knowing what he'd done.

When Durst testified about buying a woman's blouse and hand-bag for his Dorothy Ciner disguise, the jury laughed. In *any* court-room, in *any* extended trial, there will be moments of humor that everyone shares, moments of sadness that everyone shares. All kinds of human emotions filter through the facts. The fact that Durst wore a wig and a blouse struck the jury as funny, and they liked him for it.

Meanwhile, Morris Black was not in the courtroom. He was not able to defend himself or amuse the jury. His suffering, his human-ity, was lost on them. He became a two-dimensional character, a "cantankerous, dangerous, threatening, unpredictable old man," as the defense defined him.

No photos of Morris Black in the courtroom—just gruesome photos of something akin to what you would see at your local meat market. Certainly nothing to connect with. It was inevitable that the jury connected with Durst and not Black.

One story the jury heard about Morris Black was that, back in 1997, he had a problem with his electricity. He called to complain and didn't like the attitude of the company rep on the phone. He flew off the handle and said, "I'm going to come down there and blow the place up." He never did it, of course.

Now, my question is, "If the guy never did anything, *why* was this story allowed to come in at all?"

Remember, the trial started in September 2003, two years after 9/11. The defense was allowed to say to the jury, "Morris Black made a terrorist threat" in their opening statement. In most states, the whole story wouldn't be admissible. Unless the defendant knew the story, it was irrelevant. Did Robert know about Black's phone-raging to the electric company? In Texas law, what Robert knew was relevant to his subjective beliefs. But honestly, did he read about Black's fight with the electric company in the North Carolina news?

The prosecution tried to turn it around. ADA Bennett reminded the jury that the defense never *proved* that Black yelled at kids, carried a stick, or attacked random strangers. As far as Black's alleged fascination with guns and the claim that he and Durst were BFF? Robert was the only one who testified about that.

The jury was allowed to take the word of a killer to characterize the victim.

Detective Cody Cazalas testified that these two were *not* the best of friends, that no one had seen them together, palling around. In all the places that were referenced by Durst as their hangouts, no one could attest to their friendship.

• **During summation, the lawyers' final argument to the jury, objections were made.** Most judges would allow "objections" during summation, and then counsel would approach the bench to argue. The idea is not to pollute jurors' minds with their version of the facts. Judges would normally remind jurors that their recollection of the testimony and not the lawyers' was what they should rely on. If there was a question, they could have any testimony reread.

Perhaps it was just Criss's personal philosophy on the bench. I don't share that philosophy. Summations are a critical point when each side gets to make final arguments without interruptions.

• **Not giving proper instructions to the jury.** During her instructions, Susan Criss made two questionable calls that benefited the defense.

One, she did not charge the jury on "consciousness of guilt." Dismembering the body, dumping the body parts, moving away, and then jumping bail were proof that Durst knew that he was guilty of committing a crime. She *repeatedly* instructed the jury to consider "the relevant facts and circumstances going to show the condition of the mind of the defendant *at the time of the alleged crime*"—the shooting. She never charged them to consider the relevant facts and circumstances and his condition of mind *immediately after* the time of the crime. It seems a rather large part of the instructions to leave out. The idiot jury did as instructed and fixated on the shooting itself, not the undeniable consciousness of guilt Durst demonstrated in abundance afterward.

Two, she didn't charge the jury that the lack of motive could be considered, but that motive was *not* required to convict. In all criminal cases, the burden of proof is on the prosecution to prove, beyond a reasonable doubt, to the unanimous satisfaction of twelve jurors, that the defendant did it. Not *why* he did it, but *that* he did it. So, of course, in their jaded playbook, the defense harped on "there was no motive." Motive, boys, is not an element of the case. They don't have to prove it or talk about it. Despite this, the defense kept saying that if there was no known reason for Durst to kill Black, the jury should be in doubt that he did. If they were in doubt, they couldn't convict.

There are many theories about Durst's motive for killing Morris. Cody believes Morris threatened Robert's freedom. But, as Cody said of Durst in *The Jinx*, "If he's cornered, he'll kill you." Perhaps Black figured out who Robert really was and asked for money in exchange for keeping his identity a secret. As we know, Durst kills when he needs to. *Something* made him need to silence Black. Shooting him and cutting off his head would do it.

As ADA Bennett told the jury in his final argument, *motive didn't matter*! "The defense wants you to believe the lack of logical objective motive is a reason for doubt in this case," he said. But motive is not essential to convict "in a case where the defendant has demonstrated the ability and the willingness to commit horrid, indescribable acts of butchery to another human being."

The jury should have been instructed, "Motive is not an element of the crime and need not be proven by the prosecution. We're here to decide the facts. Did he commit murder or did he not?" The questions were, "Did he *intend* to kill?" and "Did he kill?" and "If so, was it self-defense or an accident?" Nothing more is required. The question, "What was his reason?" is irrelevant. Does anyone really know why John Wayne Gacy put on a clown suit and killed boys? He *killed* them. Who knows why people kill. The only ones who give a damn why are the shrinks.

DA Kurt Sistrunk said in his summation, "If the sole fact that Robert Durst severed Morris Black's head at the sixth vertebra convinces you beyond a reasonable doubt that he intentionally and knowingly murdered him, and it was no accident and it was not self-defense, that's it. If the facts of dismemberment and flight together convince you he's guilty of murder, that's all it takes."

But the defense countered that if Robert Durst didn't have a *reason* to kill Morris Black then it couldn't *not* be self-defense. It was a negative upon a negative upon a negative. Brilliant!

The prosecution *didn't* have the head. They *couldn't* prove it *wasn't* an accident.

So, if Black *wasn't* murdered, according to trusty Bob, then the dismemberment *didn't* matter.

All those negatives were a disturbing echo and reminder of Michael Struk and the NYPD's attitude about Kathie. They *couldn't* prove she *didn't* run away. Therefore, she did.

• **Did the jurors not hear Durst's lies?** There's a Latin expression, *falsus in uno, falsus in omnibus,* meaning "false in one, false in all." As a judge, I repeatedly charged jurors to consider the credibility of the witness. Did they consider:

- How Robert said he was a disengaged loner in high school, but actually he'd been on the soccer club, the aviation club, the camera club.
- How he told a landlord he was a botanist, a writer, a lumber worker, that he had a Ph.D.
- How he told police he was visiting his daughter at college.
- How he lied about his sex, his age, his name, his ability to speak.

In his final argument, Bennett listed all the aliases he'd discovered:

- Dorothy Ciner
- James Klosty
- Jim Turst
- Robert Klosty

- Morris Black
- Maury Blauch
- Emilio Vignoni
- G. Paren
- Diane Winn
- Everett Ward
- James Cordis

The most offensive of his lies was using Kathie Durst's Social Security number to get an American Express card.

Then there was the blatantly ridiculous story about Durst running down the street, banging on doors after the murder, begging people to call 911, and that he tried to call it himself from a pay phone (again, with the pay phone?) but the woman using it turned her back on him.

Are you kidding me? A frantic man, covered in blood, screaming, "Call 911!" was ignored? It never happened.

Or how about the falsehood about the two gunshots heard by witnesses that night? If the shooting was an accident, the gun would go off only once, people. To explain the second shot, Durst came up with the story about Black shooting an eviction letter he'd been sent by the landlord. The cops found that eviction notice—without a bullet hole in it. The defense argued, "Black shot at the notice and missed." In a small room? The guy they say was obsessed with guns and went target shooting with Robert? It was all a charade to show that there was only one gunshot, even though people heard two. How best to cover it up? By saying the previous gunshot was already there.

Or this huge credibility issue: There was dramatic evidence of a cleanup. No fingerprints in the apartment at all, not even in Durst's apartment. What did *that* tell you? Why was he cleaning his *own* fingerprints in his *own* apartment? Why? So he could say he never lived there. And why pay Morris Black's rent for the next month? Why? So that no one would know that Morris was missing or even that he left there.

How about the obvious lie that Robert didn't remember anything, like cleaning up the apartment or dismembering the body? Really? "If you don't remember the cleanup how can you get up there and testify that you didn't clean the blood off the gun? You can't, it's a lie, he *does* remember, he remembers everything," said ADA Bennett.

The biggest lie of all was the defense's claim that Durst didn't know what he was doing when he dismembered Morris. Bennett described it in detail: "It's clear that he was not cut up with an axe. An axe is not going to do this. [The weapon of choice had to be] a knife or some sharp instrument where he could cut the skin, cut all the muscle all the way to the bone, pull the tissue and muscle, and get to the bone, and saw it off so he could dump the body."

The prosecution brought in a medical examiner who said whoever dismembered Morris Black knew what he was doing. "Smooth cuts with a sharp object through skin and muscle," testified the doctor. "The bones appeared to be sawed." The head was severed cleanly at the sixth vertebra.

What? Durst claimed he was wasted on Jack Daniel's and pot and in an Asperger's dissociative state. How could he have cut so precisely? I remember Cody saying the same thing during my Galveston tour. When he saw Black's torso and limbs, he instantly thought it was a clean cut and not a panicked hack job.

None of this is relevant to his guilt?

It was *all* relevant to guilt.

What about the bruises on Morris's body? He had marks on his left side, the right side, his shoulders, the middle of the back, the inside and outside of his arm, the elbow, and the top of the shoulders from multiple blows. The medical examiner testified that the bruises were fresh and dark purple. There was also aspirated blood in the lungs, consistent with a man's being beaten about the head and neck while he was alive, before he was shot.

"We have evidence of *multiple* trauma, multiple contusion, multiple areas. He was beaten repeatedly. Those injuries are *not* consistent with someone falling on a flat, plane surface, these are deep-tissue bruises," said Bennett in his argument. "Morris Black is speaking to you loud and clear. He is telling you, 'I was beaten repeatedly before I was shot, before I was cut into pieces and dumped in the bay.'"

But Durst told the courtroom that the bruising happened in the scuffle for the gun. And the judge did not charge the jury to consider his credibility, but to "place yourselves in the defendant's position at the time and view this from his standpoint alone."

If Black's body was speaking to the jury, they weren't listening. Why? In effect, Judge Susan Criss told them not to.

The only question was whether the gun went off on purpose or by accident. The only way to prove that was by examining the head. One juror said he had to acquit because the head was never found.

Guess what, idiot? Who do you think got rid of the head? Why wasn't it with the rest of the body?

In my years as an ADA, I got convictions in murder cases on circumstantial evidence. Circumstantial evidence is no less reliable than direct evidence. Prosecutors rely on circumstantial evidence all the time, particularly in murder cases. Every day in courtrooms across the country jurors draw logical inferences from circumstantial evidence, inferences that can point indelibly toward guilt. It's not like every thug waits for a video camera or eyewitnesses to commit his crime; it's usually done in secret. So should we reward the guy who hides the evidence?

If he bought a bow saw in advance, if he lied about everything, if he fled, if he chopped up the body, it was evidence. As far as I'm concerned, the prosecution met their burden. They did everything they could have done. They brought a lot of witnesses in. But between this judge, and this jury, and this defense team, the deck was stacked too high against them.

• **The defense's manipulation of the jury.** Mike Ramsey started the final argument for the defense and actually mentioned a juror by name, Joanne Gongora. He singled her out and complimented her copious note taking, making her feel important. In more than three decades in courtrooms, I have never heard counsel mention a juror by name, let alone flatter her.

During Chip Lewis's final argument for the defense, he told the court that he'd been keeping score of the prosecution's word choice. "Eleven times, we heard the word 'butchery.' Seven times, we heard 'cut up.' We heard 'run away' repeatedly over and over again."

Well, I kept score, too. In their final argument, defense attorneys Ramsey and Lewis mentioned Judge Criss fourteen times by name (as in, "As Judge Criss instructed you, a presumption of innocence alone is enough to acquit"), and ten more times by title (as in, "Thank you, Judge"). Saying her name over and over again was a ploy, another aspect of the show. It communicated to the jury that the defense and the judge were on the same side—and the jury was with them, too.

"What you give us by being here is a window to the world because we all know each other," Ramsey said, speaking directly to the jury, in his argument. "We are friends. We know the police officers. . . . The judge comes from our ranks. I hate to say that about the judge, but she does." We're all in this boat together, on the same level, and on the same side. "We are friends," he said.

It was pure pandering! They created an "us" against "them" mentality. And who was the "them"? Me.

It was a kind of brainwashing, convincing the jury that Durst was their friend. The evidence that it worked? The jurors said after the verdict that they could relate to Robert.

I never would have allowed it. And, because it was so blatant and improper, the judge should have corrected any misimpression the jury might have gotten.

• **The mischaracterization of yours truly.** The defense attorneys acted like puppeteers, not officers of the court. They wrote a play and molded their client into a sympathetic character. They created an antagonist in an ethnic, ambitious New Yorker that simple Texan folk were sure to despise.

Ramsey's final argument:

> *I get to finally talk about Ms. Jeanine Pirro. She's a DA in West-chester County who took a case that is no case. There is no case pending involving Bob Durst and the disappearance of his wife Kathie. There is no indictment after over two and a half years of releasing poison into the media. No charges because there is no case there. No self-regarding district attorney is going to try a case by going to the* New York Post *and releasing to them the fact, "We have got a suspicion about an old case." And unless you have seen your picture on the front page of the newspaper being accused of having something to do with the disappearance of a loved one, you don't know what it feels like. You don't know what it feels like, the person in the frame of mind that Bob Durst was in certainly.*
>
> *What corroborates this business about Pirro? You heard me cross-examine the Pennsylvania officer at the car search. I asked, "You know what? She didn't break a nail in that search, did she? She didn't really pop out into a sweat while you were searching the car?" [He said] no. She was there for a photo op. She was there*

*in her limousine with her driver to get on television. One of the
officers actually testified she was in TV makeup. She is there at the
extradition hearing in Pennsylvania to get on TV again. She even
comes to Galveston to get on television. She has got no case. There's
no case pending, never has, never will be. That is what started
this whole chain of events here, a woman getting on television for
whatever reason she has to get on television, whatever drives those
kind of people who are media hungry to get on television, to get into
the newspapers, and to cause this whole thing to start, to drive Bob
Durst out of New York, to drive him into hiding, to drive him to
not wanting to be Robert Durst, to want to be someone else, to be the
person that you have seen in court.*

*[The prosecution is] married to the position that he did it as a
part of a cool, calculated, well-planned, orchestrated event. Now
you believe that, you know, we can sell you a bridge in New York.
[The murder] just happened that way. Now, it is tragic and Bob has
expressed regret for it. He said, "If I just hadn't left the gun in the
apartment, then none of that would've happened."*

*If Ms. Pirro had kept her mouth shut, none of this would have
happened.*

The *hate* that came from Ramsey's mouth in his final argument
was not unfamiliar to me. Insecure people of his generation could be
so uncomfortable with a younger woman in a position of power that
they were reduced to criticism of the lowest kind. His moral compass
is clearly lacking an arrow.

I laughed with pure incredulity while watching this on Court
TV. For *any* judge to allow that bile to be heard by the jury was an
outrage.

What does "popping a sweat" conjure up in your mind? Maybe a
woman having sex?

How about "breaking a nail"? Maybe a woman doesn't have a brain, she's just out there trying to look pretty?

My alleged TV makeup? Are you kidding? When I showed up in Pennsylvania, I was scrub-faced. But even if I had had on an inch of makeup, what did that have to do with Morris Black's murder?

And the "limousine" comment. Since when is a government Tahoe a limousine? The L-word was code for a rich woman riding around on her high horse. *Come on!* Virtually every DA has an unmarked police car.

Ramsey's whole speech was sexist and offensive. A man calling for a woman to "keep her mouth shut," to be mute like Dorothy Ciner, or silenced like Kathie and Susan Berman? It was hate speech. No judge I know would have ever allowed that.

And it was irrelevant! What did my arrival in Galveston in October or in Pennsylvania in December have to do with Durst's "righteous shooting," as Ramsey loved to say, in September?

The trial was a *charade*! It was upside-down justice.

I remember thinking at the time: *The jury will never buy that.*
But they did.

They bought it all. They believed the unsupported, unproven story that the dream team of DeGuerin, Ramsey, and Lewis spooled out for them.

Many judges are consumed by the idea that they don't want any of their cases to be reversed. They fret about wrongful convictions, especially in the DNA era. Insecure and inadequate judges don't worry about wrongful acquittals. To preserve their records and prevent reversals, they'd rather bend over backward in favor of the defendant, even facilitate a murderer going free, than seek truth and justice in their courtrooms.

Lady Justice was turned on her head in Galveston. She wasn't only wearing a blindfold. She was in chains.

• • •

THE JURY.

Dear God.

Those eight women and four men were an egg carton full of stupid.

After deliberating for twenty-six hours over five days, they decided unanimously that Durst murdered Black in self-defense because he was afraid of me. The defense story was tailor-made for gun-loving, stand-your-ground Texans. Durst said he found Black trespassing in his apartment. By all means, shoot the bastard.

Unbelievable.

The jurors gave a press conference after the acquittal. In a room packed with reporters, one juror, Deborah Warren, a surgical technician who worked at a hospital delivering babies, admitted that the deliberations gave her agita. "People cried. People fussed and argued. We had paper all around the room. My stomach is still knotted up." The jury voted a few times before reaching their unanimous decision. "The prosecutors did the best that they could with what they had. We did the best that we could with what we had," Warren said. "I wouldn't ask him to escort my daughter to her senior prom. [But] Durst isn't the only crazy person in Galveston."

You can say that again, lady.

Just look in the mirror.

The juror who seemed to be most terrified of "Jeanine *Py*-ro" was Joanne Gongora, the one singled out by name by the defense. This woman ran a consulting firm for nursing malpractice lawsuits. She knew just enough of the law to be truly dangerous. She said, "The burden is on the prosecution to show how the event happened, and we didn't see that. It wasn't proven. Based on the evidence presented to us, there was reasonable doubt. It was a big struggle for all of us." She said then—and she's been saying it ever since, on Anderson Cooper's

CNN show on *The Jinx*—that she *related* to Durst's panicked reaction. "I could understand his panic. I could understand his life," she said at the press conference.

How could some middle-age, middle-income woman begin to *understand* Robert Durst's life? How could she relate to him in any way, shape, or form?

Another genius, a juror named Robbie Clarac, a business manager, told the press room that Robert Durst's four days on the witness stand were taken with a pound of salt by the jury. They knew he was a liar, and yet they set him free. "We took Durst's story completely out of the picture," he said. "We took the evidence that was presented to us. We went on the facts that were presented to us. Based on the evidence, it wasn't there. We could not convict him."

So let me get this straight. He knew Durst was lying on the stand. He knew he'd killed and chopped up Black. He knew he fled. And yet he couldn't find him guilty. Nice reward!

I needed a forklift to get my jaw off the floor.

Once again, I could only cringe at the irony of this circus. The jurors who were so turned off by the media-thirsty creature Jeanine Py-ro proceeded to make the rounds on various TV shows, local and national, after the verdict. Deborah Warren, Joanne Gongora, and Chris Lovell are *still* doing it, and sticking with their stories despite everything we know now about Durst and his lawyers.

Can't you just imagine Joanne Gongora getting all gussied up, putting on her best red lipstick, pulling out her curlers, for her debut on the *Today* show? She told Matt Lauer, "The public can't get over the shock and horror of the dismemberment. The charge we had to determine was how Morris Black died. Was it intentional or was it an act of self-defense? The dismemberment and the bond jumping all came later. It was the actual act of what occurred in the apartment . . . that one moment in time. And, so, based on the evidence that was presented to us, there was reasonable doubt."

There is no reasonable doubt that she and the other idiots of the jury were influenced by the judge, impressed by Durst's wealth, and wowed by his defense.

I previously mentioned that one juror, Warren, said that it seemed like the prosecution didn't put in much effort. But the defense pulled out all the stops.

Was she serious? Durst *paid millions* for all those bells and whistles and the full table of stuffed-shirt lawyers. Her tax dollars paid for Sistrunk and Bennett. Financially, the prosecution was outmatched. And she faulted them for it.

To this day, I'm convinced that something untoward was going on. One juror in particular came under serious scrutiny. Chris Lovell appeared on *The Jinx*, grinning and recalling what must have been the most exciting time in his entire life. I imagine the whole jury felt important to be a part of it. They were small people from a small town. They looked at Durst and DeGuerin and thought, *These are rich, powerful,* famous *people. They're paying attention to* me. *Making eye contact with* me. *They make me feel important and powerful, too.* The jurors felt not just an allegiance—"We're friends!"—but as if they *owed* the defense something. And they gave it to them.

Lovell was smitten with Robert Durst. Warren told the press that the jury demonstrated (more theater!) different scenarios for how the gun went off. I would bet my eyes that Chris Lovell played Durst. When the trial ended, Lovell wasn't ready to leave the circus. He just had to prolong his proximity to power and wealth.

So he started visiting Durst in prison. He claimed it was to prove to himself that Durst was innocent. You'd think he could put his own mind to rest after, say, one or two visits. But he went back, for a third, fourth, and *fifth* time. He brought his wife to meet Durst in prison.

Recently, I spoke to a sheriff's investigator in Galveston, Randy Burrows, who monitored Durst's visitations in jail. "Lovell's visits started right after the acquittal in 2003," he said. "When Judge Criss got wind of Lovell's visits (from a bailiff and a corrections officer), she brought it to our attention and expressed her concern. We opened an investigation into whether money exchanged hands," said Randy. "During those visits, Durst and Lovell sat face to face with a panel of glass between them. They spoke through a speaker, and we recorded those conversations. It was obvious to me that Chris was trying to become friends and attach himself to Durst to get some money out of it. Durst picked up on that and was very careful how he talked to Chris. Their conversations reminded me of a younger child trying to become friends with an older child."

Lovell kissed Robert's ass. "He was flattering to Durst. Buttering him up," said Randy. "He admired his wealth and asked questions about how he obtained it."

Was Lovell not paying attention for the six weeks of the trial? Durst was *born* rich. He obtained nothing on his own.

Back to Randy. "Durst was apprehensive. He was willing to talk to Chris, but he didn't give up anything."

A month or so after his flurry of prison visits, as Randy recalled, "Durst was renting a house in [nearby] League City. I was told that an alarm went off at the house. Durst was in jail, and obviously not there. Police responded to the alarm and they found Chris Lovell. He was living there. He might have been working on the property."

I also heard from a source that the Lovells vacationed with Durst in Mexico.

While the investigation never resulted in any charges against Lovell, as far as I'm concerned, that man should've been locked up in a cell right next to his idol.

AFTER THE ACQUITTAL, I really felt for the prosecutors. DA Sistrunk told the press he was "disappointed and dismayed." Joel Bennett and Sistrunk did a masterful job with the investigation, nailing down every painstaking detail about the murder, the dismemberment, the flight. They were eloquent and decisive in their arguments. But in that kangaroo court, they were too logical to get traction. One only has to read the trial transcripts to see what they were up against.

They also lacked the one piece of evidence that would have truly been a slam dunk for the DA: the head.

Cody's theory about the head: Sergeant Gary Jones secured Durst's car when he was arrested in Galveston. Cody Cazalas took possession of Durst. In the car, along with serial killer gear—false IDs, two .38 guns, a black zipper bag, latex gloves, live ammo, rope, a box cutter, a wood-handled knife, scissors, a drop cloth, earplugs (the dismemberment sawing noise must have irritated him)— detectives found cash, weed, and a receipt from a New Orleans dry cleaner, dated one day earlier. Cody called the dry cleaner and was told Durst's item was still there. So Cody jumped in the car with Detective Jason Chide and drove forthwith to New Orleans, six hours each way.

Knowing he couldn't get there before the dry cleaner closed, he called Vernon Geberth, a legendary homicide investigator from the NYPD, author of *Practical Homicide Investigation: Tactics, Procedures and Forensic Techniques*, the bible on most detectives' desks, and a lecturer to cops all over, and asked if he knew anyone in New Orleans. He did. His cousin was a lieutenant with the NOPD who went to retrieve Durst's item, a comforter. Unfortunately, it'd already been cleaned, making it too late for forensics.

The blanket had been brought to the dry cleaner with a big red stain.

In that route from Galveston to New Orleans, Cody and Jason Chide drove on bridges over the bayou. Cody believes Durst dumped the head in a bayou. The son of a bitch knew the head would give him away, so he fed it to the gators.

Durst is so cheap, he was not about to throw the comforter into the swamp with the head. He took it to be dry cleaned, and kept the receipt. Just like the glasses he put a deposit on. And the Laundromat in Ship Bottom. Why didn't he just throw stuff away?

Upon his return to Galveston from New Orleans, Durst stayed at the Holiday Inn in room 208. A subsequent search of the room found a prescription for Viagra for Robert, a green canvas bag, a green shaving cream kit, and, of course, green pens.

I got a lot of requests from the media to comment on the verdict. I gave all outlets the same statement: "The Texas jury has spoken. We accept the verdict. It does not affect our investigation into the disappearance of Kathleen Durst."

It killed me to say it, but it's what I believed. You respect the jury's verdict. Right or wrong, you don't have to agree with it but that is our system.

I would say that anytime a case was lost, even in my office.

Unlike DA Sistrunk, I wouldn't describe my feelings after the acquittal as dismayed or disappointed. I was angry and disgusted and troubled by what this miscarriage meant for our judicial system as a whole. The Durst verdict came on the heels of the sensational trial of O. J. Simpson, another wealthy wife-beater who got away with it. Everyone was saying, "What's going on with the criminal-justice system?" If you had money and power, you could buy your freedom, even for murder.

After O.J., I remembered walking into the trial bureau and asking my ADAs, "So what's going on in court today?" There was nothing better than hanging out with the ADAs and chiefs. I would rather be running an investigation or in a courtroom any day of the week than in my office.

One ADA said, "Boss, you are not going to believe it. I'm on a robbery case, picking a jury. And this woman says, 'I won't convict anyone without DNA evidence.' " That was the legacy of the O. J. Simpson trial. In the robbery case, the defendant stuck a gun in someone's face, said, "Give me your money." The woman identified him in a lineup. Now we need DNA, too? What DNA should we produce?

The justice system was going backward.

Our job in law enforcement was to fight that trend. We had to level the playing field. It was about what my mother taught me growing up, shopping for the blind, washing the hair of the infirm, caring for the sick, and protecting the vulnerable. We had to seek justice with passion *and* objectivity. And we couldn't give up after a setback.

The criminal-justice system is wrongly named. It should be called the *victim's*-justice system. We fight on behalf of the person who never chose to be a part of the system in the first place. The person who was going along in his or her life, never expecting a trauma. We serve the family of the victim. A *criminal* made the decision to victimize. So why does the accused have all the constitutional rights, not the victim? Why are we so concerned with how to treat the criminal when it's completely legal and encouraged to disparage the victim?

Morris Black was labeled a violent, cantankerous terrorist.

Kathie Durst was called a drug addict, a slut, a drunk.

In untold thousands of other cases, the victim's skirt was too short, or she was mouthing off, or she "asked for it."

Kathie Durst's case represented everything that was wrong with the *criminal*-justice system. The victim came from a humble background. The criminal used his family's wealth and influence to sweep her disappearance under the rug. This young, professional woman with everything to live for fell off the side of the earth. Those in positions of power didn't lift a finger to protect the powerless. They

Robert Durst and Kathie Durst's wedding. *(Courtesy of the Galveston Police Department)*

HE KILLED THEM ALL

Morris Black as a young man. *(Courtesy of Gladys Saslaw)*

Susan Berman, Durst's friend. *(Gerardo Samoza/Polaris)*

Photo of Robert Durst in the late 1960s found in his car after his arrest in Pennsylvania.
(Courtesy of the Galveston Police Department)

"I live to eat, other things are just to get through the day. What DD is doing to me, puts me in the same place, as what Kathy [*sic*] did to me." Note in green ink found in Durst's car in Pennsylvania. DD thought to be Douglas Durst.
(Courtesy of the Galveston Police Department)

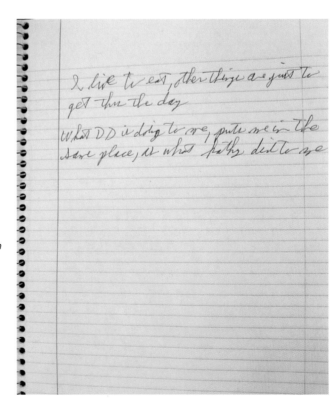

Kathie's diary, where she writes how Robert would bring women into their apartment and where she says Robert's brother believed he was embezzling funds. *(Courtesy of James McCormack)*

While district attorney, meeting with Westchester county executive Andrew O'Rourke to discuss a Westchester police helicopter. *(Anthony Vitulli)*

Announcing new domestic violence legislation at a press conference in the DA office's library. Governor George Pataki and other legislators were in attendance. *(Author's collection)*

As DA in 1999 at the beginning of the Durst odyssey. *(Getty Images)*

An old photograph of Debrah Lee Charatan found in Durst's car after his arrest for murder in Galveston. *(Courtesy of the Galveston Police Department)*

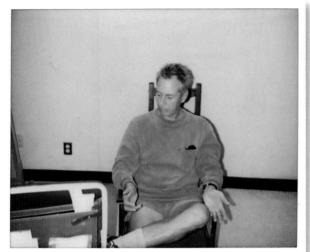

Durst being processed by the Galveston Police Department for the murder of Morris Black on October 9, 2001. *(Courtesy of the Galveston Police Department)*

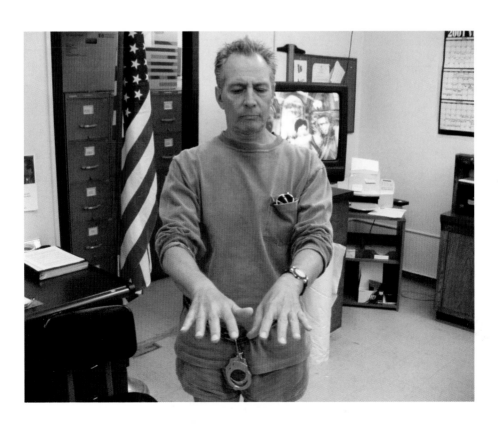

Detective Cody Cazalas of the Galveston Police Department. *(Courtesy of Cody Cazalas)*

With my security detail, left to right, investigator Tim McAuliff, Chief Mike Duffy, and investigator Pat Spatafore. *(John Vecchiolla)*

With investigator John O'Donnell (left), investigator John Fitzsimmons, and senior investigator Bob Donnelly. *(Courtesy of the author)*

A page found in Durst's car with circled and crossed-out paragraphs. Preparing for a psychiatric defense? *(Courtesy of the Galveston Police Department and Colonial Regional Police)*

The calendar from Durst's vehicle with significant dates, including those for when Susan Berman was killed and the day he assigned power of attorney to Debrah Lee Charatan, circled in green. *(Courtesy of the Galveston Police Department and Colonial Regional Police)*

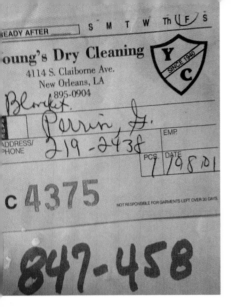

The New Orleans dry-cleaning receipt for the blanket with a red stain (believed to be from blood from the head of Morris Black), which Durst dropped off one day before he was arrested in Galveston. *(Courtesy of the Galveston Police Department)*

One of the trash bags that contained Morris Black's severed limbs. *(Courtesy of the Galveston Police Department)*

The gun used to shoot Morris Black: a Ruger .22 semiautomatic pistol. *(Courtesy of the Galveston Police Department)*

At dinner after the worldwide premiere of *The Jinx* with Cody Cazalas and director Andrew Jarecki. *(Startraks)*

circled the wagons and protected their own, so that Durst could kill and kill again.

If justice had been served in 1982, Susan Berman and Morris Black would not have been killed.

So, no, I wasn't discouraged by the verdict. I was motivated by it.

| DOUGLAS DURST,
THE DEVIL'S BROTHER

The acquittal was a blow. But we didn't give up the fight.

We had low-keyed our investigation during the Galveston trial because of the gag order and because we expected Durst to be convicted. Putting Durst behind bars for the murder of Morris Black for the rest of his life would be a win even if we didn't get all the answers we wanted. Of course, I would have loved to indict him in New York, but the dots weren't yet connected. We weren't there yet. We didn't have much more than they had in 1982, other than an additional twenty-one years of witnesses' memories fading, lost opportunities, and minus one central witness. And no, I'm not saying that they couldn't have gone further in '82. I am saying that they didn't go further, they didn't follow up, they didn't re-create the crime scene, didn't interview essential witnesses.

So I put the investigation back on the front burner and started pushing for cooperation from the Durst family. I reached out to Thomas, the younger brother, the one who told the McCormacks "this meeting is over" back in '82. He lived in California in 2003, and we talked by phone.

The conversation was short but cooperative. I said to him, "This guy's dangerous. Do you understand that? Whether my case convinces you or not, there are a lot of dead bodies in this guy's wake." He wasn't too forthcoming with information about Kathie's disappearance and how his family handled it at the time. But I definitely impressed upon him that he'd better watch his back. Thomas hired bodyguards for himself and his family.

I tried to speak with Robert's sister, Wendy Durst Kreeger. She lived in Westchester County, right near me in Rye.

Wendy and my then husband, Al, actually had a bit of a run-in. Al was building some spec houses across the street from hers, and she and her husband showed up at Al's presentation before the Rye planning board. The Kreegers objected to various details about the project, the height of the houses, etc. They were able to temporarily stop construction. At one point, according to Al, either Wendy or her husband indicated that they were tripping him up because he was married to me. Al's frustration was understandable, but he got his approvals in spite of the Kreegers' efforts.

Next on my list was Douglas Durst. The ruler of the kingdom.

What did Douglas know about Kathie? What had deceased Seymour known? I'd wanted answers to those questions since 1999. In late 2003, I was emboldened by the acquittal to go to the source to find out.

ANDREW JARECKI TRIED TO get answers from Douglas in 2013 while filming *The Jinx*. He called Douglas's office repeatedly to request an interview. Douglas's surrogates turned him down flat. In January 2015, a month before the series' airdate, Douglas filed a petition against Jarecki in state supreme court to force him to disclose how he got sealed video depositions of Douglas from 2006.

To say Douglas did not support *The Jinx* was putting it mildly.

The petition stated, "Douglas Durst is worried *The Jinx* will be a violent broadside against the family name and history."

Understandable. He was right. He had to know that *The Jinx* was not *only* about Robert, but would also consider the Durst family's involvement, if any, in a cover-up to protect Robert.

Jarecki's film explored the role of Robert's family beginning with the time of Kathie's disapperance. Jarecki located Ed Wright, whom Scoppetta hired to investigate Robert's account of that Sunday night in January 1982.

For those keeping score, this made a grand total of three simultaneous investigations: Struk's, Gilberte's, and Ed Wright's.

Until *The Jinx*, I had no idea that Wright had looked into the case. It was a shocker for me, a welcome one. More than ten years before the show aired, my office found the same inconsistencies Wright enumerated in his 1982 report titled, "Discrepancies in the recollections of various principals"—the flip-flopping doorman and the phone call Robert claimed to have made from various locations. What was most fascinating to me was not what Wright discovered since we'd unearthed the information, but that he'd been hired by Scoppetta to investigate his own client, clearly not a trustworthy character, when the body, assuming there was one, wasn't even cold. And certainly one might conclude that the Dursts became aware of what Wright determined.

Of course, Robert claimed Scoppetta was hired by his family to help find Kathie. This makes no sense. If this high-profile criminal defense attorney was hired to find Kathie, why didn't he speak to the McCormack family, Kathie's friends, students from medical school? Why was he investigating Robert?

Did the Dursts have an inkling what Robert really was? Did they *know*?

According to Wright in *The Jinx*, "When Kathie disappeared and her family members were pointing fingers, Robert's father, who was, you know, a millionaire many times over, contacted [Scoppetta] to represent Robert. Nick contacted me to do some work and that's what I did."

Detective Michael Struk was also in the dark about the secret investigation by Wright, an ex-cop, formerly with the New York State Organized Crime Task Force, on behalf of the Dursts. "When Wright was telling these people there was deception on the part of their son and brother, I would think that, behind the scenes, there was a great deal of alarm concerning this matter," he told Jarecki. "The Durst family never offered to help us and never said, 'Look, we have a private investigator on this. Anything he finds, he'll share with you.' They just further backed away."

What does that tell you?

Although Robert lies like he breathes, he said in *The Jinx* that he had ten or a dozen meetings with Wright—and that five or six of those meetings were held *with Douglas present.*

If what Robert claims is true, one could easily believe Douglas knew about the inconsistencies in Wright's report in 1982 and also feared it would come out when HBO aired *The Jinx* in February 2015.

As that date approached, Douglas had to be furious, fearful, and frustrated. His refusal to participate hadn't stopped the filmmakers. His petition against Jarecki and his high-powered lawyers didn't slow this train. So, as I see it, Douglas decided to launch a preemptive strike. He sat for an interview with the *New York Times* to cast himself in a sympathetic light, just before January 1, 2015, before the series debut. Interestingly, instead of speaking to investigative journalist Charles Bagli, who had been reporting on the story for years, he talked to columnist Jim Dwyer.

Why Jim Dwyer? Did he think he would have a better shot controlling the story and not being challenged? And why talk about his brother now? What changed? Why was the guy who was so unwilling to talk to law enforcement for decades suddenly so interested in sitting down with the *New York Times*?

Along with sharing bizarre details about Robert—he kept a

sharpened wrench in his desk at work; he routinely pissed in waste-baskets; he stole from the company payroll—Douglas told Dwyer, "Before the disappearance of my sister-in-law, Bob had a series of Alaskan malamutes, which is like a husky. He had seven of them, and they all died, mysteriously, of different things, within six months of owning them. All of them named Igor. We don't know how they died, and what happened to the bodies. In retrospect, I now believe he was practicing killing and disposing of his wife with those dogs." Wow. Did you just figure that out? How did it come to you? In a dream, revelation, or epiphany? Or was it when he heard that Robert told Debrah Lee in those Pennsylvania prison tapes that he wanted to "Igor Douglas"?

As an animal lover, I was horrified by this. I love dogs and have had as many as five at a time. I raised two pigs. One lived to be eighteen years old. (RIP, Wilbur.) I've had lovebirds, turtles, gerbils. I wanted to get a goat. Since I couldn't look them in the eye, I decided not to.

As DA in 1997, I wanted to start an animal-cruelty unit when I investigated dogfighting and cockfights in Mount Vernon, and the illegal gambling that went along with those fights. I was told in no uncertain terms that my job as a prosecutor was to protect humans as victims, and not animals. In my research and my preparation for the presentation to the county, though, I found that pretty much every serial murderer began his career with the abuse and torture of an animal. When I heard that Durst might have killed his own dogs, it didn't surprise me.

Why didn't Douglas inform the authorities about the Igors in 1982, or 2000, or 2001?

Maybe he would have, but law enforcement didn't even bother to speak to Robert's family. Then again, nor did they offer to speak to police.

People have asked over the years, if Seymour, Douglas, and/or Thomas Durst suspected or knew foul play might be involved in the disappearance of Robert's wife in '82, why weren't they more involved with the investigation?

From where Douglas sits now, I'm sure he wishes he had.

At the time, Seymour was in a battle with Mayor Ed Koch for control of Times Square. The Dursts were pressing their influence hard to secure their place at the very heart of New York City. They and their attorneys appeared in front of planning boards and commissions. *Not* a good image to have a felon, a murderer, a wife-beater, as part of the Durst Organization.

What's more, Kathie Durst was doing some digging into the Durst Organization's business practices herself. There was a scene in *All Good Things* that had "Karen" collect evidence of wrongdoings and send it in a package to the New York senator. The senator's aide received the file and gave it to the senator. The senator instructed him to return it to "Sanford Marks," saying it was a family matter.

Recently, I spoke to Jim and Sharon McCormack, and they both had vivid memories of Kathie describing a similar situation taking place right before she went missing.

According to Jim, Kathie told him she'd collected information about a suspicious fire at a building owned by the Dursts. Someone died in the fire. Apparently, Kathie created a dossier about the fire and sent it to Daniel Patrick Moynihan, the U.S. senator from New York. Kathie told Jim that her dossier was then returned to Seymour Durst by Moynihan's office.

Two weeks before her disappearance, Kathie went to a baby shower for Sharon McCormack, who was pregnant with her daughter Elizabeth. Sharon told me that during the shower "Kathie was carrying on, very emotional, and said repeatedly, 'I'm petrified of Seymour and Bobby. I think they're going to kill me. If anything happens to me, look into Seymour and Bobby.'" She had a few glasses of red wine at the shower, but Sharon said Kathie was not drunk. "Just very emotional. She was very scared of her husband's father and her husband. There were sixty people at the shower, and everyone was concerned." Kathie wound up spending the night with Jim and Sharon. "We said to her, 'Leave Bobby. Just walk away.' But Kathie thought she had all this information and she was going to use it. She told us, 'Bobby and I have been married for nine years. I deserve more than he's offering.' She was a feisty woman and she was not going to just walk away. She wanted more."

Sharon remembers Kathie as a classy, beautiful, and generous person who planned her and Jim's rehearsal dinner before their wedding and sent her flowers to the hospital when Elizabeth was born (one week before Kathie disappeared). Kathie always thought of others. Sharon told me a story I'd never heard before. "When Kathie was a nurse, she led the campaign to get rid of nurses' caps," she said. "They were always falling down or distracting her. So she waged a campaign to end the requirement and it worked. No more caps."

This gutsy, fearless New York Irishwoman was willing to wage another battle with the Dursts. She was one tough woman.

In 2003, I'd been obsessed with the Kathleen Durst case for four years. In all that time, I'd never had a single conversation with Robert. If I couldn't get to my prime suspect, though, I might be able to get something out of Douglas. It'd been twenty-two years since his sister-in-law vanished. He'd never once, not even after the murders of Susan Berman and Morris Black, talked about Kathie publicly (or privately, apparently). Maybe his conscience was starting to crack? It was worth a try to find out.

My primary objective was to get as much information as I could. Robert Durst worked in the organization until '94, twelve years after Kathie's disappearance. Maybe Robert Durst said something or did something incriminating that Douglas hadn't recognized as incriminating *at the time*. I hoped to find out.

My second objective was to tell Douglas to his face, "Robert is a dangerous guy. He's a serial killer." I'd said the same thing to Thomas, and to Debrah Lee Charatan during our cigarette break on the fire escape in 2001. I was even *more* worried about Debrah. She hadn't grown up with Robert. She didn't know the essence of this murderer the way Douglas had to.

My third objective was to satisfy my curiosity. I wanted to look this man in the eye and see what he was made of. I'd been convinced for years that he helped his brother cover up Kathie's murder, if not in action, in gross inaction. Would sitting across the table from him give me any indication if I was right? What would it be like to break bread with the Devil's brother?

I put in a call to Douglas's office and requested a face-to-face. His lawyer called back with the date for a meeting—with the lawyer himself.

Uh, no.

"I want to talk to Douglas Durst," I said when I called back.

"What is this regarding?"

"Well, in case you haven't noticed, his brother is the target of several investigations and I would like to speak to Douglas Durst about them."

Douglas, I was told, didn't want to see me. But, if I so desired, I could send the lawyer my list of questions and he'd . . .

"I'm not going to ask questions through you. I need to see *him*. I need to talk with *him*."

We went back and forth for a week. It started to look as if this meeting wouldn't happen at all. And then I pulled out the big guns and told the lawyer, "We can do this a nice way or we can bring your client into the courthouse. Sometimes, the press sees people they recognize coming in. I don't know how they find out to be there at the right time . . . So, he can come in voluntarily or we can put him in front of the grand jury and force him to testify under oath. What works for you?"

The next day, Roseanne came into the office and said, "Douglas Durst on the phone for you."

That was fast. I picked up the phone and said, "Hello?"

He said, "This is Douglas Durst. I understand you want to talk to me." His voice was soft but clear. No gravelly muttering and odd inflections like his brother's.

"Yes, I do."

"I'd rather not come to your office."

Understandable. "Okay. Where do you want to meet? Someplace quiet." I was willing to accommodate the guy because *I* was the one who needed something from him.

A few hours later, he called back with a date and a time, but not a place. "I'll let you know where to go on the day of."

So it's going to be like that? It felt like I was in *The Godfather*, like Clemenza is going to drive me to a secret location for a sit-down with Sonny.

I called my driver James (O'Donnell, not Clemenza) and told him, "We have a 7:30 a.m. meeting."

"Where, Boss?"

"I don't know."

"In Manhattan?" he asked.

"Probably."

In the morning, I got into the car, and Durst's people finally sent an address on West Forty-Third Street. Neither James nor I recognized it. I assume it was a building the Durst Organization owned.

James pulled to a stop at the curb. The door was unmarked. He said, "Boss, I don't want you to go in there alone." These guys were loyal to me and very concerned about me. When you're the DA, you get death threats. I didn't take them nearly as seriously as my security detail.

"What's he going to do? Kill me?" I said.

But James insisted. He walked me in.

The door opened into a restaurant, Le Madeleine. New York is full of places like this that only a select few even know about. The décor seemed very south-of-France, with grapevines hanging from the ceiling. The tables were covered with starched white tablecloths and silverware. It was nice. Clean. Eerily quiet.

Except for James and me, the place was empty.

What now? I thought.

A waiter appeared and walked toward us. He nodded at James and said to me, "This way, ma'am."

He walked me over to a booth in the back. I took a seat. A few minutes later, Douglas Durst came into the restaurant and walked straight over to the booth.

He was average height, maybe a bit shorter, but not as puny as Robert. He was average weight, maybe a little heavy. Short brown hair, sloppily cut. He was kind of nerdy. If I saw him on the street, I wouldn't have been impressed. He was just kind of schleppy. Although he was, without a doubt, a master of the universe, he did *not* come across as one. I didn't notice any family resemblance to Robert. But, then again, when I last saw Robert in a Pennsylvania courtroom, he wasn't in a suit like Douglas. He was in an orange jumpsuit and shackles.

Douglas sat down. The waiter took our orders. All I wanted was coffee. I wasn't in the mood for breakfast. In fact, I couldn't believe that I was sitting down with the Devil's brother in a restaurant, albeit closed. Not quite what I was accustomed to when interviewing potential witnesses. I was polite but firm.

I said, "You know we're still investigating the Kathie Durst case. I have a couple of questions."

"Ask your questions," he said.

"What can you tell me about your brother?" I always started with a very general question.

"My brother doesn't work for the company anymore," he said, trying to distance himself from Robert. "He hasn't for some time."

Really? Does he think I'm stupid? I thought. I went on.

"What was his marriage to Kathie like?"

"It was a long time ago and I don't remember that much about it." Again, distancing himself.

Okay, I see where this is going . . .

Then, he turned the tables and asked me a question. "What can *you* tell me about my brother?"

I hadn't anticipated that Douglas would come into this meeting with the same agenda that I did: to get as much information as possible. It was clear he'd agreed to do it so he could learn what I knew about the case, and about him, not so he could give me information to ease his guilty conscience or to solve the case.

The conversation was circular in that way. It reminded me of my chat with Debrah Lee Charatan. All the people in Robert Durst's life were cagey. I told him that I knew his brother was a very dangerous man.

He asked, "What's going to happen?"

"I don't know. I'm trying to find out from you. What can you tell me? Your brother Thomas is afraid of Robert. Are you afraid of him? Are you taking precautions for yourself and your family?"

I knew already that Douglas had hired bodyguards after Robert went on the lam in 2001.

(Comically, in *The Jinx*, when Robert was interviewed in prison as to why his brother had hired protection, he said, "Because he's a pussy." Douglas's reply to that was quoted in several sources: "If that makes me a pussy, then I'm a pussy." Okay, then.)

In 2003, he didn't strike me as a wimp. He was nonplussed by my warnings, and canny about what he said and expressed. He was the kind of guy who sat at a lot of negotiation tables and played a lot of poker. His strategy was to be soft-spoken and understated. Not macho at all. He showed strength with stealth.

Maybe he and his brother had some things in common after all.

I made it clear that I was speaking as the DA, and that I was not done with Kathie's case and would look to impanel a grand jury and, if I did so, he would be called. I always try to give people the benefit of the doubt. Hopefully, their civic responsibilities would kick in. More often than not, I am disappointed. I was threatening him, and fishing. I thought if he believed we'd convene a grand jury, he'd start talking to me right there, in that French restaurant. It was largely an empty threat. But that didn't stop me from making it.

Douglas hadn't risen to the top of the Durst Organization because he's stupid. He had to know that my mission wasn't necessarily to help him. It was to prove my case.

"I'd like to see my brother put behind bars as much as anyone," he said. "He's a danger to me and my family, and to society at large."

I thought, *Don't give me this hogwash!* Of course, it was in his interest to get this guy locked up *now*. The whole country wanted him locked up. He was acquitted after dismembering a human being, to universal public outrage.

I wanted to say, "If you were so intent on getting Robert locked up, why didn't you do more in 1982? Or 2000?"

Instead, I asked him straight, "Why was Scoppetta hired? Why wasn't Kathie's disappearance on the front page every day? Why wasn't there more attention on the case?" I was trying to tee him up. That's what we do.

"There *was* a lot of attention on the case."

I was an ADA in Westchester, running a domestic violence unit, training NYPD about the signs of spousal abuse, and I never heard of it.

"Scoppetta?"

"I didn't make that decision."

"What advice did he give you?"

"I don't remember."

"Were you at the meetings?"

"I don't remember."

Perhaps Douglas had Asperger's, too.

"Did your family block the NYPD investigation into Kathie's disappearance?"

He said, "No."

"Was there a Durst Organization cover-up?"

"No."

"Where is Kathie?"

"I have no idea," he said.

"Do you recall having any thoughts when it happened?"

"No."

He wasn't going to say *anything*. Neither was I. The meeting was over before it even began.

I wouldn't call it a waste of my time. The coffee was excellent.

My breakfast with the Devil's brother lasted half an hour tops. I didn't even finish my coffee. We ended it politely. I asked that he take precautions and to notify my office if he heard from Robert. "If anything comes up, the door is always open," I said. "Please stay in touch with me."

Although it was tense at points, the meeting never got heated. It was poker. He was looking at me and I was looking at him. I was the one with the power. He had the most to lose.

But Douglas played the game very well. If he thought I was going to confront him with new evidence, he was wrong, and probably extremely relieved. He agreed to meet me only because he wanted to know what I had. He probably kicked his heels up when he walked out of the restaurant.

I got back into my DA car with James, disappointed.

The grand jury idea wasn't going to pan out, I realized. I'd just get more denials and claims of ignorance. Without hard evidence, there would be no point. I didn't think I had enough to convince twelve people beyond a reasonable doubt that Kathie's murder had to be *intentional*.

Why intentional? Why was that a sticking point?

People have often asked me, "Why didn't you charge him with manslaughter?"

Manslaughter is a brutal accident, like they had a fight, she was drinking, he pushed her, she hit her head. He could say anything and get away with manslaughter, not that it would matter. New York had a statute of limitation on manslaughter—five years. To charge Robert with manslaughter, I needed a time machine to take me back to 1987.

It had to be intentional murder or nothing. And people have criticized me for not pursuing a lesser charge.

Everyone thinks he's a fucking genius.

IN JANUARY 2015, ELEVEN years after it happened, Douglas described our legendary meeting to Jim Dwyer of the *New York Times*. He said that I arranged the meeting. True. After that, our recollections differ.

He said, "[Pirro] told me that, based on what happened in Texas, Bob was not smart enough to make his wife disappear and I must've helped him. I told her that if I had any way of getting my brother behind bars, I would do everything I could, but there was nothing I could do."

I never would have said that Robert was too stupid to do anything. Based on what happened in Texas, the guy *proved* that he was smart enough to kill people and get away with it! It was always my contention that Robert was a chess player, planning his moves long in advance. He might make stupid mistakes, but he was by no means an idiot.

Was the Durst family complicit in the suppression of evidence and in using their influence with the NYPD? Was there a cover-up from the get-go? From the start, I saw an ample basis to pose these questions.

• The elevator operator and the doorman at 37 Riverside Drive who claimed to have seen Kathie that night and the next morning were both employees of the Durst Organization and had jobs to protect.

• The Dursts hired a high-powered criminal defense attorney when Robert was never considered a suspect or under arrest.

• No one in the Durst family gave interviews to the police at the time. The police didn't even ask for an interview with any of them.

• Robert's college buddy became the family spokesperson. Why didn't they use the in-house PR guy, Marty Matz, to handle press? Was it because a pro would have encouraged them to offer a decent reward, not the ten thousand dollars Durst put up, or to start a Kathleen Durst Foundation to help solve missing-persons cases? He would have organized a citywide search and put Robert on TV, begging the public for tips. Did that never happen because the Dursts had to know, or at least suspect, that Kathie would never be found, and that Robert could not pull off being the aggrieved husband?

Do I know for sure that there was a cover-up? Can I pinpoint specifics of proof, how someone gave an envelope full of money to this person, or made a hushed phone call to that person, or gave an arm-twist to someone else, and so on up the chain? No.

What I do know is that the Dursts were heartless in not reaching out to the McCormack family to express support or sympathy, especially to Kathie's then seventy-year-old mother.

I also know that the daughter-in-law of the family that built the landscape of New York disappeared and they were satisfied with a half-assed police investigation, including a detective and a lieutenant who believed she probably just ran off with another guy.

Instead, after all these years, until *The Jinx* was upon them, the extended Durst family essentially dared not speak the name Kathleen. Wendy's son Evan Kreeger said as much in *The Jinx*. Whenever he'd tried to ask his parents or his uncle Douglas about his aunt Kathie, he was told by the older generation that it was something they did not talk about.

At the very least, it's a conspiracy of silence.

As far as I am concerned, Douglas Durst is not the man he wants the New York City real-estate world to believe he is. He presents himself as a patron of education and the arts, donating to the New School and the Roundabout Theater Company. He bought an organic farm. On *The Jinx*, he was given an award from Children's Rights, a welfare-advocacy group. But Douglas and his family failed to protect Kathie from the psychopath who is their son and brother. And, even if they managed to be blind to Robert's nature prior to Kathie's disappearance, their failure to act afterward as Robert went on to kill again . . . and again, is unforgivable.

Douglas's brother Thomas suspected from the start that Robert had killed Kathie. The report of Scoppetta's investigator made clear that Robert was lying. Robert says Douglas was at meetings with the investigator. Douglas says he never spoke with the investigator. I believe he did. But whomever he spoke to, I do not believe that the heir to the kingdom had no clue that a major crisis was unfolding in his own office. I find it remarkable that when he spoke to the *New York Times*' Dwyer thirty-three years later, he admitted that he suspected Robert, although he was uncertain. "Even though he wasn't my favorite person in the world, it was hard for me to believe—to completely believe—that he had killed her." Given what's at stake, why didn't an incomplete belief incite Douglas and his family to action?

Certainly the family is quick to act to protect themselves from attack. As I was finishing my edit of this very chapter in July 2015, I received a letter from Richard Emery, Douglas Durst's lawyer. It was a warning to me, and to Simon & Schuster, that if I wrote anything in my book that defamed him, Douglas would sue.

Douglas sued Jarecki on the eve of the airing of *The Jinx* to determine his sources and to express his concern that the documentary wouldn't be fair to his family.

Then he threatened to sue me.

Douglas and his family have all the money in the world. They have used it to defend a psychopathic murderer. They have used it to protect their name. But as far as I am concerned, there is simply not enough money in the world to buy them free of their failure, whether by action or inaction, to do right by Kathie Durst and ultimately Susan Berman and Morris Black.

| ALL BAD THINGS

Although he'd been acquitted of murder, Robert Durst served time in federal prison for bail jumping and tampering with evidence (aka Morris Black's body). He was released in July 2005. Counting the time served while awaiting trial in Galveston, he spent three years total in prison, a pale and anemic comparison to the ninety-nine years he should have served if it weren't for that judge and jury.

After his release, he was put on parole for two years and allowed to serve it in Houston, where he had a home. Of course, Durst did what he so loved to do: returned to the scene of the crime. He drove from Houston to Galveston to visit the flophouse at 2213 Avenue K, where Durst did the wet work on Black's body. I have no idea how long he hung out on Avenue K, or what he did there. Probably sat in his car and replayed the disgusting memories.

He also violated the terms of his parole by going shopping in a Houston mall. In an ironic twist, he bumped into none other than his salvation, Judge Susan Criss.

Can you imagine that awkward run-in?

Criss: "Hello, Robert. I didn't expect to see you at Victoria's Secret."

Durst: "Hello, Susan. Did you get the check I sent you? Consider it a gift."

In all seriousness, Criss described their mall encounter to journalist Pamela Chelin of the website Mashable as "friendly." Apparently, she spotted him first. When he noticed her, he dropped his phone. As he was trying to put the pieces back together, she said, "Hi, Bob."

"And he said, 'I can't believe you're talking to me,' " she told Chelin. "I said, 'It's a job. It's not personal and it's just a conversation,' but I was wondering how I could end this and get away from it. It was the first time I had seen him in the free world and he's not a dangerous-looking person, so I said, 'Happy holidays,' and walked off."

Then Judge Criss reported him to the parole board. Durst found himself back in federal prison for another couple of months.

While in prison for his last stint in 2006, Durst settled his lawsuit with the Durst Organization, cutting his last thin thread to his family. He'd sued Douglas and Jonathan Durst, a cousin, back in 2001 when they tried to limit Robert's access to his family trust funds after they learned about his secret marriage to Debrah.

Robert settled the suit for $65 million.

A month after that windfall, he walked out of prison a free man in every sense of the word.

So in June 2006, a few months after Durst was released from his second round of probation in Houston, Judge Susan Criss called the Galveston police in a panic, saying someone left a cat head in front of her house. One of the first cops on the scene was Sergeant J. Caldwell. According to his report, "She believed this to be the work of Robert Durst."

Officer Garrett Groce examined the gray tabby's "fully intact head along with the two front legs." The cat was *on the road*, seven feet from the sidewalk.

Criss told Groce she didn't recognize the cat and thought it'd been put there by Durst "in order to make her feel in fear of her safety," per his report.

A good investigator, Groce proceeded to interview Criss's neighbors and quickly learned that the tabby did, in fact, belong to one of them. Indications were that it had been run over by a car but in light of the judge's concern, the cat remains were sent to Texas A&M for further analysis, including DNA testing of the claws, X-rays, and a total necropsy of the poor animal, who'd already suffered enough.

The findings were consistent with the roadkill scenario. No human DNA in the claws. No suspicious fiber or blood. The lab doctors determined that the body was torn apart—*not cut* with a knife or a saw à la Durst.

The matter was closed. And yet, after *The Jinx* aired, and media requests came pouring in, Susan Criss went on TV and exaggerated the facts. As she recounted to *Inside Edition* in March 2015, she found a "perfectly clean and preserved cat head cut up by someone who knew what they were doing."

Instead of the world loathing and mocking her for the way she ran her courtroom, she tried to turn herself into one of Durst's victims. This judge was hardly a victim. She was investigated for ethical violations and in the years after the trial pocketed cash donations from Dick DeGuerin and Chip Lewis. According to Joel Bennett, she was written up in private reprimands—one for threatening to keep polls open after their closing times—and overstepped her rights. If she had served as a judge in Westchester, I would have filed grievance after grievance against her.

She dusted off her nine-year-old cat-head story, which by all indications was hogwash.

It makes me livid that so many of the players have accused *me* of using this case for media attention, when, in truth, it was exactly what they were doing themselves.

They still are.

What's the saying, that you always recognize the traits in others that are the least appealing in yourself?

Look, I can understand Susan Criss's state of mind in 2006. She spotted a dead cat in the road, knew Durst had just completed his parole, and got a little nervous. But the exhaustive investigation—I have to believe never before (or since) in the history of Texas had roadkill received so much attention or cost the taxpayers so much—should have proven to Criss that she had nothing to worry about. And yet, when she sniffed out an opportunity to get back in the spotlight, she went on TV and said Durst chopped off the head of a cat with surgical precision, just like Morris Black's, and left it on her very doorstep as a warning that he was coming to Igor *her*.

Do you not feel the *drama*? This woman had to beat a dead cat for more attention.

She also told *Inside Edition*, "I believe that Robert Durst is a serial killer."

Really? Ya think?

Not to belabor my point that Criss didn't belong on the bench, but she recently tainted a jury and set free a child pornographer.

Oh, yes.

I did a whole segment on this case on *Justice with Judge Jeanine*. I'm very proud of what I wrote, so here is my summary of the case:

> *Imagine a judge arresting a prospective juror because he requests a religious exemption. Prospective Juror No. 48 in Texas tells Judge Susan Criss he can't look at evidence of child pornography for religious reasons, generally an acceptable excuse for not serving on a jury. Now, additionally, the juror tells Judge Criss that as a Jehovah's Witness it is not his place to judge.*
>
>   *Criss, however, wasn't hearing any of it. Her response was, if a child could suffer through the abuse, then an adult can certainly*

watch the video. "So if it grosses you out, you can take it out on the person in punishment. That's what my God tells me," Criss said. She then tells Juror 48 what she will do if he refuses to look at the evidence, saying, "So you want to find out what I'll do? You'll find out what I'll do. You want to find out what my God will tell me to do? Let's test it, buddy. Let's test it." Criss continues on her tirade, saying, "If you get picked on this jury, you get picked on this jury. And Jehovah can visit you in jail."

Now, at that point, she directs court officers to arrest Juror 48 and remove him from the courtroom. The judge's outrageous behavior toward this juror created the basis for a reversal of the conviction of the child pornographer of a fourteen-year-old. The appellate court found fundamental error: "The religious beliefs of the citizens of the state of Texas—whatever they might be—are far too important to be subjected to mockery, derision, ridicule or criticism by any of the trial judiciary of this state." The court reasoned that actually arresting the juror and putting him in handcuffs in front of the other prospective jurors had a chilling effect on the jury and it precluded the defendant from getting a fair trial.

Way to go, District Judge Susan Criss from Texas, for creating grounds for reversal of the conviction of the lowest of the low in our society.

That was in May 2015. She has since left the bench. Everyone in Texas can now breathe a sigh of relief.

While Durst was in prison and on parole, I was going through a tumultuous time in my own life. I made the decision to leave the DA's office in 2005. It had nothing to do with fear of losing a bid for a fourth term. I felt thirty-two years in law enforcement was enough.

I don't believe that government should necessarily be a lifetime employment just because it's comfortable or because someone thinks he or she is entitled to it. I believe in term limits. There are none for the Westchester DA. I imposed the limit on myself.

I walked out of the DA's office with a stellar record—and I don't believe a woman should downplay her accomplishments. She should crow about them.

• Four hundred thousand cases were prosecuted during my tenure as DA.

• My office had a 98 percent conviction rate for felony cases at the superior court level.

• Under my watch, there was a 15 percent increase in convictions . . .

• And a 10 percent drop in crime.

• I founded the Domestic Violence and Child Abuse Unit, the first of its kind in the nation.

• I founded the High Technology Crimes Bureau, the first of its kind, to catch Internet pedophiles, and did. Over a hundred of them.

• I created the "no-drop" policy of pursuing domestic violence crimes, even if the victim wanted to drop the case.

• I prosecuted rapists, murderers, wife-beaters, deadbeat dads, embezzlers, slumlords, racketeers, wiseguys, white-collar criminals, animal torturers, sexual deviants, crooked cops, hate criminals, pedophile priests, robbers, thieves, kidnappers, and drug dealers, among other scumbags.

Of course, there was one case I wasn't able to indict, let alone prosecute. Durst was my white whale.

I'd been accused of being politically ambitious by every one of my critics without having made any noise about seeking higher office. But after decades in law enforcement and four political campaigns, the attorney general's race seemed like a logical next step.

I'd chased a psychopath for years, and the chase had taken a toll on me. At no point did I ever think, "Just drop it. Forget about it. Distance yourself from it." Absolutely not. If there was any stone to turn over to get Durst, any worms under that stone to pick through, I'd do it, in or out of office.

Naturally, when my term as DA ended, no-level Ellen Strauss blasted me in the press for leaving office without indicting Durst and for caring more about my relentless pursuit of publicity in other states than meeting with the McCormack family in New York.

All police investigation is a team effort. We were all doing our part. Everybody was. For my part, I interviewed Debrah. I created the tristate task force and searched Durst's Chevy personally. I met with Douglas, as uneventful as that was. I got the DAs in Los Angeles and Galveston on the phone. I kept the money flowing into the investigation. And, yes, I spoke to the press. There were times when the McCormacks were frustrated and disappointed by the pacing of our investigation. They wanted an arrest ASAP, but we weren't in a position to make one. They'd been waiting since 1982, seventeen years longer than my office had been involved. Despite my assuring the family we were doing everything we could, Jim McCormack in particular would complain, "You're not doing enough."

He didn't understand the legal ins and outs. There was no point in indicting until I knew I could get a conviction. Meanwhile, Joe Becerra was encouraging the McCormacks' impatience, telling them, "We're ready."

If there was such a solid case, why didn't the DA who followed me indict Robert? She's got more evidence than I had in 2005. I didn't indict, and she hasn't either, because until Durst's bathroom confession, there was no way in hell we could get a unanimous guilty verdict for intentional murder on the evidence we had.

The worst possible outcome would be for Robert Durst to be acquitted. That would mean we would lose all chance to get justice for Kathie. And Robert Durst would skate on another one.

Even as a private citizen, no longer a member of law enforcement, I vowed to track Durst and keep both eyes peeled. If he so much as pissed himself in public (which he finally did, and got arrested for, in 2014!), I'd know about it. If he came into my neck of the woods, I'd hear about it.

Another twist: When Durst did come to Westchester, he stayed at the Ritz in White Plains, in the same complex Al was living in for a while. A friend then always called to give me the heads-up, "Durst's in town." He came often. I learned he was there in July and December 2009 and March 2010. Whenever Durst was a guest at the Ritz, female staff were not allowed on his floor without security. A source who works there told me about this precaution and Durst's gruff manner and secrecy. He rarely went out and talked to no one.

Still, time to lock the doors, set the alarm, and load the guns.

THE DAY AFTER I lost the election for attorney general of New York State, Warner Bros. Productions called. I didn't even have an agent. They wanted me to do a courtroom show called *Judge Jeanine Pirro*.

I'd been thinking about doing TV for a while. In fact, as a sitting DA, I'd been approached. That would have been inappropriate, of course. But the timing of the Warner Bros. call was serendipitous. With law enforcement and politics behind me, I turned to entertainment. I wasn't concerned about being unemployed. I just saw it as my next great adventure.

We developed the show for a year, and then premiered in 2009. *Judge Jeanine Pirro* was syndicated and did quite well. I even won an Emmy for it in 2011. At the same time, I started working for Fox News as a commentator. When *Judge Jeanine* wasn't renewed, I created a one-hour news-format show called *Justice with Judge Jeanine* on Fox News.

Andrew Jarecki's feature film *All Good Things* was released in 2010.

I'd practically forgotten about that guy.

He'd come to our offices in 2003 after the acquittal and met with David Hebert. He said he was working on a movie about the case. He wanted access, records, interviews, our entire file on an open case. After meeting with Jarecki, David didn't think this project was an attempt to understand and explain the reality and banality of evil. Jarecki was captivated by the psychology and morality of a scheming, violent individual and he wanted to explore that creatively. It sounded to David like Jarecki's movie might show Durst in a sympathetic light, and we wanted nothing to do with it. It would not further the interests of law enforcement, period. So David gave Andrew the brush-off, saying, "Thank you for coming in. It's an open and pending case and we generally do not release investigative material. We're going to pass, but do stay in touch."

And that was that.

Or so I thought.

A nosy ADA in our office named Kevin Hynes got wind of the Jarecki inquiry and asked a lot of questions about it. I should have known to be wary.

Some background on Kevin Hynes: He worked in my office from 2002 to 2004. When I hired him, Durst was in prison in Texas, awaiting trial. Kevin was *not* in my office in 1999 when the lake and the

South Salem cottage were searched, or when we interviewed Kathie's friends and family. He missed the murders of Susan Berman and Morris Black. Given that he had some previous experience as a prosecutor, we had him take a look at the Durst file when he started in my office. He had fresh eyes. He might see something.

As it turned out, he had nothing to offer about Durst, or to law enforcement in general. I never should have hired him.

To my misfortune, after I'd hired him, I learned he was peddling a book project about John F. Kennedy Jr. Hynes and Kennedy worked in the Manhattan DA's office together. After John died in that horrific plane crash, along with his new wife and her sister, Hynes intended to exploit their supposed friendship for profit. I have since gotten my hands on a copy of his book proposal. The entire package was a sick exploitation of Hynes's just-buried so-called best friend. Not too surprisingly, it went nowhere.

I should've been on alert when I heard this story and questioned Hynes's character. But his father was Charles "Joe" Hynes, the Brooklyn DA, a friend of mine. He said his son was smart and would be an asset to my office. I had a great deal of respect for Joe and believed him. I had met Kevin several times socially and found him to be impressive, quick, witty, and articulate. Coincidentally, Kevin had also written a letter of support for Al after his conviction. He'd done good work with defense attorneys in Westchester. At first glance, he was extremely ballsy, a not-afraid-of-anything, outgoing guy.

You hire different people for different reasons. He wouldn't be a good investigator, but I thought he would be great in a courtroom. I was always on the lookout for a fearless prosecutor with the gift of gab who could convince a jury to convict. So I hired him.

Terrible mistake.

Almost immediately, he managed to make enemies out of just about everyone. It's telling that a truckload of fancy furniture arrived before he did. He cared a lot about the trappings. How his office looked was more important than what he did in there. He cut corners, and took shortcuts, which you don't do in law enforcement when you have to chase down every tiny lead and present precise facts and figures. The ballsy quality I liked? It had an aggressive edge.

And then there was an incident with Hynes that had me boot him—with both Manolos—out of my office.

One night in July 2004, Hynes took out one of the county's cars, a 1997 Mercury, crashed it into an embankment in Armonk, and left the scene of the accident without reporting it. The police found the wrecked car with the airbags deployed and an empty Heineken bottle on the seat.

He left the scene of an accident with alcohol in the car. My staff and I had spent the last decade visiting high schools in Westchester, lecturing kids about the dangers of drunk driving. I was known as a notoriously tough judge when it came to teens and alcohol, and anyone arrested for DWI.

That one of my own had been engaged in such conduct was a black mark on my office, and I was livid.

It gets worse.

At 5:00 a.m.—one hour before the police found the crashed car—Hynes walked into a nearby Texaco station. According to the police interview with the man working the late shift there, Hynes walked in and tried to buy beer but was refused (in Westchester, we had a cutoff time for alcohol purchases). He had a black burn mark on the right front pocket of his pant leg. He then asked for a straw, while shifting on his feet nervously and repeatedly wiping his nose.

We all know what that means.

The station cashier said Hynes looked intoxicated, on drugs, or both. He took his straw and left, only to come back in later to buy a Coke, and then loiter in the parking lot in a daze for half an hour. It seemed shady to the cashier, so he reported it.

It gets even worse.

Hynes was picked up in the Texaco parking lot by another investigator, who denied doing so. Did these two really think that as the DA, I couldn't figure out what happened? I learned the truth about their movements from pings on their cell phones.

Hynes would claim he left the scene of his accident because he was afraid for his safety—in Armonk, a wealthy suburb. Ridiculous. *He* was the most dangerous man in Armonk that night. He eventually did call in the accident and admit to being the driver, but he didn't go to the police station for a Breathalyzer test for a period of time that would have allowed alcohol, if any, to be metabolized out of his system. Leaving the scene of an accident was a lesser charge than DWI, which he knew all too well.

Chief investigator Casey Quinn unearthed that Hynes wasn't alone that night. He was with another person. Many suspected it was a married female ADA with whom he had an extremely close friendship.

I moved the Hynes matter to another prosecutor's office because I clearly had a conflict. Eventually, he was charged only with leaving the scene. Although witnesses had attested to his drunken appearance that night, the prosecutor couldn't prove how drunk he was given the time lapse, so no additional charges were filed against him.

Hynes wisely resigned a few days later. He knew I never wanted to see him again. I ended up asking the investigator who lied about picking him up at the Texaco to leave the office, and got his retirement paperwork on my desk promptly.

In my press statement, I said, "It is well known that my office has been at the forefront of combating the problem of the illegal use and sale of alcohol. As public servants we are held to a higher standard."

Months later, I went to see my dermatologist, Amy Newburger, whose brilliant daughter was an intern in my office. She said, "Too bad about Kevin Hynes."

I said, "What's bad about it? He was drinking and driving and he lied about it. Good riddance."

She said, "I thought you knew he had a drinking problem. He used to drink at lunch. He took my daughter to the Cheesecake Factory in White Plains and drank heavily."

She thought I *knew*? I had no idea! I would have fired him as soon as I found out! It wasn't bad enough that he was drinking at lunch. He took a young intern with him.

Kevin told people I'd be sorry for firing him one day. He and Joe Becerra were best pals (perhaps Kevin should write a book about *their* friendship?), and I'm sure they bonded over their common hatred of me.

Hey, I didn't get drunk and drive a car into a shrub. I didn't leave the scene and wander, wasted, into a Texaco and ask some kid behind the register for a straw while repeatedly wiping my nose. But here's another guy who had it out for me because I refused to clean up his mess.

I was not the cleaning lady.

I was the Boss.

It was difficult for some fully grown boys to accept that. If anyone disrespected the office of the district attorney, he was gone. Kevin had a truck come get his furniture, and that was the end of him. I never liked that furniture anyway.

So fast-forward to 2010. *All Good Things* (the name of the Vermont health food store that Robert and Kathie once owned) was released. My son Alex saw it and was *furious*. "It made you look really bad, Ma," he told me. "Really bad."

Alex lived through those years with me, and he knew what it was really like. How hard I worked, how frightened Al was for our safety. Apparently, Jarecki reduced it all to a cliché. He turned me into a cartoon character of a media-obsessed dragon lady. He was Dick DeGuerin in a Hollywood hoodie and goatee.

I didn't see the movie in theaters. But then curiosity got the best of me, and I bought the DVD.

About halfway through, actor Diane Venora made her first appearance as "Janice Rizzo." The name alone was Italian baiting. Why not have my character carry around a box of spaghetti and a jar of tomato sauce instead of a briefcase? Really?

If only I had the power to indict, I'd charge Diane Venora for overacting.

Jarecki made the character look shady. There was a scene when she was barking demands at her office lackey with her high heels up on her desk, like she had nothing better to do than schedule television appearances and file her nails. The last time I filed my own nails was when I was in grammar school. This character wasn't me. She wasn't on a mission to protect women from domestic violence. She wasn't a passionate advocate for the underdog. And if you saw what my desk really looked like in 2004, covered in case files, the phone lighting up 24/7, you'd know how absurd laid-back "Janice Rizzo" was.

I worked my tail off. Try spending fourteen hours working in Manolo Blahniks and not put your feet up.

I was furious about the depiction of my breakfast meeting with Douglas.

I can't prove it, but I believe Hynes reached out to Jarecki on his own after he resigned in 2004 and told him about that meeting. No one outside my office knew it'd taken place. Kevin sat in an office adjacent to mine. I must have told him something about the meeting. But what was presented in the movie was nothing like what actually happened.

The actor who played me walked into a deserted restaurant and sat down at the table with the actor who played Douglas. Then "I" said, "How can I help you?" It suggested to the viewer I was there to play ball with the Dursts, and that he bought me off to stop the investigation into Robert's crimes.

Hog.

Wash.

It was infuriating that my career in law enforcement had been reduced to a vapid, one-dimensional caricature. "Janice Rizzo" was a cartoon in an okay suit.

I couldn't have expected Jarecki to make me a three-dimensional character. But even in his vulgar depiction, he could have given the character *some* depth. The movie was just another example of a man slamming a woman in power. He played into the public's fear of an "ambitious LADY." Not just me. *Any* woman in power was someone to be feared—and criticized out of existence. It was easier to make Durst sympathetic than to make a powerful woman decent.

But I didn't dwell on it. I had a TV show to do and many other things to deal with. I thought, *Done thinking about that. Moving on.*

Everyone got a bad shake in *All Good Things*.

Jim McCormack, played by Nick Offerman, came off as a bumbling idiot.

Susan Berman was portrayed as a strung-out party girl.

Douglas was portrayed as a vain, cold, heartless schemer. That didn't ring true to me. My take on Douglas was "brilliant coward."

The worst offense: Kirsten Dunst as "Kathie Marks" was a coke-snorting glutton for punishment.

My stomach turned watching love scenes between Kirsten Dunst and Ryan Gosling as "David Marks." Was Jarecki going for a psycho-romance?

Never before or since has a shirtless Ryan Gosling made me throw up in my mouth.

As a whole, the movie made a lot of leaps over some perilous chasms. Spoiler alert: "David Marks" was portrayed as a misunderstood victim of his domineering father and helpless in his fight against his worst impulses. Jarecki implied that Seymour Durst, played by Frank Langella, helped Robert dispose of Kathie's body. We don't know that he didn't, but it did seem like a bit of a stretch that the old man would do the dirty work. The Morris Black character, "Malvern Bump," was construed as the shooter of Susan Berman. That was just preposterous.

Who in his or her right mind would actually pay to see this (besides me)?

Not a lot of people did, actually.

It didn't annoy me that the few who did buy a ticket or rent the disc got the wrong impression of me. What disappointed me was that my son saw it and felt offended on my behalf.

The one word that has always motivated me is not "ambition." It is "justice." I used my high profile to get justice. It was an arrow in my quiver, one of many. Jarecki bought into the superficial narrative that some had been pushing.

Apparently, Andrew's erroneous opinion of me changed when he confronted the facts of the case, put aside the fiction, and made *The Jinx*.

You can't take a psychotic, entitled, narcissist serial killer *anywhere*.

Postprobation Robert Durst seemed hell-bent on getting himself in trouble. His latest flare-ups with the law were bizarre and gratuitous.

In August 2013, Robert stalked Douglas's Manhattan town house. He was caught by a surveillance camera peering in the window, as was his usual play. Douglas had warned his brother (through attorneys) to stay away from his family. When Robert was spotted twice at the West Forty-Third Street residence of his nephew Alexander, Douglas's son, you can only imagine how spooked Douglas must have been.

So he had Robert arrested for trespassing, and he was released on $5,000 bail.

Charles Bagli reported in the *Times* that, coincidentally, the L.A.

bureau of the FBI was looking at Durst for Susan Berman. The trespassing arrest came at a particularly sensitive moment, but he wound up skating on this charge, too. In December 2014, Robert was found not guilty of trespassing. His lawyer, my old friend Steve Rabinowitz, whom I met in the Queen for a Day talk with Debrah Lee Charatan back in 2001, argued that the Durst family security guards didn't properly inform Robert to stay away.

In July 2014, Robert was arrested in Houston, his old stomping and dismembering grounds, for unsheathing himself and urinating on a candy display and a cash register at a local CVS. He claimed in court that he had a medical condition. Or maybe he just really hates gummy bears? He paid a fine of $500 and replaced $150 worth of candy.

I, for one, was asking people in my office at Fox News, "What on earth is Durst going to get arrested for next?"

In only a few months, I'd have my answer—and it would be a doozy.

| OKAY, NOW LET'S ALL WATCH *THE JINX* TOGETHER

I heard from Jarecki again in 2011, when I was in Chicago doing my syndicated courtroom show for Warner Bros. He reached me by phone and asked me to participate in *The Jinx*, a documentary he was making about the case.

He had some set.

I said, "Why would I participate? You didn't play me so well in the Ryan Gosling movie."

But I liked Andrew and I agreed to meet him for lunch or breakfast. He always came off as sincere, low-key, no big deal, an "I'm not going to harm anybody" kind of guy. He told me how the documentary project came about, that Durst himself volunteered to be interviewed after seeing *All Good Things*. Why would Jarecki devote more time, money, and effort to make another movie about the case? He'd been on it for five years already. If he hadn't lost interest or gotten frustrated by now, he might be a lifer, like Cody and me. We would never stop looking at Durst until justice was served.

But I said no. I was busy and I still didn't see what good it would do for the case or for me personally.

Andrew wore down my reluctance over a two-year period. Lots of email exchanges and lunches. He seemed to be passionate about the subject matter, with decent intentions.

When he came to my office one Saturday, we caught up, and, again, he made his pitch. "The documentary will be about right and wrong in the criminal-justice system," he said. "We might be in totally different fields, but we're focused on the same thing—justice, the truth, and settling scores." Jarecki reminded me of his previous documentary, *Capturing the Friedmans*, about a family that was destroyed by false accusations of child abuse run amok. "Whether it's *Capturing the Friedmans* or the Durst case, my goal is about getting to the truth," he said.

He seemed to be pruriently fascinated by the investigations, but I also thought he had a strong sense of right and wrong. I realized that Andrew and I *were* on the same side, that there might be a benefit to participating in this documentary after all.

My "no" changed to "maybe."

A few months later, we were having lunch at the St. Regis in New York. Andrew said, "I want you to see something." Jarecki took his iPad out of his cross-body-strap messenger bag and cued up a short video.

He gave me the tablet and I pushed play. It was Chip Lewis, one of Durst's lawyers in Galveston. Lewis said, "It was very easy for us to make her the enemy. We created this mythical creature—Jeanine Pirro. And we took liberty with how directly she was involved in the pursuit of Bob. That message played well. The jury ate that one up."

I couldn't believe my eyes and ears. He actually said, in no uncertain terms, that they knowingly played fast and loose with the truth about me in court. Why would he admit it? He must *really* think that he's a bulletproof superstar and that revealing their strategic deception would bring him to the next level or something. I would be *ashamed* if I perpetuated a fraud in a courtroom. Lewis acted proud of it.

"Son of a *bitch*."

That was it. Jarecki knew the Lewis clip would make my blood boil.

"Maybe" changed to "hell yes!"

I said, "I'm in."

The only stipulation was that I could speak to no one about the project.

Gagged again, but I had no problem agreeing this time. I didn't discuss *The Jinx* with anyone, not even Cody, who I knew was also participating in it.

My son, Alex, was upset that I was cooperating with the man who'd been so wrong about me in his previous effort. "After what Jarecki did to you in *All Good Things*? How could you ever work with him?"

I said, "He's evolved on it."

"He's just going to make money on the case again."

Many people have made money on Robert Durst (none more than his legal team). He was a cottage industry. For the record, I have been asked many times over the years to write a book about my involvement in the case, and always refused. Until Episode Five, I didn't see the point of writing a book, because Kathie's story didn't have a satisfying conclusion.

I said to Alex, "This case has been a thorn in my side for more than a decade, and if this documentary sheds more light on the Kathie Durst case, I'm happy to be a part of it."

In advance of my taping, Andrew sent me a three-page list of questions. It was well organized and thorough, starting with my personal background ("Where did you grow up?" "What was your path to becoming the DA?") and moving into Kathie's missing-persons case and our investigation into it.

He specifically asked, "New York City case versus Westchester case?" I got an inkling that Jarecki truly understood the issue. He must have seen the original files and deduced for himself that the original investigation by the NYPD had been botched.

One question on the list made me groan: "How did all the media affect the case?" Part of me wanted to talk about how the media leaks jeopardized the case and how DeGuerin had played the media like a fiddle, but I didn't.

Regarding the Susan Berman murder, he had the question, "Did you think it was at all connected to Bob and Kathie?"

Uh, *yeah*!

In the section of questions about the Galveston trial, he included, "What did you think about Bob's choice to use your investigation as part of his defense? [Pirro's name doesn't show up in the press until after Susan's murder, so Bob's story isn't true.]"

Wow. He figured it out. He actually read those papers. It proved to me that by adding that revelation to the show, Jarecki and Smerling were sticking with the facts and ditching the fiction this time around.

The last question on their list was, "Were you surprised that Bob reached out to us about telling 'his side' of the story? Bob has much to lose. Knowing something about him, can you imagine why he might do that?"

Why indeed?

Robert Durst is a narcissist. He believes the world revolves around him, and he simply couldn't resist putting his stamp on Jarecki's interpretation of the case. He is frustratingly slippery, always one step ahead of being caught. He's the kind of guy who loved to dance on that edge. He clearly got off on it. I believe he agreed to do *The Jinx* so he could feel superior, smugly smarter than Jarecki and Smerling, and that he'd get to put one over on the viewing audience. Or maybe he did want the truth to come out. On some level, it was possible that he wanted the world to know how he'd gotten away with murder. O. J. Simpson, another egomaniac, wrote a book called *If I Did It*, trying to get credit but take no responsibility. It was to be his last act. Maybe the playacting Durst had learned in Texas convinced him he could con the world as well.

• • •

We taped my interview in the fall of 2013. Jarecki, Smerling, and a crew came to my house and set up in the morning. Filming took place in the library. I was asked to sit in my big burgundy leather club chair even though I was wearing a red-orange dress. Apparently, the light was good in the library. Jarecki sat across from me, conversation style. He knew *every* fact, *every* detail, *every* aspect of the case. He kept a three-ring binder on his lap, his bible of the case, and flipped through it as we talked. The tone was polite, professional, and efficient. There was never a glitch or tense moment throughout the day. There were no egos involved. It went very smoothly. By midafternoon, they packed up their equipment and left. Start to finish, it took six hours.

I believe I was one of the last people interviewed on camera. Of course, Durst's second interview was the very last one recorded. Jarecki organized his schedule just as I would have, starting on the outside, learning the facts, and slowly working his way in, peeling that onion to the core.

The questions they'd sent and my prepared answers weren't nearly as important to them as catching on film my raw reaction to things Durst had told them. They asked me plenty, and we discussed all the facts about the case, including the defense strategy. But I could tell they were really waiting for the right moment to show me something, or tell me new bits of information they'd unearthed.

At the very end of the interview, Jarecki handed me a copy of the cadaver letter, which I already knew by heart. Then he handed me another paper and said, "Take a look at this." It was the envelope addressed to Susan on Durst's Wall Street stationery that Sareb Kaufman found in a box of his mom's things.

But I didn't know that at the time.

I asked, "Where did you get this?"

Jarecki just shook his head and said nothing.

I looked at the envelope.

It took a second for me to react. I read it and said, "Beverley," noticing the misspelling. Then I studied the envelope for a second longer, saw the handwriting similarities, and said, "Son of a bitch!"

In my head, thoughts were exploding. "Oh, my God! Here it is. All these years. Here it is. We can prove it now. We can convict him now. He did it. *Of course*, he killed her, too."

I'm sure my thought process was very similar to Robert Durst's experience of seeing the two Beverleys side by side, both of us quietly contemplating what we were looking at. I felt hot all over, flushed and glowing.

Durst's blood must have run ice cold.

Holding the envelope was like being lost in the desert and then suddenly seeing an oasis in front of you.

I'd thought I'd found a few oases before with the Durst case. But they were mirages. The two Beverleys were not a mirage. They were the ocean.

When I looked up at Jarecki and Smerling, they were looking at me intensely, and then with slight grins, probably because they knew they had gotten a genuine reaction they could use in the film. I looked at these two guys and thought to myself, *Oh, my God. They did it. They got him.*

And then another thought struck me. *God, would I love to try that case.*

I have always believed that, ultimately, the truth comes out. I said it repeatedly in the case. The Durst truth took a lot longer than most. But seeing the letter proved that patience and determination will always win in the end. Good for Jarecki and Smerling.

Good for *everyone* who fought for justice, myself included.

• • •

I WAS INVITED TO the premiere party in New York City on January 28, 2015, to watch the first episode, or "chapter" as they called it. Cody and I walked into the Time Warner Center Theater at Columbus Circle. We were both a bit wary. I didn't know what to expect. A few celebs were there—Barbara Walters, Diane Sawyer, Regis and Joy Philbin, Rosanna Scotto, Greg Kelly, Cindy Adams and Dan Abrams, and some others I had worked with from Court TV. It had a very newsy, legal vibe.

I spotted Andrew. He didn't dress too fancy for the party. He wore his jeans and zipped sweater—with a tie.

We greeted each other with a friendly hug and kiss. I said, "Congratulations!" His premiere was years in the making. It was a huge accomplishment and I hoped he was enjoying the moment.

He said to me, "There's going be closure. You will be satisfied with the outcome."

Well, okay, then. Now I could enjoy the moment, too. Cody and I sat together with absolutely no idea what was coming.

Some things that jumped out at me as I watched the first episode. Here—watch it with me:

| EPISODE ONE: A BODY IN THE BAY

• **Cody looks great!** Not only had he done excellent police work to catch Durst in Galveston, he basically narrated his odyssey and how he struggled through the crazy facts of the "female" Dorothy Ciner living at 2213 Avenue K. At the end of the episode, he summed up Durst's killer instinct perfectly: "He's not the kind of man who kills for the thrill of it. I don't believe he takes any particular pleasure from killing. But if you back him into a corner and threaten his freedom, he'll kill you."

• **Dick DeGuerin looks** *horrible*. Fat, gray, with an unflattering pop-injay lavender plaid shirt. He said, "You try to make judgments about whether you're getting the truth. I believed Bob. I believed him from the very beginning." Yes, he believed that Bob was a murderer from the very beginning, but since he could pay a defense fee in the millions, Dick would work with that.

• **Oh, my God, the Debrah Lee Charatan deposition video!** I was riveted. Instantly, I flashed back to our conversation on her office fire escape and remembered how quick-witted she was. Before she answered any question—to me and on that deposition—she had worked out all of the landmines that she might stumble upon. I was reminded of her self-confidence and condescension, which, I heard from sources in her life, were lifelong traits. Debrah believed not only that she was smarter than everyone but told many that she could be president.

The Debrah video piqued my curiosity again. What was she doing now? And was she still married to Robert?

Debrah is married. Yes, she and Robert are still married, but they don't talk. She begged him not to do *The Jinx*, and when he did it anyway, she stopped speaking to him. But she's still selling property for him, including his Fifth Avenue apartment and a house in Bridgehampton, to the tune of twenty million dollars.

Debrah is rich. Filthy rich. With millions of Durst's money, she started BCB Property Management, Inc., with her formerly estranged son, Bennat. They are buying and selling property all over the city and the Hamptons and making millions in commissions.

Debrah is in love. She lives with Steven I. Holm, a real-estate lawyer who has represented Robert in some deals. Their love nest is a luxurious Fifth Avenue apartment. Together, they run the Charatan/Holm Family Foundation, through which they donate tens of thousands of dollars to Jewish charities each year. (Side note: The foundation donates regularly to Albert Einstein Medical School.) We found a copy of the *Park East Synagogue Chronicle* from 2014 that mentioned "Mrs. Debrah Charatan Holm."

She's using her live-in boyfriend's name in temple. She never refers to herself as Mrs. Debrah Durst. That tells you all you need to know about whom she considers to be her true husband.

Debrah may be in deep shit. There's been some noise about arresting her for trying to help Robert in his failed attempt to go to Cuba. She could be charged with "aiding and abetting an attempted unlawful flight to avoid prosecution," "conspiracy to commit unlawful flight to avoid prosecution," "attempt to conceal a person from arrest," and "conspiracy to conceal a person from arrest." Each conviction could get her five years. I have no idea if she will be charged. But if she is, and she goes to prison, she will be running the place in no time. And, if she is, there is no need to cut a deal for her, since Durst has dug his own grave.

• **Why include that vintage clip of DA Morganelli and me in Pennsylvania?** John Morganelli held a press conference in Pennsylvania before Durst was extradited back to Texas in 2001 and invited me to join him to talk to the swarm of reporters. I was wearing a very tailored Chanel cashmere jacket. I loved that jacket. I gave it to my daughter, Kiki, who is now a lawyer at Kirkland and Ellis in New York City. Morganelli asked me to join him to talk to the swarm of reporters. I said, "There's no question. We'll find out what happened to Kathleen sooner or later." In my seat in the theater, I remembered thinking, *Why show that clip in episode one?* It was a nice bit of foreshadowing. By the time the series finale aired, we *would* know what happened to her.

After the premiere, Andrew and Marc sat on the stage. They insisted that Cody sit with them, and the three of them took questions.

Although there were other Durst players in the audience, only one person was brought onstage to sit with the filmmakers. It was clear that they had both respect and affection for Cody.

For the next month, I watched new episodes every Sunday on HBO, mostly at home with Lance and Mickey. There were periodic outbursts from me. I yelled at the TV screen, jumping up and down on my sofa, and frantically texted comments as new facts and inconsistencies were revealed. Cody and I watched some chapters together, both looking and commenting at the same time. Seeing all the familiar faces was sort of like a family reunion. I got to judge them all, as in, "Oh, God. This one didn't age too well," or, "She looks good." If I do say so myself, I didn't look half bad.

It was fascinating to see the attention *The Jinx* was getting. People young and old, from different walks of life, my kids, their friends, their bosses, my mom, Esther, eighty-three, were mesmerized by the case.

The following few pages are like a viewing guide of *The Jinx* and how I reacted to key moments while watching the episodes. So cue up the series again and read along, as if we were binge-watching on the couch together.

| EPISODE TWO: POOR LITTLE RICH BOY

• **Did Robert always speak about himself in the third person?** Just add it to the long list of "Ways Robert Durst Is Creepy." He explained his reasoning for finally doing an interview with a journalist after ignoring countless requests for thirty years. "I will be able to tell it my way," he said. If his version causes viewers to see "a different story to what's been put in the media, they'll have an opportunity to believe it." Or to know he's full of baloney. Or, as it finally played out, that he was an unapologetic, lying, violent serial murderer.

• **The blinking!** I have learned from body language experts that there are ways to tell whether someone is speaking the truth or lying. Great detectives swear that body language, eye shifts, and mannerisms speak louder than words. When I tried cases, I was often some distance from the person I was cross-examining because of the layout of the courtroom. The witness stand was immediately adjacent to the judge's bench, yet distant from both the defense or prosecution tables. I was always cognizant of the layout because I wanted jurors to be able to assess directly a witness's credibility. And, although there were times when I would be an in-your-face cross-examiner, I was always told to pull back by the judge. So, watching *The Jinx* was a pleasure because I could plainly see the tiniest shift in Durst's eyes. His eyes *always* shifted or blinked when what I knew were blatant lies came out of his mouth. But, to give the Devil his due, he was good.

I read fan theories online about the blinking. Some commenters believe he was wearing Japanese contact lenses called "Doe Eyes" that make the whites of the eyes appear smaller and the irises larger, giving an innocent, baby deer gaze.

Another costume! The theater never ends.

• **And the twitching!** The guy couldn't keep his facial muscles under control, which indicated to me that he was trying to project a false front. It was very distracting, how he constantly fidgeted and picked his hair. I shouted at the TV, "Stop twitching, you freak! You're twitching because you're worried, dirtbag!"

• **Bernice Durst's suicide.** I have a theory (of course) about why she did it. She had four kids under the age of seven, including a brand-new baby. Was it possible Bernice was suffering from postpartum depression? And did Robert's father really take him out to wave at Mommy and watch her jump from the roof? Did Seymour think that was a smart thing to do?

• **Jim McCormack described Robert as "Prince Charming."** True, he did have a Prince Valiant hairstyle in the late 1970s. Maybe he was a prince *then*. Kathie went to live in Vermont with him after only two dates.

• **First appearance of Gilberte and Eleanor Schwank, another one of Kathie's loyal friends.** Gilberte died on July 26, 2015. At least she lived long enough to hear Durst say it, although I know from speaking with her a few weeks before her passing that she still hoped to find out where Kathie's remains were buried.

• **Detective Michael Struk's apathy.** I threw the phone at the TV when Struk said, "Not that you're jaded about the effort you're going to put forth, but it's like maybe she's shacking up or she's just tired of this guy. He's a banana, and she doesn't want to involve herself with him anymore. And she took off."

Speaking from personal experience, perhaps, Detective Banana?

Every utterance from Struk enraged me. How could this so-called gold shield detective have the nerve to go on TV and rationalize his sexist, inept, and uncaring investigation?

When Struk was advised that there were problems in the marriage, he concluded that she must have run off because "that happens all the time." This man, instead of being a detective, should have been a relationship counselor.

When he heard that Robert Durst lied to him about the phone calls and having the drink with William Mayer, Struk concluded that maybe *the neighbor* was wrong. Really?

When the women met with Struk to relate the incidents of violence, the threats, and the destruction of her books and her clothes, he didn't bother to take notes. His condescension to the women, who were better investigators than he was, was reflected in his response to them. " 'If anything happens to me, blah blah blah,' " he said. The more evidence he received of foul play, of domestic violence, the more firmly he concluded that there was no reason to suspect foul play? You got it backward, buddy. Your words are *blah, blah, blah*!

When he was presented with the dig/shovel to-do list, he asked, "What are you going to do with a shovel in South Salem in February? You're not going to be able to dig a hole to bury somebody."

He dismissed the possibility of foul play. "No corpse, no crime scene. This is a missing-persons case." In Struk's world, if you're smart enough to get rid of the body, you can get away with murder. No questions asked.

The fact that Struk didn't even think about looking at the car of Robert Durst is astonishing. Wouldn't a detective want to pull out all the stops to impress one of the wealthiest families in New York City? Wouldn't he want to show his law-enforcement gravitas? Of course he would. So, why? Why no search of anything, anywhere? Because if you didn't bother to preserve a crime scene, there was none?

He didn't question Durst's lack of an alibi. There were no interviews with anyone from the Durst family in the original case folder. And yet Struk remained nonplussed when a criminal defense attorney called to tell him to refrain from speaking to his client. His antenna didn't go up then. Maybe he doesn't have one.

Lieutenant Gibbons, Struk's superior, told Jim McCormack that there are two ways to look at this. Kathie was "either dead or she voluntarily left, and I wouldn't be surprised as to the second, as a matter of fact." How could a lieutenant with no evidence support a claim that a fourth-year medical student within months of graduation who was pursuing a divorce from her husband ran off? What evidence supports his conclusion?

Or is it, as Struk explained, that maybe she was "shacking up" or "tired of this guy"? That was definitely the simplest way to explain a woman's vanishing: She's a slut. She's shacking up, and it makes perfect sense.

What's even more infuriating is that Struk, to this day, sticks by his theory.

That an NYPD detective and a lieutenant could do so little and draw such conclusions based on information provided by Robert Durst's spokesperson and employees of the Dursts was reflective of a society that felt women were disposable.

• **Eleanor Schwank seemed to throw epic shade on Ellen Strauss.** Eleanor was describing the efforts of the "entourage of girls" to locate Kathie or get a bead on her, canvassing the train and hospitals with her photo. Then she seemed to sigh and said, like an afterthought, "Anyway, Ellen became involved," referring to Ellen Strauss. After hearing from Gilberte about Strauss I found this hilarious.

• **Ellen Strauss, annoying and as fake as ever.** She opened her diary and said, "Ah, March 7, 1982," like a snooty wine sommelier. "Ah, 1982, a very good year." So fake. So self-important. Gilberte told me on her deathbed that Ellen Strauss did not participate in the garbage collection at the South Salem cottage. In *The Jinx*, Ellen claimed to have been there, waiting in the getaway car. Was she too prissy to do the dirty work? Gilberte generously described Ellen as "my partner in crime" in the episode. They were using each other. Ellen used Gilberte for information.

Gilberte used Ellen like a secretary.

• **Seymour and Douglas probably discouraged Robert from going to the police.** Robert said, "I got a call she hadn't been in class for several days. I went to talk with my father and my brother Douglas. And they all said, 'You two have been having arguments for so many years. She's probably just over there, over there. You go and report it to the police, they're not going to do anything, but you're gonna get all this press dealing with the family.' They discouraged me from reporting it to the police until it got to be Thursday night. Then I just felt like, 'I'm worried. This is what I should do.' And I did it. They discouraged me."

I don't, as a rule, believe anything he says, but this rang true to me, sort of. I believe he consulted his family about how to handle the situation, and they urged him to keep it quiet.

What they knew about Kathie's fate is an open question.

• **"That puts her in the city."** Robert's attitude with Struk was dismissive and packed with lies. Did he lie because he believed there would be no follow-up? Regarding his many lies—he didn't have a drink with the neighbor, he didn't call her that night, and so on—Robert said, "What I told the police—I was hoping it would make everything go away." And he further explained, "They wanted to hear, 'What did you do?' So I told them, 'I did that.' It was like a negotiation. You tell somebody something; that's it. They don't go back there. They don't look back there or 'why is he telling me this?' kind of thing. I thought that would get them to leave me alone, accept a missing person like that. Now the police are going to leave me alone. I said, 'I called her from a pay phone and she answered.' That puts her in the city."

Emphasis on "puts her in the city." Meaning, he shifted her disappearance to Manhattan, to keep South Salem, Westchester County, the actual crime scene, out of it. He just admitted to obstruction. Circumstantial evidence was piling up. I was infuriated that he could be so cocky about his falsehoods. But they were all caught on camera. He couldn't take them back.

| EPISODE THREE: THE GANGSTER'S DAUGHTER

• **The Kathie Durst case is now prosecutable.** When Jarecki questioned Robert about my investigation into Kathie's disappearance, he asked, "Why do you think they searched [Lake Truesdale]?"

Durst said, "I guess they were looking for body parts."

Body *parts*.

Not "a body."

Not "my wife's body."

Body *parts*. That sealed it for me. He might as well have stood up and declared, "I chopped up Kathie, just like Morris, just like the Igors."

This is an admission. No one was talking about body parts. In 1982, police were looking for a body, a wife, a missing person. No one even suspected that Durst was capable of chopping up a body until Morris Black. This suggests that Kathie's body was not just disposed of, but disposed of in pieces.

• **There's Eddie Murphy**! I love this man. On camera, he was direct. His charming honesty came through. You can imagine what a pleasure it was to hire him and have him working in my office. He mentioned that Susan Berman became the self-appointed spokesperson for Robert, and then Charles Bagli made the excellent point that, with Susan planting ideas out there—"the doorman saw Kathie," "the dean took a call," "she had a late-night male visitor"—it was hard for the press or the police to find out what really happened.

• **There's Kevin Hynes?** What was he doing on the show? The fact that he was included in the series confirmed my suspicion that he'd ingratiated himself with Jarecki in 2003 or 2004 and probably told him about my breakfast meeting with Douglas, which had been so inaccurately portrayed in *All Good Things* and, to my mind, again by Douglas in 2015 in the *New York Times*. Here on *The Jinx*, Kevin's inaccurate portrayals continued. He acted as if he were a major player in our investigation. Really? He wasn't even on our staff until two years after the investigation. John O'Donnell, Eddie Murphy,

Clem Patti, and Steve Bender ran the case. Kevin was just a new set of eyes on the file—years after the investigation opened.

• **The collect calls from Ship Bottom.** Durst tried to wiggle out of having made the collect calls from the Laundromat in Ship Bottom by claiming a Durst client had a beach house down there, and it wouldn't be unusual for the receptionist to accept those calls. We knew the calls were from the Ship Bottom area and along that coast, but how would he know about these collect calls unless he was the one making them? Does he want us to believe that he rifled through the telephone bills of the Durst Organization to identify collect calls made in the spring, summer, and fall from that area? He knew collect calls were made. He knew because he made them.

• **"I gave them a map to her door."** Ellen Strauss talked about her Internet searching to get Susan Berman's address and how she gave it to my office as if it were some huge break in the case.

We already had Berman's address. We had every address she'd ever had. We had her income taxes. We had interviews with her neighbors. We practically had the contents of her refrigerator.

We did not need Ellen Strauss's computer printout.

• **Sareb Kaufman's denial.** It's sad that Sareb, Susan's adoptive son, clung to his faith in Durst when virtually all of Susan's friends didn't trust him. The one exception: Kim Lankford, who took a trip to Palm Springs with Robert after Susan's murder to "mourn her" and remember her together, as she said to me on my show *Justice with Judge Jeanine*, without Robert bothering to tell her that he'd married Debrah. Sareb said, "It never made sense to me, even for a second. I knew how Susan felt about him. People explained the theory [of why Robert was suspected of shooting Susan] and said, 'There's no such thing as coincidence.' Of course there's coincidence!" No,

Sareb. There's no coincidence with Durst. There's only plotting and scheming, like how he plotted to keep you docile and quiet by offering you one hundred thousand dollars for college.

| EPISODE FOUR: THE STATE OF TEXAS VS. ROBERT DURST

• **It's the idiot jurors!** Chris Lovell and Joanne Gongora came back for another helping of pseudo-celebrity. Those two never missed an opportunity to get in front of a camera. Lovell said, "It's shocking," referring to the dismemberment of Morris Black. So why did you fall in man-love with Durst? He said, "I felt in my gut it was murder." So why didn't you go with what you knew to be true? Small minds were easily swayed. These two were wooed by DeGuerin, Ramsey, and Lewis to go against their own better judgment, assuming they had it.

Pathetic.

Later in the episode, Gongora said, "[Pirro] was really out to get him. He was running away. I can't fault him for that." He was a murderer on the run covering his tracks!

I thought, *You idiot. You've been played and you don't even know it.*

Why on earth was this woman so terrified of me? You know what? Maybe she should be.

• **Ramsey's mold.** I am still reeling from the cavalier attitude to the defense about the scripted drama they directed in court. Ramsey said, "Bob had intelligence and wit. He'd been through the mill. I had to look past that and see this lump of clay I'm going to have to mold into the shape I want him to be before we go to a jury." He also admitted to molding the victim so that the jury would believe that, as he said, "He had it coming. Morris Black was such a bad guy.

We touched on so many ways we could prove it." But they never did prove it. They called zero witnesses to corroborate their assertion.

But again, the idiot jury bought it.

• **Lewis's myth.** Referring to DeGuerin and Ramsey, he said, "We created this mythical creature—Jeanine Pirro." Bingo. He's right! "We took liberty with how directly she was involved in the pursuit of Bob." Disgraceful. Lewis also created the myth of Robert's faulty memory. "It was a concern on our part that the way he sometimes described things without emotion, hearing him describe the technical dissection of the body, would lead someone to believe he was a cold-blooded killer," he said. He's right. It would. Because Durst *is* a cold-blooded killer! Lewis's instructions to Robert? "Say, 'I don't remember.' Your memory is very fuzzy. Your memory is suppressed. It's very common you don't remember the details. Don't try to." Again, he admitted on camera that he essentially coached his client to lie on the stand.

• **"I got this idea that I could cut it in half."** Durst said this on the witness stand to explain why he dismembered Black. I took notice of his use of the word "it." Morris Black was not a friend or even a man to him. Morris Black was an "it." Serial murderers dehumanize their victims. It's what they do. They don't think of them as people.

• **Cody's testimony.** DeGuerin cued him up by saying, "It's the prosecution's burden to disprove self-defense. You found no evidence that would disprove it." All Cody could do was say, "No, sir." Cody would later say, "The victim is not there to tell his story. You are there to represent the victim. To tell his story. You're doing that for God." He got choked up on camera and said, "Can we stop?" Only those closest to Cody knew what he went through after the acquittal. He carried the guilt and shame for years. I told him the prosecution should have been on their feet objecting, saying, "That's for the jury to decide. It's a question of fact. It's a conclusion. Your Honor, without the head, we can't tell." Despite what I and his family told Cody, he blamed himself. Watching the last episode with him, I could see the one-hundred-pound weight fall off his shoulders. Thank you, Andrew.

• **"No one tells the whole truth."** Again, Robert was gleeful about how he lied to get away with murder. He didn't tell the truth *at all*. He described to Jarecki his faulty interpretation of the phrase "The truth, the whole truth, and nothing but the truth." He decided to remove "the whole truth" from the oath. "If you want to leave out something that makes you look bad, try it!" he said.

One, the definition of "the whole truth" was for the jury to decide.

Two, it was a conclusion, not a fact.

Three, it was a vague interpretation.

During a break in filming, Durst practiced different ways of saying, "I did not knowingly, intentionally, purposefully lie. I made mistakes. I didn't tell the whole truth. No one tells the whole truth." It was picked up on his hot mic. I wondered why they left that in. It was enough, to me, to hear him say it at all. Why was it necessary to catch him rehearsing his prepared line with the hot mic?

Of course, now we know. It was for the purpose of showing that he had talked on a hot mic previous to that final admission. He can't be excused and say, "Gee, I didn't know the mic worked when I'm alone."

| EPISODE FIVE: FAMILY VALUES

• **Dick DeGuerin's rationalization.** He said, "Do I think it's unfair [that the rich are at an advantage defending themselves]? Well, this is a capitalist society. The people with money can drive a Cadillac. Those who don't have as much money make do with a used car." Translation: "For freeing a serial murderer, I can go buy myself a Cadillac." No one is saying DeGuerin, Ramsey, and Lewis shouldn't get paid for their work or that defendants are not entitled to a fair trial. My issue is they knowingly got a guy off for murder using smoke and mirrors and mythical characters, and they did it for only one reason: money. It didn't look like DeGuerin and Ramsey felt a smidgen of regret on *The Jinx*. They were probably *proud* of themselves. They knew what they were doing the whole time. But the difference is, now *everyone else* does, too. We all know that *they* knew their defense wasn't ringing true. Their egos are simply too inflated to get a perspective on the bigger picture of what that does to our society. Men like DeGuerin and Ramsey—and obviously Durst—think women are disposable. They can be battered. They can be disappeared. They don't matter.

• **Ed Wright's secret investigation.** Until I watched *The Jinx*, I was unaware that Nick Scoppetta had hired Ed Wright, a criminal investigator for the New York Organized Crime Task Force, to look into Robert's version of events on the night of Kathie's disappearance. Wright interviewed the same witnesses as Detective Struk. Yet Struk and Wright drew far different conclusions about Robert's veracity.

Durst, reflecting on the hiring of Wright, clearly understood the importance of his being "able to get lots from police." Durst knew that Wright knew police and police liked him. He was able to get information that theoretically was unavailable. Who thought what, who said what. If, as Durst alleges, the criminal lawyer was supposed to find Kathie, why would it be necessary to get investigators who could find out information that wouldn't be available to anyone?

Robert needed to know, and, according to him, the Durst family needed to know, if his lies could be unearthed.

This was proof to me that members of the Durst family suspected Robert was involved from the beginning.

Take it logically. If Robert alone worked with Scoppetta, why agree to hire Wright? Robert already knew his own story was bullshit. Hiring an investigator would just prove that. But if Seymour had doubts about Robert, he might want Scoppetta to hire an investigator secretly to confirm his suspicions. Certainly Wright did more than justify any suspicion that Robert was involved in Kathie's disappearance. Then Wright left the case, and Scoppetta called Struk and informed him that Robert was represented by counsel. Makes perfect sense.

• **Andrew's ambush of Douglas at the Children's Rights charity event.** Andrew came across in that scene exactly the way he is. Just a polite, decent fellow, trying to get all sides on the record. After his two-minute talk with Douglas, the camera stayed on Durst. If you look closely, you can see that Douglas is visibly *sweating.*

• **"California is a pretty big state."** Robert's line when asked about his presence in California the week of Susan Berman's murder. He smirked when he said it, and then had to wipe his mouth with his sleeve on both sides. He was literally salivating over how close to the edge he came that time and how great it was that he got away with it.

• **Sareb finds the "Beverley" letter in a box of Susan's stuff.** Shocking. It's absolutely shocking that the LAPD didn't go through those boxes of Susan Berman's stuff back in 2000. She was a homicide victim. Why didn't the police search her files after they received the cadaver note? They knew the whole thing rested on handwriting, but they ignored her saved paperwork and letters? It was shoddy police work. I can only assume they didn't do a thorough search because Susan Berman was marginalized.

In Westchester, we would have gone through every scrap. You can solve hard cases and get the evidence, but you have to dig deep.

• **Sareb's realization.** Upon finding the "Beverley" letter, he said, "It was clear enough that I might be dancing with the Devil." Ya think?

Sareb defended Durst for years, and convinced himself he wasn't dancing with the Devil. He broke down on camera because he finally let himself see the truth that had been staring him in the face for thirteen years.

I believe Sareb believed Durst. When he stumbled on the letter, he could have destroyed it, or gone to Robert with it—probably with a big payday. But he loved Susan and wanted her killer caught. Thank you, Sareb, for making the right decision.

I'm not faulting Sareb. He didn't do anything wrong. He took the money from Robert and visited him in prison and defended him because that was what he needed to do, financially and emotionally, in order to survive. I hope he's in a good place, and I wish him well.

| EPISODE SIX: WHAT THE HELL DID I DO?

• **Watching my reaction to the two Beverleys.** Seeing it for the first time on TV was just as satisfying as holding it in my hand. It's like the feeling you get when you hear "guilty" at the prosecutor's table. It's not happiness, or pride. It's not another notch in your belt. As the DA, I would walk into the felony trial bureau and ask ADAs where we were on cases. It was always personal with me. Every prosecution was personal. And that's the problem—people don't take crime personally enough. Someone lost *everything* because some dirtbag decided to end his or her life. The trial bureau was our battle station. It's where we went to war. That Beverley letter brought back those feelings, the passion and the fight.

I said, "Oh, Jesus!" when recognition kicked in. It was a bit like a prayer, an acknowledgment of the tragedy of Susan losing her life.

Then, fired up again, I said, "Son of a bitch!" That was my celebration, like, "You piece of garbage! You can't get away anymore! Damn you!"

• **Chip Lewis reacting to the two Beverleys.** The expression on his face was priceless. I thought he might pass out on camera. He paused for a few beats and looked like a guy who had an actual conscience for a second there, like he might express regret, or apologize for going too far. He'd helped a serial killer go free. He was, literally, the Devil's advocate. But, alas, no. He muttered, "I don't know about handwriting to be anything other than dangerous. I see similarities. I see differences."

• **The hot-mic admission.** Well, I described that sensational moment in Chapter One of this book. It was amazing, shocking, fascinating. Andrew played him perfectly. He said, "Did you write the cadaver letter?"

Durst said, "No."

Jarecki said, "You wrote this but you didn't write this." He showed him the two Beverleys side by side. "Can you tell me which one you didn't write?" I couldn't wait for the answer.

Durst said, "No." Completely defeated. He knew he was cooked.

Immediately after this episode aired, I did a Fox News special. Defense attorney Chip Lewis, to his credit, called in for a quick phone interview. I asked him what he thought of the bathroom hot-mic admission. He said, "I was a bit underwhelmed. The lead-up and the buildup . . . honestly, you and I are flamboyant people who speak their minds. [It would] lead you to say things under your breath that you probably didn't mean. L.A. County has a case and we'll address those facts in the courtroom." More defense-speak. "We're eager to get to Los Angeles and hear if there's any new evidence but the mutterings in the bathroom."

As if that wasn't enough.

WHAT AMAZES ME, LOOKING back, is that Jarecki and Smerling had been able to keep the admission under wraps since the taping two years ago. They claimed that they didn't know they had it until around nine months before airing. An assistant chanced upon the tapes, and history was made.

In the aftermath of the last two episodes of *The Jinx*, a lot of arm-chair pundits questioned the ethics of not turning over such explosive evidence to police sooner. As I've said before, Andrew Jarecki and Marc Smerling were not obligated to tell anyone anything. We do not have Good Samaritan laws in New York or in the United States. Other countries have Good Samaritan laws. We don't. The only mandatory reporting laws are those requiring that child abuse be reported. No law requires people to inform other people they're solving a crime, let alone reporting one, that's relevant to them, or might relieve them of their sadness. In our society, chances are, if you inform someone of something you think he or she has a right to know and you're wrong, you'll get sued.

When Jarecki and Smerling located the letter, they got excellent legal advice. In their capacity as journalists, they could sit on the letter until they confronted Durst with it. They took such pains to film the "chain of custody" of that envelope, with Marc on the phone with an upset Sareb, then Marc in Sareb's apartment, opening the box and seeing the letter. Then you see Andrew at the bank, putting the letter in a safety deposit box. They secured the evidence.

By keeping quiet, they were protecting themselves from being agents of law enforcement during the second interview with their subject. If they'd turned it in, consistent with law enforcement, and then confronted him, they would have been required to inform Durst of his right to remain silent. It would have opened the door for Durst to accuse them of entrapment. They eliminated all that by keeping the letter to themselves.

We should be *grateful* they didn't turn it in, or there would have been no bathroom admission at all.

What about their journalistic integrity? These guys are moviemakers, investigative reporters. It's their right not to reveal their sources. They could have sat on the evidence for all time. But, instead, they shared it on their documentary, for maximum creative and journalistic impact.

Some might have a problem with that. I don't.

If you're not working at the behest of or in cooperation with law enforcement—and the filmmakers were clearly not—you are not legally obliged to share evidence with anyone, in your capacity as a documentarian.

Jarecki told the *New York Times* that L.A. authorities knew about the evidence *well* in advance of the screening. When Robert was arrested for trespassing at the Durst home on West Forty-Third Street in 2013, the FBI was looking at Robert for the murder of Susan Berman.

Why would the FBI pick up that case after all this time?

Don't assume for one minute that the LAPD or the FBI heard about the letter and the bathroom admission at the same time as the rest of the world.

I'd guess that law enforcement knew about the evidence since 2014. Sometime between filming that scene with Durst in 2013 and *The Jinx* airing in January 2015, they informed L.A. they were sitting on a powder keg. Law enforcement quietly reopened the investigation into the Berman murder, started watching Durst, and got their ducks in a row for an indictment. The pace picked up when *The Jinx* debuted and Durst set the wheels in motion to flee again.

I don't give a crap when they turned over the evidence. I'm just glad that they found it in the first place.

Now, as for my legal opinion about whether the second Beverley letter and the bathroom tape will be admissible in court:

The hot-mic stuff? Absolutely.

Durst was not in custody when he made this admission.

He was not being interrogated.

He knew he had a mic on.

Every time he was interviewed, he signed a waiver.

He voluntarily agreed to engage in videotaped discussions with the producer and director.

Durst is no dummy. He knew he was wearing a mic in the john. It was clipped to his clothes! He could have seen it in the mirror if he washed his hands. If he hadn't been reminded about being recorded with a mic on in a previous chapter, by his own attorney, one might argue that there was an expectation of privacy in the bathroom, if he were actually urinating. But he had been reminded, and from the recording, it didn't sound like he was actually using the john.

It's another "pushing the envelope" moment, another opportunity to see how close to the edge he could dance. I believe it's a spontaneous statement, he blurts out an admission of guilt. After the reality of seeing the handwriting on the wall—or, in this case, on the envelope—Durst's devious, calculating mind knew it was over.

To me, the only gray area is whether "killed them all" referred to just Kathie, Susan, and Morris, or to more people we don't know about.

As for the admissibility of the second Beverley letter, you bet it is.

Jarecki and Smerling were extra careful to protect the chain of custody. Jarecki not only preserved the evidentiary value of the envelope, but he has also protected himself. By filming it all, he's covered from claims of tampering. Jarecki's not a dummy, either. He does his homework. *Capturing the Friedmans*, his previous documentary about the flaws of the judicial system, also included original witness interviews and the discovery of evidence.

Anyone who complains about how the evidence was gathered and when it should or shouldn't have come to light should sit down and shut up.

You can't have it both ways. You can't say, *"The Jinx* cracked the case" out of one side of your mouth, and say, "Shame on them for not turning over the evidence sooner" out of the other.

The McCormacks had been suffering for thirty-three years before they heard Durst's admission. I can tell you, as someone who was in the room with Jim and his wife, they were glad to hear it *at all*. Sure, they would probably have liked to know two years earlier. But it wasn't up to them. Jarecki and Smerling deserved to have their brilliant surprise ending. And, man, did they get it.

I told the media, "They did, in eight years, what law enforcement in three states couldn't do in thirty." Kudos. Jarecki and Smerling and their team nailed the bastard.

They landed the one-two punch of evidence and that should be able to keep him behind bars for the rest of his pathetic life, alone with not one of the benefits that wealth provided him, with nothing to plan for, scheme for, and hopefully, no pens with green ink. No, I take that back. Lots of pens with green ink to remind him of all the money had had and blew.

| CRAZY IS MY COMFORT ZONE

On March 14, 2015, one day before *The Jinx* finale aired on HBO, Robert Durst was arrested in New Orleans. The FBI tracked him to Louisiana, to the JW Marriott Hotel on Canal Street, with a warrant for his arrest in the murder of Susan Berman in Los Angeles in December 2000. It took them fifteen years to indict him, and two days to find him.

Durst went on the lam, again, on March 12, leaving his apartment in Houston unlocked and ditching his cell phone. Agents got a bead on him when he used a pay phone (the guy is addicted to pay phones) to check his voicemail. When they got to the JW Marriott, they asked the concierge if Robert Durst had checked in. No? How about James Klosty? Emilio Vignoni? Diane Winn? Everett Ward?

Hilariously, they were running through Durst's aliases when guess who walked through the lobby on his way back from dinner at NOLA, Emeril Lagasse's restaurant in the French Quarter? I would have doubled over laughing to see Robert's face when the FBI arrested him in the lobby, right under the arched entryway.

A search of his room yielded classic Durst booty: pot (five ounces, enough to last him at least a few days), a .38 caliber handgun, forty-four thousand dollars in cash, a passport, fake IDs, a map of Florida and Cuba, and, bizarrely, a latex mask. It was spy stuff. When you put it over the head, it changed the surface of your face to make you unrecognizable. They also found a UPS tracking number for a package that, when it was found later in New York, contained another $117,000 and a pair of sneakers.

If that didn't say "run," I don't know what did.

Regarding the UPS package, my first thought was, of course, Debrah Lee Charatan. She was his usual cash supplier. But the FBI tracked the package to another mysterious woman: Susan (*another* Susan, number three in this crazy story) Giordano of Campbell Hall, New York. She claimed to be a "longtime friend" of Robert's. For the life of me, I can't understand why any human, let alone any woman, would want to be his friend. She admitted to the FBI that she mailed the package on March 12, several days after the two Beverleys revelation on *The Jinx*. When the police searched Giordano's house, they found boxes of Durst's personal papers in her cellar. It was her house where Jarecki and Smerling had been during the sixth-episode party. She claimed that none other than Debrah Lee Charatan had shipped Durst's boxes to her!

Debrah handing the Durst baton to Susan Giordano? Why was there always another woman waiting in the wings? What is wrong with these people?

After the FBI arrested him, Durst was thrown in jail and then moved to the hospital wing due to his various illnesses. Hydrocephalus. Esophageal cancer. I wondered if his diseases were real, or if they were another trick. If they turned out to be real, would I feel pity for this sick old man who was being locked up?

You should know my answer by now.

Whatever he experiences in that hellhole is better than what Kathie Durst, Susan Berman, and Morris Black got.

As the DA, I had followed him to Texas and Pennsylvania. On April 6, I flew down to Louisiana to cover Durst's preliminary hearing, this time as a correspondent for Fox News. I'd done several segments on the case during the run of *The Jinx*. My audience was itching to see Durst punished for his crimes. Me, too. And, if I were lucky, I'd get a good seat.

The charges were illegal concealment of a gun and possession of firearms with a controlled substance. The issue at hand for his hearing was whether he was a flight risk.

What in this man's history pointed to his *not* being a flight risk?

He'd run from Galveston, forfeiting $300,000 in bail.

Obviously, he was planning to disappear to Cuba with his fake passport, cash, mask . . . and sneakers.

But the system is the system. You have to go through due process.

I like to respect protocol, so I called the New Orleans DA's office before I went south as a courtesy and had a conversation with Chris Bowman, the chief assistant. I asked him whether there was a separate press entrance to the courthouse. I'd covered Casey Anthony, George Zimmerman, and Drew Peterson, and had gotten used to the media's sometimes preferential access.

He said, "This is New Orleans. We don't do special treatment for the press. We're so corrupt down here, unless you know somebody, you're not getting anywhere."

"But now I know you!" I said hopefully.

He said, "You can come to my office in the morning before the hearing."

I flew down alone and checked into the Saint, a boutique hotel only two blocks from the JW Marriott. My producer Tim Lauer got there before me. He met me at the Saint around 8:00 p.m. We went to Acme Oysters and I ate fried soft-shelled crabs with sweet potato fries, which I would absolutely order again. And again. And again. My mood at dinner was flying high. I was just bouncing off the walls with excitement that the judge would finally lock Durst up and throw away the key.

In the morning, as planned, I met with Chris Bowman. It was kind of interesting going into the Orleans Parish DA's office. They had the same kind of cubbies, the same type of coffee mugs, the piles of paperwork and hardworking, good people with family photos on their desks. It made me a little nostalgic. It didn't matter if you were in New Orleans or in NYC, you felt the diligence of the cops and ADAs, and the pain of the victims on whose behalf they crusaded. It was comfortably uncomfortable, like having déjà vu.

I told Chris, "You know you have the best job in the world." He didn't disagree.

We chatted in his office while he drank some coffee. It was super-early, 7:30 a.m. I'd already done a hit for *Fox & Friends* and was in full makeup. Durst wasn't scheduled to appear in court for another two hours.

"My boss said he'll talk to you," announced Chris, and he brought me into Leon Cannizzaro Jr.'s office, which also reminded me of my old one in Westchester.

The DA, a cool guy, went over exactly what was going on. He spoke in a language I understood. Los Angeles had an indictment for murder. Cannizzaro hadn't yet indicted him for drug and gun charges. If he did, it would most likely delay Durst's extradition to Los Angeles.

If I were in Cannizzaro's shoes, what would I do? I would *love* to see Durst stand trial for Susan Berman's murder. But, then again, Cannizzaro had the bird in hand—bird in *cage*. Durst couldn't finagle his way out of the gun charge if it were made against him. I hesitated to use the phrase "slam dunk," of course.

I told Leon about the odyssey I'd been through with Durst, from reopening the case to the present day. Cannizzaro and I had a long, good conversation. At the end of it, I said, "What do you think you're going to do?"

He said, "I don't know. We can get some good time on the gun here if we indict him." Ten years, maybe twenty if his history was taken into consideration. Durst would be eighty-two when he got out, if he lived that long.

I said, "Well, yours would certainly be easier than the murder case."

We agreed on that.

I said good-bye to Chris and Leon and joined Tim to walk over to the courtroom. I saw some of my media pals who, like me, had traversed the country chasing these stories. It was colder than expected (wasn't Louisiana supposed to be hot in April?), but I felt a certain warmth among the producers and reporters I'd gotten to be close with over the years. They all knew what Durst's downward spiral meant to me, personally and professionally. It felt real this time, as if nothing was going to stop the inevitable. I wasn't the first journalist to arrive, but I got a spot in the front row.

The New Orleans courtroom was large, with a lot of deep, rich mahogany, right out of *Midnight in the Garden of Good and Evil*. On the wall was their slogan, "Union, Justice, Confidence." The room was oddly organized. You entered behind and alongside the judge's bench, and the counsel tables were off to the side. In front of the defendants stood a glass partition. They waited there for their turn in court. The spectators sat opposite the counsel tables. The layout was different from what I was familiar with. But who cares? It was a courtroom. I'd rather be here than anywhere else.

I hadn't personally eyeballed Durst since Pennsylvania in 2001. *The Jinx* was filmed two years ago. I was curious to see what he looked like now.

Right on time, Durst was brought into the court with several other prisoners. They stood together behind the glass partition in their orange jumpsuits and shackles.

Durst looked alarmingly small. Just *minuscule*. There was nothing to him. Had his bulimia flared up again (did he live on Metamucil or had ipecac been shipped to him from Susan Giordano?), or was his weight loss due to the cancer treatment? Either way, he appeared weak. A kitten could take him. I stared at my nemesis, this pathetic, bald, broken-down codger. He seemed to have aged twenty years since *The Jinx*.

If his insides festered with evil, it showed on the outside.

He did his usual thousand-mile stare, not making eye contact with anyone.

I knew he had a shunt in his head to drain the fluid in his brain, but I couldn't see it from where I was seated.

And then I spotted Dick DeGuerin, no cowboy hat today, cheeks and nose spotty and inflamed, reminding me of every alcoholic I've ever known. He saw me and scowled, radiating contempt.

I thought, *This guy is* still *pissed off?* He won his case by selling me as a "mythical character" to the half-wit Texas jury. I had every right to be furious at *him*. But the fact that I was still nipping at his heels was too much for his ego. He seemed to resent me, and the world that couldn't keep women down on the farm or in the barn.

I grinned at him, and he turned beet red. Maybe he had high blood pressure. Maybe he swilled too much moonshine. Maybe he sat in front of too many campfires. I don't know! I did wonder if he was going to have a heart attack, and if it might be insensitive to film it for my show.

Durst took a seat next to DeGuerin, and the hearing began.

The prosecutor stood up and told the court that we'd gathered to determine if Robert Durst was a flight risk, a danger to himself and others, and should be denied bail.

"Good morning, Your Honor," said DeGuerin suddenly. "May we make an opening statement?"

The defense and the ADA went back and forth, standard bail-hearing-type stuff. I loved the ADA, Mark Burton. He could have been any one of my guys, Murphy, O'Donnell, Duffy. Sometimes, it seemed like every guy in law enforcement was Irish, whether they were in New York or New Orleans. The fighting Irish. God, I love 'em.

Magistrate Judge Harry Cantrell, a large, tall, bald black man with a graying mustache and glasses, asked to hear the prosecution witnesses. ADA Burton said, "Well, we only have Investigator O'Hearn." The investigator who'd worked with the team that arrested Durst.

O'Hearn took the stand. Burton said, "Can you tell us about this case?"

The investigator said, "Well, back in 1982, Mr. Durst's first wife, Kathleen Durst, was listed as a missing person . . ."

He went on and gave a brief history of Durst's thirty-three-year crime spree. I sat there thinking, *What does any of this have to do with gun charges in New Orleans?* My antenna went up.

Burton asked, "Jeanine Pirro. Who is that?"

Oh, shit, I thought. *Did I just hear my name? Why is my name even being mentioned? What is going on?* I told myself to relax, it's nothing. It'll pass, like a bad cramp. *What was he bringing me up for? I have nothing to do with New Orleans.*

Forget the antenna. The bells of Notre Dame were clanging in my head now.

O'Hearn said, "She was the Westchester district attorney in the office at that time."

"And she made statements that it was going to be reopened?"

I never made any statements! Becerra talked to the press, not me. I tried to remain calm. I had to tell myself to stay seated, because I was ready to jump up and shout, *"You're wrong!"*

The next question from the prosecutor was, "At that time, did the *New York Times* do an exposé?"

O'Hearn answered, "Yeah, the *Times*, the *Daily News*, and *People* magazine."

"And it was public knowledge the case was being reopened?" asked Burton.

At this point, DeGuerin said, "Excuse me, Your Honor. I wasn't aware the questioning was going to take that turn."

You and me both! I thought. *For once, I may agree with you.* Before I could give him credit for that, he proved himself to be as full of Texas horseshit as ever.

He announced, "There is a potential witness in the courtroom—Jeanine Pirro. I'd like to have her sworn and placed under the rule."

Whatever does that even mean? Under the rule? Did he want me to be sequestered, like a witness?

Apparently so. Judge Cantrell said, "All right, Mr. DeGuerin has filed a motion for sequestration. If Ms. Pirro is going to testify, I'm going to ask you to step outside."

You? How does he even know I'm here? Remember, the bench was in front of me. Unless he had a third eye on the side of his head, how could he know I sat in the courtroom?

Burton said, "I'm not going to call her as a witness."

DeGuerin said, "Well, *I am*."

What the fuck is he going to call me about? I had no knowledge of the gun at the Marriott.

It was completely surreal. Was I in a New Orleans courtroom or the Twilight Zone? I knew some voodoo shit was going on.

The judge asked DeGuerin, "You are?"

Dick straightened himself up and said, "Yes."

I was stiff with rage. *I'm a witness for the* defense? *Fucking A!*

Everyone in the room was looking at me, so the judge knew where to turn his head to actually see me. He said, "You'll have to leave the courtroom."

Well, I grabbed my Chanel bag, smiled, and walked out, thinking, *I've been thrown out of better courtrooms than this sideways dump!*

I kept my head up, maintained an air about me, and went outside into the hallway. Immediately, I started working my phone. I called Dianne Brandi, a lawyer for Fox, and got her voicemail. I called Bill Shine, the head honcho under Roger Ailes, and got his voicemail. Then I called Rich Weill, my former chief ADA, who knew this case inside and out and now worked with one of the most famous attorneys of our time, David Boies, and got *his* voicemail. *Pick up your phones, people!*

Dianne called back and I explained what had happened, not that I had any clue what the hell had just gone down in there. She asked, "Why would they call you?"

I said, "I have no idea! I can't take the witness stand right now. I have to look at reports! I have to refresh my memory!"

Dianne said, "Leave the courthouse. They may very well serve you."

"No!" I was not going to be chased out of there by Dick DeGuerin. He'd tried to make me a witness in the Galveston trial and he was doing it all over again. Why does this guy have so many issues with me? That time, I was ordered to stay quiet. This time, I was not going to be silenced. I wasn't afraid of them, and I was not leaving. I'd come down to see Durst and to cover the story. This was my *job*.

She said, "Jeanine, leave the courthouse."

"I'm not leaving!"

This went back and forth for a while.

She said she'd send local Fox lawyers to the courthouse to help me.

Meanwhile, Rich Weill called back. He said, "They can't throw you out. They have to serve you. And if you're a former prosecutor or member of law enforcement, you're entitled to a certain number of days' notice. *And* you're there as a reporter, so you have First Amendment rights."

I said, "Absolutely." You go, Rich!

There was a commotion in the hallway. DA Leon Cannizzaro was walking toward the courtroom door, surrounded by ADAs, bodyguards, the whole entourage I used to travel around with. I shouted "Leon!" to him, but he breezed straight into the courtroom. I assumed he'd gotten word of what had just happened and came to check it out for himself.

A reporter from ABC approached me with a camera crew and asked for an interview right now. So did a crew from NBC.

A reporter from the *Los Angeles Times* popped up and asked for an interview, too.

I said, "I'm not talking to anybody until the judge makes a decision."

She said, "We can go right outside! We can go in a corner!"

My adrenaline was skyrocketing. I politely told them all I had other things to deal with at the moment.

Tim Lauer, the producer, was on his first trip with me. He didn't know what to do. "Here's my credit card," I said. "Buy me some chocolate, a Peppermint Pattie, Junior Mints, anything, just get me chocolate!" He turned his head to leave and I yelled, "Tim! Forget the chocolate. Get in the courtroom and find out what they're saying!"

Right about then, the local attorneys hired by Fox, a woman named Mary Ellen Roy and a gentleman by the name of Dan Zimmerman, found me in the hallway.

"What do you want to do?" asked Mary Ellen. "You have a right to be in that courtroom. Do you want to go back in?"

I said, "Of course!"

Chris Bowman suddenly appeared in the mayhem, and said, "I have an application for the court!" He held up a few sheets of paper. "I'm going in, right now," he said, ready to present his hastily composed memo to the judge. The guy was my knight in shining armor.

He let me scan the paper. It was a thing of beauty. He made four main points:

1. **There is no indication that the putative witness has been served with the motion.** Basically, that means that I hadn't been properly served.
2. **The information sought from Ms. Pirro does not constitute "essential" information.** That means that whatever I knew about the far-reaching history of Durst's crimes was irrelevant to the issue of whether Durst should be denied bail.
3. **The defendant has made no affirmative showing that the purpose of the subpoena is not to harass Ms. Pirro.** The dream team did this throughout the Morris Black pretrial and trial (and are still doing it).
4. **The defense has made no affirmative showing that the information cannot be obtained through practical alternative means.** This point is that DeGuerin was trying to keep me out when he simply didn't have to, just to be a blowhard.

It was splendid. In Galveston, I'd been used and lied about by the defense. The jury, the judge, and the media bought it. As I looked around at all these people in New Orleans who refused to let DeGuerin pull his stunts in their city, I realized that the tide had turned.

I couldn't wait to get back into court. I said, "Let's hit it!"

Tim was stunned by me in general, and he sure hadn't seen anything like this before. He looked terrified. I told him he could now go to the newsstand and get those Peppermint Patties.

I followed Chris back into the courtroom. A half hour had gone by since I was ejected.

As I came through the door, the court officer whispered to me, "You're not allowed in here."

I said, "Watch me," with a smile.

Since I entered behind and alongside the bench, it took a while for the judge to realize I was there. They were in the middle of testimony. I walked around to the front so he could see me and said, "Your Honor, my lawyers are here. We need to have a legal argument."

Judge Cantrell looked over his glasses at me and said, "Didn't I order you out of the courtroom?"

I said, "Yes, but I'm a lawyer. I'm here to argue."

He said, "No you're not."

My Fox lawyers from Phelps Dunbar came forward and said, "Your Honor, I'm Mary Ellen Roy. I represent Jeanine Pirro." I liked her. She stepped right up like she owned the place. My kinda gal.

Chris Bowman piped up, too. "And, Your Honor, Chris Bowman for the state of Louisiana. You had sequestered Ms. Pirro. The state of Louisiana is objecting to any subpoena or order to call her as a witness because the defense has not followed the code of evidence." I made eye contact with Leon Cannizzaro in the bullpen. He nodded at me.

At this point, Judge Cantrell said to me, "You have to leave." There he goes again!

I got thrown out. Twice in one hour. It was a record.

Seriously, I'd never been thrown out of court in my life. But I ran a court and knew how I would have handled this. I would have listened to the arguments and made a thoughtful decision. I hoped this judge would do the same.

I went back into the hall for another twenty minutes, angling my way as close to the door as possible to try to hear something, while my two lawyers and chief assistant Chris Bowman were arguing inside. Meanwhile, I fielded calls from a few Fox executives who didn't want me to be served and therefore unable to cover the hearing or any of Durst's upcoming trials.

The courtroom door opened, and Mary Ellen came out. She said, "The judge is off the bench. He's considering our request." She told me that DeGuerin argued that I'd been "dogging Durst," and had to be put on a leash. I needed to be on a leash? Is that how he thinks women should be treated?

Another twenty minutes went by before the judge returned to the bench. He called all the lawyers up and he announced, "Ms. Pirro has a First Amendment right to be here."

Word got around. The doors opened.

I grabbed my Chanel bag and walked back in, with, as ABC's David Muir said the next morning, "the faintest of smiles." That was for DeGuerin's benefit. (He looked straight ahead, too chicken to look at me.) I took my seat in the front row and arranged my skirt just so. And then the court went back to the hearing.

I sat there, writing everything down, scribbling away on my note-pad as if nothing had happened. My heart was racing, though.

I stared at Durst. He leaned back in his chair as if he were barely paying attention, probably thinking, *I've got another sixty million to get through this.*

At the end of the session I walked up to the judge's clerk and I whispered, "Just tell the judge I said, 'Thank you.' "

He gave me a little nod and a smile and said, "I will."

It was only forty minutes between my being thrown out and my being invited back in. But those forty minutes felt like a microcosm of the last fifteen years on this case.

One of my favorite moments in a long time was walking into that courtroom in the middle of testimony and just saying, "Your Honor, I'm here to argue." I walked straight into the well of the courtroom.

That was my comfort zone, right in the middle of a heated battle of words. I realized that was where I felt at home.

• • •

DEGUERIN'S FOCUS ON ME seems to go beyond any legitimate defense tactic. I'm convinced he's one of those men who I've come across throughout my career who can't deal with an intelligent, assertive, stand-on-her-own woman, or at least he knew I had his number and didn't like it. Look, I respect defense attorneys. I do not respect Dick DeGuerin and his ilk. They take the truth and turn it inside out. In his pompous southern drawl, he sells lies and snake oil to jurors in a place where people swear on the Bible to tell the truth, in a place where the sign on the wall reads "In God We Trust." The stench of people like DeGuerin, who laugh about distorting the truth and in many ways come close to perjury, should be an outrage to good, law-abiding Americans. I believe in truth and justice. I've dedicated my career to the fight for a level playing field for victims who never chose to be in the courtroom in the first place, and for the victims, like Kathie, Susan, and Morris, who couldn't be.

The New Orleans prosecution needed to determine if my office investigated Susan Berman, and if my team went to Los Angeles. They wanted to prove that Susan knew we were coming to question her about Kathie, and that Susan told Robert about it. If so, then the legal interpretation of his actions—marrying Debrah, planning this trip to L.A., and so on—would be that he was "lying in wait."

If Durst knew that she was about to talk to us, he was "lying in wait" to shoot her to prevent her testifying. In that case, the murder becomes death penalty eligible.

In L.A., if there is a trial, I suspect the defense is going to say that Susan Berman did *not* get a grand jury subpoena from me (she didn't). But DeGuerin doesn't know whether I spoke with anyone close to her, or what information we might have kept in our back pocket. He doesn't know much of anything about our investigation of Susan

Berman. By trying to get me on the witness stand, he intended to find out. So far, he's out of luck.

The judge, clearly a genius, denied bail for Robert. Since then, the feds have indicted Durst for federal felony gun charges and DA Leon Cannizzaro has dismissed his charges. Durst is housed in St. Charles Parish's Correctional Center. His case is scheduled for hearing in January 2016. The L.A. case will proceed after that.

Meanwhile, Durst's lawyers are throwing things at the judge in New Orleans, trying to make something stick. But U.S. Magistrate Judge Sally Shushan isn't falling for it. DeGuerin and company asked for the handwriting comparisons that the prosecution will be using against him in California, no doubt to figure out a way to discredit them. Judge Shushan ruled that the prosecution does not have to turn them over, that the defense can make do with a detailed document that summarizes the history of the comparisons.

In the spring of 2015, they couldn't wait to get to Los Angeles. Now they're stalling with pretrial hearings.

Even if this one doesn't go his way, DeGuerin and company must be salivating about a trial in Hollywood. He's probably shopping for new cowboy boots and hat right now.

And I will definitely be there, in the front row with my notebook, my Chanel bag, and in that bag, Peppermint Patties.

| ANALYZING ROBERT DURST

John Sharp, MD, an adolescent and adult psychiatrist, is a faculty member at Harvard and UCLA with clinical practices in Boston and Los Angeles and more than twenty years' experience. He's been a friend of mine and has appeared on *Justice with Judge Jeanine* as an expert on human behavior. Dr. Sharp was kind enough to travel from Boston in August 2015 to talk with me about the mental health and behavior of Robert Durst.

Me: Thanks for speaking with me today, Dr. Sharp.

John Sharp: My pleasure, Judge.

What the hell is wrong with him?

His behavior is consistent with someone who has a major personality disorder, specifically, an antisocial personality disorder.

What are the specific characteristics of someone with an antisocial personality disorder?

Just to mention a few: deceitfulness, repeated lying, use of aliases, conning others for personal profit and pleasure, impulsivity, irritability or aggressiveness, reckless disregard for the safety of others, constant irresponsibility, lack of remorse.

A stronger determinant than anything else is a total disconnection from emotion. The only emotion we see in Robert Durst is on the dimension of irritability to outrage. It's a very narrow band. Inside his own mind, he doesn't connect to the full range of feelings. He's out of touch with his own emotions. The flip side of the same coin, he's out of touch with the feelings of others. It strikes me how fully Robert Durst meets the criteria.

Other people—Gilberte Najamy and Jim McCormack, for example—observed that he and Kathie were madly in love in their early life together.

His "madly in love" was in a primitive form. He was fascinated with someone who was synchronous with his needs at the time. Other people look at their relationship and see love, but they were attributing normal emotions to a man who doesn't have them. He doesn't have the capacity to truly love.

What about his great friendship with Susan Berman? Many people talk about how close they were.

They both had childhoods with special circumstances that related to each other's. But their apparent fondness was utility driven. Susan Berman and Robert Durst were useful to each other when they met in college. On an operational level, he needed friends. They shared an understanding of growing up with wealth and power, so she was a wise choice. When her usefulness to him ended, so did their friendship, and her life.

He was known to have a lot of sexual relationships. He had affairs with Prudence Farrow and possibly others while he was married to Kathie. He was with Kim Lankford when he was married to Debrah, and presumably others. He took Viagra and is clearly a sexual being.

He cannot be a considerate person. His sex life was probably mechanical, not different from pleasuring himself. As for his ability to have affairs, he was a man who lacked remorse and empathy. He could do anything. He's not in touch with his feelings, which makes him an incomplete. That said, he is also free from the constraints of legality and morality. The concerns of others—a wife that he be faithful, a lover that he be considerate—do not concern him.

You're describing something that's more animal than human being.

He has operated like an animal in the wild. If something or someone poses a life-and-death threat to him, he kills. When the threat is gone, he just goes on his way. There was a wonderful book by Robert Sapolsky called *Why Zebras Don't Get Ulcers* that illustrates my point. You'd think, living in the jungle, grazers would be nervous wrecks all the time. But researchers determined that they sense their threat level. They deal with it—by running away, or fighting the lion—and then, when the threat is gone, they return to normal.

Durst did the same thing. He had no qualms about dealing with a threat by killing his wife. And then, when the threat was gone, he went back to his other business.

But back in 2000, how did he react to me? Did Durst take me seriously as a threat?

He couldn't be business-as-usual when you, Judge, entered the picture. You raised the threat level to a unique high to him, one he couldn't dispose of. He said in *The Jinx* that, in 2000 when *you* reopened the investigation, everything changed. You had authority and power. All of a sudden, the threat (or the lion) isn't going away. You kept saying, "Sooner or later, we're going to know the truth." He knew when he saw you, it was not ever going to be fine. The lion wasn't going away.

He never tried to eliminate me as a threat—that I know of. He did visit the Ritz in White Plains very close to my home several

times, though. **But he didn't dare come here. Even in the mob, you don't kill prosecutors.**

I would think it crossed his mind to kill you, and he decided he couldn't pull it off. There's no way it didn't occur to him.

What about Gilberte? She'd been saying he was a murderer for eighteen years. Wasn't she a threat?

He didn't think of her as a real threat in the sense that she didn't have power or authority. She was a witness, and he probably detested her—hate falling on the same narrow band of emotion with irritation and outrage—but what could she do to him in practical terms? She'd already told police what she knew. She'd been arrested for drugs. She had no clout and her claims could be dismissed. You were someone with power and clout, someone he perceived of as on his level.

Growing up in his family, he learned early on that power and clout were to be respected. He learned from them to do what he needed to do.

Susan Berman and the cadaver letter. If he has no conscience, why did he send it? Some people interpreted it as his way of making sure her body didn't decompose before it was found, a way to express his affection for her.

There is no way he had a guilty conscience, but he may have been troubled by her body lying there. She had to go, and he took action. But then he might have thought that he'd be respectful. The letter could have been a code of honor, like "honor among thieves," something he owed to her. Sending it could have been a coldly calculated move, but it was definitely not an emotional one. He lived in a world without remorse.

Since the defense never asked an actual doctor about Asperger's, let me put it to you, Dr. Sharp: Do you believe Robert Durst has Asperger syndrome?

For starters, Asperger's no longer exists. The fifth and latest edition of the *Diagnostic and Statistical Manual of Mental Disorders* doesn't list it. It's been dismissed by experts as a kind of autism that doesn't merit a unique name.

Now, is Robert Durst autistic?

Autism is a totally different way people can be out of touch with themselves and the feelings of others. But autistic people are not disconnected or lacking in empathy. They are relatively insensitive to interpersonal cues.

It was a good idea to use it in the defense. Durst's lawyers took his problem with human interaction and reframed it in a socially acceptable way. No one blames a kid with autism. They say, "The poor kid can't read human cues."

What about the dissociative state the defense said Robert was in when he dismembered Morris Black? They compared it to the fog of war, that Robert was traumatized by the shooting, went into a fog, and can't remember anything about it.

The dissociative state defense is too Hollywood. You can find cases, but it's exceedingly rare that people can't remember a thing.

When you look at people who have been through traumatic events—like soldiers who fought in an actual war—they don't have global amnesia, or completely forget what happened. Transient global amnesia, temporarily forgetting everything, is related to head injury.

And he couldn't have been overcome by emotion. The only way to have a traumatic reaction is to feel. He's not a feeling person. He's like a machine. He doesn't have emotions to overcome, so he couldn't have had a traumatic reaction.

Durst did primal scream therapy in the 1980s. What is that, and would it have changed him?

Primal scream therapy is no longer practiced. It's long been dis-
credited. The theory was to connect with trauma by screaming.
Robert Durst could scream primally every day of his life and it
wouldn't make a difference.

**Could Durst have been treated with another therapy and been
cured?**

Antisocial personality disorder is considered untreatable. I'm a
therapeutic optimist. If he were my patient, I would require him
to stop smoking marijuana and use cognitive behavior techniques
to manage his personality. I'd look for underlying unconscious
pain that could be at the root of his problem and then try to see if
he were capable of addressing that. A tiny percentage of antisocial
personality disordered people have some capacity to tolerate the
pain driving their disconnection. But the odds of successful treatment are infinitesimal.

What's it like inside Robert Durst's head?

Dark rooms with paper-thin walls. Cold. He's only partially
aware of where he is and where he's going. He's unmoored,
like he's floating around the world. Thoughts come in and
go out.

**He'd marked up pages from a book about adults with ADD. Is
there any validity to ADD explaining his crimes?**

A guy this disordered? His is not an ADD-level problem. It
doesn't touch on the depth and power of this true nature.

**He once described what sounded like a traumatic reaction to
learning that I'd reopened the Kathleen Durst investigation. He
told his sister that when his family's PR agency was receiving
calls from the tabloids, he felt sick to his stomach, went to the
bathroom, and threw up. Then he went to sleep.**

He felt outrage. It's on his narrow band of emotion. Since it's as
easy for him to lie as it is to tell the truth, I wonder if he really
threw up.

Maybe he ate some bad caviar. Or maybe he made himself throw up. There is a history of Robert dealing with bulimia.

Most bulimics are struggling to maintain control of their feelings. But, as someone who matches up with the traits of antisocial personality disorder, his bulimia must have been more methodical, a cleaning ritual perhaps. Or it was vanity based. He wrote once that he lived for food. Food would satisfy his base-level pleasure drive—food, sex, sleep. Like an animal in the wild, he organized his life around them. He enjoyed eating and wanted to stay slim, so bulimia would have been a quick and calculated strategy, not the result of intense feeling or emotional distress.

Robert said he enjoyed prison life.

That might be his survival instinct. He said that the prisoners respected him. It's the same thing we see when people project their own emotions onto Durst. He didn't show fear or appear intimidated in prison, so the prisoners might have thought, *Wow, he must be a tough guy not to be intimidated in here.* His lack of feeling would help him in prison. In normal life, it was a deficit.

Was he born a psychopath?

Many experts believe psychopaths are born that way. He could have had an early-childhood experience that led to it. Seeing his mother going off the roof was a big injury. His father favoring Douglas was another injury. He might've been born fragile and then some serious stuff happened, and he ran away from feelings and closed himself off to protect himself. By disconnecting fully and going through life in an uncaring way, you become a psychopath.

He talked in *The Jinx* about the shock of seeing his mother buried when he was seven and saying, "Get Mommy out of the box."

Well, I'm sure that made an impression on him. But it's totally unrealistic for a seven-year-old—one who claimed to have seen his mother's broken body on the ground—to think that they were actually burying his mother alive. A three-year-old, yes. But a seven-year-old? He clearly had a pattern of being unable to square off with reality. I can imagine his feeling overwhelmingly outraged at her death—sadness and bewilderment at first, but the outrage even more.

I understand that he has a narrow band of emotion. But does that protect someone from being disgusted by the grisly work of dismembering a body? After he cut up Morris Black, he went out and got a haircut.

Why wasn't he grossed out? Medical students who choose to dismember a body for all the right reasons, who volunteer to do it, are grossed out. But Durst was disconnected from his feelings. He didn't empathize with Morris Black. He was like a butcher, approaching it as a job that needed to be done. He did the work mechanically.

He doesn't feel sad or guilty or remorseful. Does he feel pride or joy?

I don't think he feels good about himself. At the most, he can feel a sense of accomplishment. He's impressed with himself.

In *The Jinx*, he complained that he was born rich and that nothing he ever did would be his own accomplishment. I wonder if that's why he left so many bread crumbs and clues. It was his way of sharing his sense of accomplishment.

His murders and his story are certain ways he's made a name for himself apart from his family. I can see him taking a kind of pride in that. Why did he contact Andrew Jarecki to participate in *The Jinx*? Only two possible reasons:

1. Pride in accomplishment.
2. He wanted to get caught.

Since he didn't want to get caught, the only logical reason is that he took pride in his accomplishments. He's so out of touch with normal that he thought he could, against the advice of lawyers, tell his story the way he wanted to, make stuff up, and get away with it.

Whenever Robert got caught, he was found with the big three: cash, guns, and pot. I always wondered why he loves marijuana so much.

Pot relaxes him, as opposed to cocaine, which would exacerbate him. Think of the narrow band of emotion he lives on. Marijuana would calm his outrage and irritation.

As for the guns and money, they've both been very useful to him over the years. With his pot, cash, and weapons, he has what he needs to get things done, to seek sensual pleasure, and to calm himself down. He's a very practical guy.

You must have noticed his twitching and blinking on *The Jinx*. He had a history of belching and farting in public.

The physical twitches are just him juggling a lot in his head, trying to figure things out. Normal people are centered by their emotions. He is uncentered and grasps for something while there's a lot of mental cross-talk and noise. Blinking and twitching are signs of grabbing things from here and there, spitting things out and reconciling things.

Belching, farting, and burping in public is a sign that he's not aware of or concerned with social cues. A normal person would learn not to do them. I believe Robert is aware of social cues, and chooses to ignore them.

Why kill Kathie?

She became more trouble than she was worth, and then she threatened to leave. That was when he realized she had to go. It might not have been as bright a line, but he couldn't think of a reason not to do it. A normal person would think, *Why not just let her go?* That was not his way of doing business. He has to dispense with the matter at hand. To him, it was quicker, easier, and more convenient to kill her and get rid of the body.

Based on what you've seen in *The Jinx* and what you've read in my book, what is your opinion about whether the Dursts wanted to find Kathie?

That's an easy one. An average person would look at hiring a criminal defense attorney, or the lack of press about the case, the small reward offered, and think, *Wow. Why didn't they do more?* They'd wonder if there was an act of suppression going on. As a normal human reaction to tragedy, the Dursts were not empathic to the McCormacks or helpful in the investigation. You don't have to be an expert in human behavior to see that. A lot more should have been done to reach out to the family and try to help locate the missing woman.

They closed ranks. Why? Three possibilities.

1. To protect themselves.
2. To protect Robert.
3. Because they're a bunch of very self-secure and self-protective people.

Now, why do you think Robert chose the disguise of a mute woman in Galveston, New Orleans, and possibly other places we don't know about?

Beyond the obvious, the simple reason he stated, that he was going for the best disguise and chose to be a woman to hide his appearance and a mute to hide his voice? He was a practical thinker.

In the study of human behavior, we think a bit deeper about the choices people make. He might not even be aware of his reasons, but his choice could tell a larger story about his true motivation.

He dressed as a woman without a voice. He might've thought a lot about wishing women would shut up, including his wife and Susan Berman. He certainly wanted Gilberte and you, Judge, to be silent. His defense went so far as to gag you. So follow the logic. He's thinking about women being silent. He's thinking about a disguise. He puts them together and comes up with the disguise of a mute woman.

He dressed up to be what he wished I were: a woman who can't talk.

Part of being good at your job is to extrapolate, and that idea wouldn't be so far-fetched to be valid. It's certainly something worth speculating about.

Why didn't Douglas tell me about the Igors in 2000, or to investigators in 1982? He said "in retrospect" he made the connection between dead dogs and a missing wife. Does it usually take over thirty years to connect the dots?

Making those kinds of connections can be delayed. You can recognize the significance over time. But the window is up to two years, not over thirty.

| FINAL ARGUMENT

Some people out there may still believe that Robert Durst is a good man who's had the worst luck in the world, and that he was driven to kill because he was scared of me. They believe that I am the Jinx. They believe that, by kicking the eighteen-year-old hornet's nest of Kathie's disappearance, I am to blame for the deaths of Susan Berman and Morris Black. They think that if I'd just kept my mouth shut, lives would have been spared.

Other people have accused me of grandstanding, or involving myself in the Durst case for personal gain and acclaim. I've been attacked by the media, by people on my own team, by the families of the victims, by jealous frauds, and by half-wit jurors.

They don't know me.

My quest for justice for Kathie Durst turned into an opportunity for people with big egos and little brains to harass a woman for doing her job. For my efforts to solve the murders of two women, they tried to make me a victim myself. Unlike Kathie and Susan, however, I'm still here to fight and defend myself.

I've made my case over the last few hundred pages, and I believe I have proven, beyond a reasonable doubt, that Robert Durst is a serial murderer, a monster, true evil.

My pursuit of this monster has always been about one thing: justice long denied. And if justice were denied for Kathie Durst, who warned everyone what was coming, you can bet the ranch that so many other women were lost in the misogyny of our society.

Women's lives are not disposable. Women's lives matter.

We have the right to speak, to lead, to fight for justice, and to be in power. The men who tried to turn me into a cartoon of ambition and ego weren't out to protect victims or to serve justice. They would rather take a murderer's dollars and fill a courtroom with smoke than do their jobs with integrity. They succeeded, for a while. But I've always believed in the long game. The truth always comes out eventually.

We have finally arrived at Robert Durst's downfall.

The Jinx would not only help put a murderer behind bars. It won an Emmy for Best Documentary as well. I would receive applause for being smiley, quotable, and knowledgeable about the case on the series. The public reaction to me in 2015 has been a lot different from that in 2000. The press that once belittled me has started calling me things like "the unsung hero of the Durst case."

They have created a *new* narrative for me: I was maligned for a long time, but I was right all along and I should be happy and grateful now that everyone knows it.

I would go on TV shows and listen to their questions—"Aren't you so glad?" "Do you feel vindicated?"—and all I could think was *You know what? I don't need your applause. I don't need vindication.*

In fact, asking if I feel vindicated is the wrong question.

It's the *case* that's been vindicated.

Our investigation has been vindicated.

I knew I was right and, with all due respect, I didn't need anyone to tell me that. The only thing I have ever wanted since I first heard the name Durst was justice for Kathie. And it looks like we're finally going to get it.

Leveling the playing field for *every* victim who is seen as disposable and as less than worthy of concern has been the driving force of my career. Kathie was only one of the women I fought for over the course of my thirty years in law enforcement. Most of them weren't "important" enough for the press to write about or report on. They weren't "important" enough to attract the wannabes and characters and theater actors that Kathie's case ultimately did. They remain, for the most part, nameless, faceless women who may not have had notoriety but were fortunate enough to have their cases handled by real cops who worked tirelessly, quietly, out of the limelight for justice. By men—like John O'Donnell and Eddie Murphy—who had a moral core, who understood the mission, and who valued the lives of every victim. By men like Cody Cazalas, who carried the burden of the Texas acquittal, who believed he worked for God.

I've fought alongside such heroes. I've led them. This book is about one case, but Kathie represents the tens of thousands of women whom I have fought for and protected and, in some cases, won justice for posthumously. The fact that a rich guy was at the end of my spear this time doesn't change the fact that I've had my spear out for thirty years—and counting.

Like it or not, that's who I am. That's what I've done. And I'd do it all over again in a heartbeat.

| ACKNOWLEDGMENTS

Thanks to the many people who helped make this book happen and generously gave their time:

Val Frankel, my cowriter, who can grasp an issue quicker than you can think it. Val, you are a lifesaver and you know why.

Mitch Ivers, my editor, who always had a smile on his face no matter how tough things got.

My agent, David Vigliano; my manager, Steve Carlis; and my lawyer, Al Pirro—yes, we are all still friends.

Gallery Books and Simon & Schuster for publishing this book— Louise Burke, Jen Bergstrom, Jen Robinson, Elisa Rivlin, and Natasha Simons.

Fox News management and Dianne Brandi for giving practical advice when I was in New Orleans and helping me fight the good fight.

Former director of public affairs for the Westchester District Attorney's Office Anne Marie Corbalis, fact-finder extraordinaire, whose research you can take to the bank.

Former chief assistant district attorney Richard Weill, one of the smartest men I know, whose advice I always take, except when I don't.

Former executive assistant district attorney David Hebert, who continues to inspire me.

Roseanne Paniccia for her memory like a steel trap.

Former chief assistant district attorney Clem Patti.

Retired senior investigator John O'Donnell, who takes crime personally. John, there should be more like you.

Retired chief investigator Mike Duffy, who has gone to the dark side as a defense lawyer.

Chief financial officer for the Westchester District Attorney's Office, Pat D'Imperio.

Retired chief investigator Casey Quinn.

Retired prosecutor Barbara Egenhauser.

Former Galveston district attorney Kurt Sistrunk and assistant district attorney Joel Bennett for their perseverance in the case.

District attorney of Northampton County in Pennsylvania, John Morganelli.

Stephen Quint for hours of transcription.

Special thanks to Carly Lee Roman, my superstar intern from the University of Pennsylvania, who will make a great lawyer someday.

And Cody Cazalas, whose encouragement helped get me through this odyssey and who consistently and generously gave of his time and energy to make sure that I had everything I needed for this book.

| INDEX